COLORADO

CONNECTICUT

DELAWARE

FLORIDA

GEORGIA

KANSAS

KENTUCKY

LOUISIANA

MAINE

MARYLAND

MONTANA

NEBRASKA

NEVADA

NEW HAMPSHIRE

NEW JERSEY

OKLAHOMA

OREGON

PENNSYLVANIA

RHODE ISLAND

SOUTH CAROLINA

VIRGINIA

WASHINGTON

WEST VIRGINIA

WISCONSIN

WYOMING

MARIO BATALI

BIG AMERICAN COOKBOOK

250 FAVORITE RECIPES *from* ACROSS THE USA

With **JIM WEBSTER**

Art Direction by **DOUGLAS RICCARDI**

Photography by **QUENTIN BACON**

GRAND CENTRAL
Life & Style
NEW YORK • BOSTON

Grand Central Life & Style
Hachette Book Group
1290 Avenue of the Americas, New York, NY 10104
grandcentrallifeandstyle.com
twitter.com/grandcentralpub

First edition: October 2016

Grand Central Life & Style is an imprint of Grand Central Publishing. The Grand Central Life & Style name and logo are trademarks of Hachette Book Group, Inc.

The publisher is not responsible for websites (or their content) that are not owned by the publisher.

The Hachette Speakers Bureau provides a wide range of authors for speaking events. To find out more, go to www.hachettespeakersbureau.com or call (866) 376-6591.

Print book interior design by Memo, NY

Interior and endpaper illustrations copyright © 2016 by Jim Datz.

Library of Congress Cataloging-in-Publication Data
Names: Batali, Mario, author. | Webster, Jim, author. | Bacon, Quentin, photographer (expression)
Title: Mario Batali Big American cookbook : 250 favorite recipes from across the USA / Mario Batali with Jim Webster ; photographs by Quentin Bacon.
Description: First edition. | New York : Grand Central Life & Style, [2016] | Includes index.
Identifiers: LCCN 2016022712 | ISBN 9781455584710 (hardcover) | ISBN 9781455584703 (ebook)
Subjects: LCSH: Cooking, American. | Local foods—United States. | LCGFT: Cookbooks.
Classification: LCC TX715 .B34359 2016 | DDC 641.5973—dc23
LC record available at https://lccn.loc.gov/2016022712

ISBNs: 978-1-4555-8471-0 (hardcover), 978-1-4555-8470-3 (ebook), 978-1-4789-7117-7 (signed edition)

Printed in the United States of America

Q-MA

10 9 8 7 6 5 4 3 2 1

TO MY WIFE, SUSI CAHN, AND OUR TWO BOYS,
BENNO AND LEO, TRUE AMERICANS WHO ARE THE
REASON I DO EVERYTHING BETTER

AND TO THE MEMORY OF GINA DEPALMA,
THE FINEST PASTRY CHEF I HAVE EVER KNOWN,
MAY SHE REST IN PEACE

CONTENTS

INTRODUCTION

WE THE PEOPLE of America's most recent vintages have been grappling with our emerging sense of self-confidence and deliciousness. For the first two centuries of our nation, much of our cooking and eating was split be tween regular everyday meals and special celebrations. The weekday meals, the ones we ate the most, very often represented time- and cost-effective "no frills" ways to gather energy and fuel our bodies. They were not considered a joyous part of our lives, but essential for simple sustenance. They were quite often approached with a workmanlike mentality, rather than a happy moment of culinary expression. In recent decades, we've become more aware of the importance of nutrition, more invested in the delight of impeccable sourcing. We've turned the act of cooking into something of a sport, but one in which both participants and spectators enjoy the thrill of victory. Our daily bread is no longer mundane; it's a pop culture icon. If mealtime used to be about "feeding the herd," now it's nothing less than tending to our very souls.

The most common celebrations of our family meals have been based on our hereditary culture and, very often, non-American traditions. The food of our religious and cultural celebrations, of our solemn moments, of our annual traditions, and of our family gatherings has often been the deepest well of our most profound memories. Much, although not all of it, was born long before we were, and in a place not very similar to where we celebrate now. The recipes for these celebration dishes have been handed down

RECIPES ARE VERY MUCH A PART OF OUR CULTURAL HERITAGE, AS SIGNIFICANT, IN MY OPINION, AS PHOTOGRAPHS OR LETTERS (OR E-MAILS, KIDS, OR EVEN SNAPCHATS).

from generation to generation, from cook to cook, from mother to daughter or daughter-in-law.

Often these recipes were not written at all, but they formed part of the oral history of many families, taught to the next generation by the venerated elders, most often women. (Men have been somewhat involved, although, historically, not often a very big part of this tradition.) Sometimes the recipes were written down, often on smudged

note cards, or conserved on well-used and crinkled pages cut from magazines or the local newspaper's food section, meticulously filed in a plain but beloved box somewhere near the pantry or stove.

Each of my grandmas kept such a box, and the treasure within was the result of infinite trial and error over years of patient practice. Some of my favorite moments in the past two decades have involved getting a note or a letter, or even a tweet in the last few years, from some happy person

THE DISHES ARE OFTEN THE DISTILLATION OF THEIR FAMILY'S ETHNIC DNA COMMINGLED WITH THE LOCAL INGREDIENTS IN THEIR FAMILY'S HOMETOWN.

who had forgotten about a dish from their family traditions, and who had just seen or read or heard me refer to it or cook the actual recipe. These are very often forgotten recipes from an aunt or uncle or grandma or grandpa or mom or dad or neighbor, and represent the very significant and emotionally satisfying bridge from the past to the present.

Recipes are very much a part of our cultural heritage, as significant, in my opinion, as photographs or letters (or e-mails, kids, or even Snapchats). They are true points in history around which we file the rest of our personal and collective memory. I can look at my grandma's hand-written biscotti recipe on the little 4-by-6 card and can

very clearly hear her voice, smell her kitchen, taste her antipasto, and remember things a photograph in an album will not bring me to. She is still very much alive on the little blue card in my wallet, and even more so when I make the annual holiday biscotti the week before Christmas with Susi and our two boys.

My family, and more than likely your family too, shares this zeal, this perspective, this honored tradition, with millions of Americans. As I have traveled around the United States over the past twenty-five years I have constantly been surprised upon the discovery of a new palette of flavors, a new list of local ingredients, a new pocket of recipes, each speaking of its own family and geo-specific tradition. The dishes are often the distillation of their family's ethnic DNA commingled with the local ingredients in their family's hometown. Recipes of the American landscape are the shared meetings of mixed cultures, each an interpretation or opinion of what was always there in the soil and the wind and the streams. The Native Americans cooked their own dishes with the fruit of the land long before the arrival of diverse immigrant cultures and the influx of international ingredients. Each culture's traditional dishes would soon be interpreted in new ways, by the new citizens. The magnificent mix of European, African, and New World gastronomies has left a delicious imprint across the entire country.

The recipes I have chosen for this book are not

in any sense trendy, modern, or in some cases, even current. These are the dishes that have struck me as speaking of the very place they are served. The vast majority of these recipes are far simpler than many of the dishes I have proposed in my previous cookbooks. These are not my interpretations of classic regional dishes, but instead represent the most common take, the dish most likely found in a local diner—not the finest or fanciest place, but the one seating the most locals eating food they love and recognize. You will more likely find a version of these recipes in the local Rotary Club cookbook than on TV.

Often I tasted a recipe after testing it a few times and thought, *Jeez, this would be good with some hot sauce, or some chopped onions, or some cayenne and lime.* I have noted these suggestions at the end of some of the recipes in orange italic type. These are little changes I might make at my house and are not meant to dismiss the greatness or integrity of the original recipe; they are just how I might adjust a recipe for my continuously jacked-up palate, always in search of a little edge or zing. You can certainly dismiss these and, even better than that, make your own tweaks and tell me about them so I can give them a shot.

I divided the chapters in this book into eight regions that are not only about contiguous geography, but also about shared cooking style and ingredient selection. Parts of New York State are in the New England chapter and yet the Beef on a Weck from Buffalo is in the Great Lakes chapter. Alabama is in both the Deep South and the Gulf Coast because the cooking there has feet on both boats.

In every region I offer up a classic cocktail, and I am justly proud of the fact that you can buy all of the ingredients for all of the drinks in any town in the U.S. You will not need a centrifuge or a smoker for any of these cocktails, more likely just a good thirst.

Each chapter has a pickle and a preserve recipe. These form the backbone of our shared frugality and pioneer experience across the country and are the easiest way to delve into a region's flavor profile.

THE MAGNIFICENT MIX OF EUROPEAN, AFRICAN, AND NEW WORLD GASTRONOMIES HAS LEFT A DELICIOUS IMPRINT ACROSS THE ENTIRE COUNTRY.

I grew up in Washington State and we pickled and canned from spring through the end of fall. The full shelves in the larder or the cellar (or, in our Seattle suburbs, the garage) represented hand-me-down recipes from more than a couple of generations. We would modify each recipe every year as we discovered a better way to keep the crunch in our dill pickles, or the proper viscosity and acidity in our strawberry freezer jam. If it was just a small change, we would scribble it right onto the existing recipe card; if it was a full overhaul, we started a new card. Full shelves also afforded a certain feel of wealth…twenty or thirty jars of blackberry jam

meant months of delicious family-specific luxury, even if just in our lunch bags at school. Once you perfect any one of the pickle recipes in this book, the best thing to do next year is to modify it to your taste, and then practice until it is the perfect expression of your family's palate. Upon perfection, it is your moral responsibility to pass the new, modified, and properly-yours recipe down to your kids or cousins or aunts and uncles.

Of course there are many crossover dishes shared by several regions, especially in the breakfast recipes. I chose the ones that seemed to be most specific to the region. In the case of biscuits and gravy, I went Deep South, although I know that the Rockies and the Plains, as well as the Mid-Atlantic regions, are well represented in the sausage gravy wars. In the world of BBQ, I celebrate much of what I consider to be the very best. I have a couple of pages of roundups to show what I feel to be the salient distinctions between BBQ from the Carolinas, Texas, Kansas City, and Memphis. All you can be sure about is that the sauce, and often the "no sauce," variations are as distinct as the meat cookery.

What fascinates me most about the regional recipes in these United States is the powerful ethnicity unique to the various parts of the country. Nearly every immigrant from Europe, the Caribbean, and Africa in the eighteenth, nineteenth, and twentieth centuries arrived on the eastern seaboard and most came through New York, Boston, Philadelphia, or Baltimore and then moved on to other parts of the country they had heard about where a relative lived. Many of the world's great cultures have informal outposts based in these great cities.

In New York City alone there are large unique and distinct communities representing immigrants from Italy, Ireland, Ukraine, Poland, more than several very specific regions of Russia and of China, Lebanon, Greece, Mexico, Central America, South America, Korea, several countries in Western Africa, the Caribbean, and Puerto Rico, and the list goes on…just in New York City!

THAT IS THE BEAUTY OF THE AMERICAN WAY WITH FOOD: THERE IS A GENEROSITY OF GIVING AND TAKING IN BOTH INGREDIENT SELECTION AND TECHNIQUE AS THE RECIPES EVOLVE.

Each of these Little-You-Name-It-Towns in the city celebrates its diverse culture with its own clubs, churches, and temples, as well as food shops, delis, bakeries, restaurants, and every single non-food category as well. Often business in these locales is conducted in the mother tongue of the immigrant population, and yet all comers are welcome, regardless of their pedigree—it is a business after all.

As the immigrants arrived, they made their decisions. Some chose big cities, some chose small towns, and some started their own communities

throughout the country. As they adapted to their new environment, they cooked up their classics, with their modifications, and their brand-new recipes. All of these recipes now form part of the new American cooking.

As these original immigrants arrived, in wave after wave, each family cook discovered an entirely new way of looking at food, a whole new palette of ingredients, and often to their dismay, the lack of a couple or even many of their favorite ingredients. This provided nearly Proustian moments, some melancholy, some joyous, during many celebrations, when the cook fantasized about an ingredient she could not find; but the need to improvise also served as a catalyst for the cook to discover new ingredients, substituting them for the traditional ones and inventing new dishes based on the New World's bounty. Recipes were changed, modified, and in many cases, so completely refigured as to defy recognition. These new recipes make up a good portion of those you will find in this book.

I am pretty sure there is not a traditional Italian version of the famous Trenton, New Jersey–style tomato pie to be found in Napoli, Italy, but there is no doubt that a Neapolitan would enjoy this new dish. There will also be some purely traditional dishes, like Cornish pasties in the Great Lakes region as well as the French Canadian tourtiere in New England. Both of these dishes, adapted for their new homes, would be recognizable in their birthplace. That is the beauty of the American way with food: There is a generosity of giving and taking in both ingredient selection and technique as the recipes evolve.

In the dessert world, this book is my most ambitious ever. These are not restaurant desserts, but in fact real home-style desserts from Sunday suppers all over the country. Certainly there are thousands of cobbler, crumble, and pie recipes in these United States and Canada, and I tried to include regional specialties along with the classic fruit varieties. But the crazy creamy sweet pies of the upper Midwest, the puddings of the Deep South, the simplest fruit crumbles and crisps of the West, are unique and so delicious, and to my mind, unheralded outside of their own regions, that they almost merit an entire tome themselves.

There is a movement in twenty-first-century cooking that demands only local, only perfect, only

THESE ARE THE DISHES THAT HAVE STRUCK ME AS SPEAKING OF THE VERY PLACE THEY ARE SERVED.

seasonal and emotionally and politically vetted ingredients all of the time. I appreciate this seemingly rigorous attention to detail in sourcing, shopping, cooking, and eating. But let's face facts—sometimes it is just not going to happen. Ideology and reality often intersect perfectly, but sometimes they don't. Do not torture yourself, admonish your friends, or convince yourself or anyone else that there is only one path. Some days the organic local product may simply not be at the store or green market or farm stand when

TO BEST ENJOY THIS BOOK, LOOK AT IT AS A CULINARY TRAVEL GUIDE AROUND THE SMALLER TOWNS AND CITIES OF THE COUNTRY.

you want it. Buying the California romaine at the local grocery, even in local romaine season, does not mean all is lost or that Nigella or Alice Waters will take you off their speed dial. Sometimes cost is a factor, or sometimes it's mere convenience, or even laziness.

Fret not if you are not the perfect high-and-mighty culinary super-being you always hoped you'd become. Life is not always lived exactly as we planned. Do the best that you can to execute your plan, your ideal, your dreamy ideological best-case scenario, but also accept an ingredient, or a menu, or a meal or even meals a few days in a row that may not be ideal; sometimes it just is what it is. There is no defeat if you are cooking at home; you have already won the war against industrially produced, mass-market machine-made food that is devoid of nutrition, fiber, and the building blocks of health, satisfaction, and happiness.

To best enjoy this book, look at it as a culinary travel guide around the smaller towns and cities

of the country. I am often at my happiest traveling by car or by train, stopping often and for irregular times, greedily touching and smelling the sweet or savory local produce at farm stands, intoxicated by the sweet yeasty fragrance of bakeries, smitten by the wafting smell of a woodburning grill, ecstatic in every sense to enjoy the music and rhythm of the locals doing it their way, the way of their families and their traditions—in short, submitting to the life force of just about any town I am in. In some towns it takes a while to crack the code: I couldn't find the real Tampa until I found my new bestie chef Greg Baker, and then… there it was. In other towns, like New Orleans or San Francisco or Charleston or Traverse City, it's hard to miss it.

There are certainly thousands and thousands of recipes not included in this small tome, but this collection represents the dishes I have noticed over four decades traveling around places that, for the most part, I found uniquely and completely delicious. The absence of your favorite dish from Enum-claw, Washington, or from Silly Little Big Town, Nebraska, does not mean I do not like it; it means I probably missed it. The selection process in creating a book of 250-plus recipes out of the 800 or 900 recipes I considered—and the tens of thousands I have not even seen yet—was purely emotional. I hope you agree with many and are starting your own list.

Thanks,

NORTHEAST and NEW ENGLAND

Maine

Vermont

New Hampshire

New York

Massachusetts

BAKED BEANS

Connecticut

Rhode Island

AMONG THE VERY FIRST IMMIGRANTS to land in the Northeastern region that would eventually be called Massachusetts were settlers from England and northern Europe. The history of the Pilgrims, their initial experiences with Native Americans, and many versions of the original Thanksgiving celebration are all well documented. Imagine the joy of the discovery of new ingredients of such depth and deliciousness as fresh local seafood like lobster, clams, flounder, and shad, or unheard of exotica like maple syrup, cranberries, and sweet corn!

Cold climates proved inhospitable to growing crops year-round, particularly the wheat of the English loaves. So corn flour, which had a longer shelf life, was used instead of wheat in the winter months to make things like Johnnycakes and Indian Pudding. The austere, simple cooking of the original settlers, particularly the English Puritans and the Germans, formed much of the spare, frill-free original food in the Northeast. But eventually the Portuguese, the French-Canadians, and the Italians would land and begin to make their mark on local food habits. From the mid-nineteenth through to the beginning of the twentieth century, about a million French-Canadian immigrants made their way south into New England. At the turn of the twentieth century, the Italians had made the Northeast and the Mid-Atlantic their new home, with many Neapolitans settling in and around Boston, Providence, and New York.

My contemporary comrades Lydia Shire, Jasper White, Michael Schlow, Ken Oringer, Jamie Bissonnette, Barbara Lynch, Ming Tsai, Johanne Killeen, and the late George Germon have interpreted these local culinary traditions in their own unique and delightful ways for the past three decades. Their intellectual and gustatory success is to our luxurious benefit as customers and as food historians.

Roadside treasures include **BLUEBERRY PIE** and **JAM** in Maine and New Hampshire; **MAPLE SYRUP CANDY**, **PUDDINGS**, and **DONUTS** in Vermont; plus **CLAMS** in a thousand ways (especially in infinite variations of "chowdah"), **LOBSTER ROLLS**, **CLAM ROLLS**, **OYSTER ROLLS**; and Italian-influenced **GRINDERS**, **SUBS**, and especially **PIZZA**—which has become its own food culture, particularly in New Haven, Connecticut.

A **CLAMBAKE** is just about as much delicious fun as you can have legally in New England; it is for me the maximum expression of this unique and delightful region. If you can wrangle an invite to the real deal, I suggest you bring something from your hometown as a hostess gift, something kind of fancy and handmade, like jam, cookies, or pickles. Perhaps you can make something from this chapter.

Paired with tart buttermilk, the funky, nutty flavor of buckwheat makes a pancake that's much more interesting than the standard. The flavor of buckwheat is so powerful and assertive that some recipes cut it with some all-purpose flour. But you should not, at least on the first try—its funk is my joy!

BUCKWHEAT-BUTTERMILK
PANCAKES

1 cup buckwheat flour

1 tablespoon sugar

1 teaspoon baking powder

½ teaspoon baking soda

½ teaspoon kosher salt

1 large egg, beaten

1 cup buttermilk

2 tablespoons unsalted
    butter, melted

Butter and maple syrup
    for serving

In a large bowl, whisk together the flour, sugar, baking powder, baking soda, and salt. Add the egg, buttermilk, and 2 tablespoons of butter, and beat until smooth.

Heat a griddle or large skillet over medium-high heat and spray with cooking spray. Pour the batter onto the griddle in ¼-cup rounds and cook for 2 or 3 minutes, until small bubbles appear on the surface. Flip and cook until the other side is lightly browned. Repeat with the remaining batter.

Serve warm with butter and maple syrup.

MAKES 8 TO 10 PANCAKES

Pickles and Preserves

When you think about the resurgent popularity of canning, it's important to realize one thing: The period of time when its popularity waned—the time it wasn't an integral part of life—was actually very, very short.

It's a concept etched in the obvious: When we have a lot, we figure out a way to save it for a time when we won't have enough. Whether your bounty comes from your backyard or a farmers' market, you can postpone the mortality of beautiful food-stuff with a little salt, vinegar, or sugar. The pro-cesses—fermenting, pickling, and making jams and jellies—are ancient. And amazing.

If you think this is a trend, just be aware that it was a "trend" that started before recorded time. Don't be intimidated by the process. Sure, it some-times takes a little bit of specialized equipment, but it isn't expensive and it's a onetime investment. After that, you can refill the jars and reuse the pots and tools forever.

Actually, you'll have to buy more jars, for two reasons. Once you see how easy it is, you'll want to can more things. And you'll give a lot of your jars away, filled, as gifts. The only way you'll get those jars back is if your recipient wants refills.

FERMENTING: This is the art of using salt to control the rate something rots to maximize deliciousness. It's science, but it's simple. Take a fruit or vegetable, expose it to salt (and maybe water), and give it time to develop plenty of lactobacillus acid, which to the tongue registers as a tang. It preserves the food and changes it. Sauerkraut (page 72) is the poster child for the process, and the beauty is you can shred almost any vegetable—beets, kohlrabi, turnips—and turn it into kraut. Add a little spice—caraway, chiles, ginger—to customize it. For Scotch Bonnet Hot Sauce (page 202), the peppers ferment for a few days to add character before becoming an ingredient in the more complex sauce. And Deli Dills (page 7) are one of the most beloved expressions, and so, so easy.

PICKLING: Vinegar becomes the agent of change in both "quick" and "putting-up" pickles. These are the ones that, when properly processed, will last on your shelf at room temperature for up to a year. The vinegar aisle is your toolbox: distilled, apple cider, sherry, champagne, white wine, red wine, rice wine. Each vinegar will have an application. You have to watch acidity levels and flavors. The vinegar becomes a brine with the addition of salt, sweet, and spice. The art is in combining the right vegetable with the right vinegar with the right enhancements. Recipes: Pickled Asparagus, page 320; Pickled Tart Cherries, page 252; Chow-Chow, page 124; Pickled Jalapeños, page 379; We Can Pickle That, page 434; Pickled Red Onion, page 471.

JAMS AND JELLIES: Fruit seasons can be notoriously short. For instance, peaches are at their peak for a couple of glorious summer months. But blink and you'll miss cherry season entirely. The beauty is that when they are available, they're abundant, and that abundance makes them more economical. So stock up and put the season in a time capsule. Sugar and a little bit of acid are the preservatives here. The balance of those things in concert with pectin, which occurs naturally in many fruits, will help you achieve the consistency you want. But it isn't really important. A thin jelly is a thick syrup and no less delicious. Recipes: Blueberry Jam, page 8; Traverse City Tart Cherry Preserves, page 253; Bourbon-Peach Jam, page 125; Orange Marmalade, page 205; Fig-Lemon Jam, page 385; Apple Butter, page 74.

You know those crazy delicious dills you can only seem to find at the deli in New York? You're never going to believe how easy they are to make at home.

DELI
DILLS

Wash 4 (1-quart) canning jars in hot water.

In a medium saucepan, heat 4 cups water, add the salt, and stir until dissolved. Remove from the heat and add 2 cups ice water. Allow to cool completely.

Into each jar, drop 2 cloves garlic, 4 sprigs of dill, 2 teaspoons pepper, and 1 teaspoon coriander. Evenly distribute the cucumbers among the jars, packing them tight. Pour the cooled brine into each jar to fill; the cucumbers need to be covered in the brine. Cover, but don't seal the jars. Either put a lid on top with no ring, or cover with cheesecloth kept in place with a rubber band.

Take a picture of your jars, because they'll be beautiful and you'll want to remember that in a couple days when they look like a science experiment gone awry.

After 3 days, the brine will be cloudy and the pickles will be half-sour. If that's your preference, put a lid on the jar and put it in the refrigerator. If you want full-sour, let them go a full 5 days before putting them in the fridge.

Either way, eat them within 6 weeks.

MAKES 4 QUARTS

¾ cup kosher salt

8 cloves garlic

16 sprigs fresh dill

8 teaspoons black peppercorns or crushed red pepper flakes

4 teaspoons coriander

4 pounds small pickling cucumbers, washed and stem ends trimmed; whole, cut in half lengthwise, or into spears

If I had some chile peppers in the house—and I always have chile peppers—I'd drop them in for a nice kick.

The mid-summer blueberry bounty presents itself at farm stands, sure, but also in U-pick fields, in backyards, and—perhaps best—wild on a random hillside. The strategy: Get as many as you can while they're here, make a pie (see page 51), and put up a dozen or so pints as jam for the eleven months of the year they aren't available fresh. You will thank me in February. (Pictured on page 23.)

BLUEBERRY JAM

6 cups fresh blueberries, rinsed, stems removed

3 cups sugar

Zest and juice of 1 lemon

½ teaspoon freshly grated nutmeg

In a large saucepan, mash the blueberries with a potato masher. Add the sugar, lemon zest and juice, and nutmeg. Turn the heat to medium-high and bring to a boil, stirring. Reduce the heat to medium-low and continue to cook for 20 to 30 minutes. Test the jam by doing a frozen-plate test as described on page 9.

Remove from the heat and skim off any foam. Carefully pour into 4 sterilized half-pint jars. Seal and process according to the directions on page 9, or search for "USDA canning guide" on the web for the latest guidelines.

MAKES 4 HALF-PINTS

To Can Jams and Pickles

Any jam or pickle recipe can be made, refrigerated, and used within a month or so without proper canning. But if you'd like to "put up" your haul, you'll need canning jars with lids and rings, a large pot, a jar lifter, a canning funnel, and a magnetic wand, most of which you can get as part of an inexpensive kit at your local hardware store.

To prepare the jars for canning, you can run them through the dishwasher on the "sterilize" cycle, or submerge them in a pot of boiling water for 10 minutes. To prepare the lids and rings, place them in a saucepan of water over low heat for 10 minutes. Don't boil those.

Allow the jars and lids to air dry while you prepare the recipe. When the recipe is ready, fill the jars, using the funnel to protect the rims. Fill to within ½ inch of the rim. Use a lint-free cloth to carefully clean the rim, then pick up a lid with the magnetic wand and place on the jar. Take a ring and hand-tighten it. When all the jars are ready, use the jar lifter to place the jars back in the pot of boiling water, and—in most locations—boil for about 10 minutes. (If you live at a high elevation, you might need to boil for as long as 30 minutes.)

After processing the jars, use the jar lifter to remove them from the pot and place them on a towel on the counter to let them cool. As they cool, the lids will "ping!," telling you they've safely sealed. If one doesn't seal, put that jar in the fridge and eat it first.

Properly processed pickles and preserves are good for about a year.

THE FROZEN-PLATE TEST: Before you start cooking the jam, place two plates in the freezer. When you think the jam might be ready, pull one plate out of the freezer and spoon a little jam on it. Put the plate back in the freezer for 2 minutes. After 2 minutes, remove from the freezer and touch the surface: It should be slightly gelled. This is like a look into the future; it's what the jam will look like after it's processed. If it seems right, proceed to the canning step. If it isn't thick enough, you can cook it more, or add more pectin, then retest using the second plate.

Like so many great debates, the Battle of Clam Chowder—cream (New England) or tomato (Manhattan)?—would be best solved by substituting "and" for "or." Both are delicious and deserve celebration. If the clams are bigger than cherrystones, I tend to go with New England style; it's the variety I grew up with and bigger chunks of tender clam seem more at home in a bath of pearlescent ivory broth.

NEW ENGLAND
CLAM CHOWDER

36 Manila or cherrystone clams

4 ounces bacon or salt pork, chopped

1 medium onion, finely chopped

2 stalks celery, finely chopped

2 medium potatoes, peeled and cut into ¼-inch dice

1 teaspoon kosher salt

1 teaspoon freshly ground white pepper

¼ cup all-purpose flour

2¼ cups milk

Put the clams in a Dutch oven and cover with water. Bring to a boil, cover the pot, and cook for 1 minute. With tongs, pull out the clams that have opened. For any that haven't, cover and cook another minute. Discard any that don't open.

Remove most of the clams from their shells, reserving 12 in their shells. Mince the clams that were removed from their shells. Strain the clam water to remove any grit and reserve.

Rinse the Dutch oven. Add the bacon and fry over medium-high heat to render some fat. Add the onion and celery and sauté until soft, about 5 minutes. Add 2 cups of the reserved strained clam water, the potatoes, and the salt and pepper. Cover, reduce the heat to medium, and cook for 10 to 15 minutes, until the potatoes are tender.

In a bowl, whisk together the flour and ¼ cup of the milk to form a smooth slurry. Whisk the mixture into the pot and raise the heat to medium-high, continuing to whisk until the chowder boils. Add the remaining 2 cups milk and whisk until smooth. When the soup has thickened, add the clams, including the ones still in the shells, and cook for 3 to 4 minutes, just to warm the clams up. Serve, prominently placing 1 or 2 of the clams in shells in each serving.

MAKES 2 QUARTS, SERVING 6 TO 8

I like more celery flavor, so I might add 1 cup celery root in ½-inch dice with the mirepoix.

MANHATTAN

CLAM CHOWDER

Put the clams in a Dutch oven and cover with water. Bring to a boil, cover the pot, and cook for 1 minute. With tongs, pull out the clams that have opened. For any that haven't, cover and cook another minute. Discard any that don't open.

Remove most of the clams from their shells, reserving 12 in their shells. Mince the clams that were removed from their shells. Strain the clam water and reserve.

Rinse the Dutch oven. Add the bacon and fry over medium-high heat to render some fat. Add the onion and sauté until soft, about 5 minutes. Add the celery and carrot and sauté for 3 minutes. Add 4 cups of the reserved strained cooking liquid, the potatoes, tomatoes, salt, and pepper. Stir, bring to a boil, cover, and reduce the heat to medium-low. Simmer for 20 minutes, then add the clams, including the ones still in the shells, and cook for 3 to 4 minutes, just to warm the clams up. Serve, prominently placing 1 or 2 of the clams in shells in each serving, with crusty bread.

MAKES 2 QUARTS, SERVING 6 TO 8

36 Manila or cherrystone clams

4 ounces bacon, chopped

1 medium onion, finely chopped

2 stalks celery, finely chopped

1 large carrot, finely chopped

2 medium potatoes, peeled and cut into ¼-inch dice

1 (28-ounce) can crushed tomatoes, pureed in the food processor

1 teaspoon kosher salt

1 teaspoon freshly ground black pepper

Crusty bread for serving

It's safe to assume that corn chowder was born on a day that someone came up empty when they went out clamming. Traditionally, this would use chicken stock, but here we get everything we can out of the corncob instead. If you can't get good corn on the cob, substitute frozen corn: Add half the kernels instead of the cobs and cob milk, puree the soup, then add the rest of the kernels.

CORN CHOWDER

In a large pot over medium-high heat, heat the oil and sauté the onion and celery until soft, about 5 minutes. Add 4 cups water, the milk scraped from the cobs, and as many of the cobs as can be submerged and bring to a boil. Cover, reduce the heat to medium-low, and cook for 30 minutes. Remove the cobs and discard. Add the potatoes and salt and cook until the potatoes are tender, about 10 minutes. Puree with an immersion blender until it is a consistency you like. Add the corn kernels and milk, stir, and simmer for 5 minutes. Season with pepper to taste and serve hot.

MAKES 2 QUARTS, SERVING 6 TO 8

2 tablespoons extra-virgin olive oil

1 large onion, finely diced

2 stalks celery, sliced very thin

10 ears corn, kernels cut off the cob (about 7 cups), the milk from the cobs scraped with the back of a knife into a bowl and reserved

2 large potatoes, peeled and cut into ½-inch dice

1 teaspoon kosher salt

2 cups milk

Freshly ground black pepper

I love adding 2 or 3 ounces of good country ham, cut into julienne, with the onion and celery. It gives a rich smoky flavor that may scare away the vegetarians…or get them to reconsider their ways.

Other than the mussels themselves, the only thing you need here is a flavorful liquid to steam them open and some crusty bread to sop up the addictive broth when you're done. Wine is classic, but no one will argue if you use beer or stock. This would be an excellent use for what is commonly referred to as "leftover wine" from another meal, a situation that has never happened at my house.

STEAMED MUSSELS

3 tablespoons unsalted butter

1 medium shallot, minced

3 cloves garlic, thinly sliced

1½ cups dry white wine

2 pounds mussels, scrubbed

2 tablespoons fresh tarragon, chopped

1 bunch flat-leaf parsley, finely chopped to yield ¼ cup

Slices of crusty bread, toasted

In a large, straight-sided skillet, heat the butter over medium-high heat. When it has melted, sauté the shallot and garlic for about 4 minutes. Add the wine and bring to a boil, then add the mussels, cover, reduce the heat to medium-low, and simmer for about 6 minutes. Remove opened mussels to a serving bowl. For any that haven't opened, cover the skillet and give them another minute or two. Discard any that don't open. Stir the tarragon and parsley into the cooking liquid and pour over the mussels. Serve with toasted bread.

SERVES 2 TO 4

It makes a lot of sense to add 2 tablespoons grain mustard when you add the wine, and maybe even ¼ cup cream to smooth it out.

You might think the New England corn muffin and Southern Cornbread (page 126) are similar. Not the case. The corn muffin celebrates the sweetness of corn by adding more sugar, and then honey for good measure. You'd have a hard time convincing a Southerner that either of those ideas was good.

CORN MUFFINS

2 cups all-purpose flour

1 cup cornmeal

½ cup sugar

2 tablespoons baking powder

1 teaspoon kosher salt

2 large eggs

1 cup milk

¼ cup honey

4 tablespoons unsalted butter, melted

Preheat the oven to 400°F. Spray the cups of a 12-cup muffin tin with cooking spray.

Combine the flour, cornmeal, sugar, baking powder, and salt in a medium bowl. Add the eggs, milk, honey, and butter and stir until well blended. Spoon the batter in the cups of the muffin tin, nearly filling each. Bake for about 15 minutes, or until they begin to turn golden.

MAKES 12 MUFFINS

I might sprinkle ½ teaspoon freshly grated pecorino Romano on top of each muffin before they go in the oven, and then call them Italian polenta muffins.

MANHATTAN

MAKES 1 COCKTAIL

The ratios have varied widely in this classic since its introduction in the late 1800s, and by some accounts this was once a vermouth drink with a little rye in it. Modern versions favor the whiskey.

3 ounces rye whiskey

½ ounce sweet red vermouth

2 dashes Angostura bitters

1 maraschino cherry is classic, but I prefer a brandied cherry

Combine the rye, vermouth, and bitters in a cocktail shaker with ice. Shake well, but do not froth up. Strain into a chilled martini glass with a cherry as a garnish.

The very shape of the clamshell invites stuffing, and anywhere you find clams, you'll find people stuffing them. In the immigrant communities on the coasts of Massachusetts and Rhode Island, Stuffies are nothing short of a signature. There is always pork, there is always bread, and there are rarely leftovers. I make two each as an appetizer, but any clam lover can consume four easily.

RHODE ISLAND
STUFFIES

Preheat the oven to 350°F. In a large, heavy pot or Dutch oven, bring 2 cups water to a boil. Drop the clams in the pot, cover, and steam for about 8 minutes, removing the clams as they open. Discard any that don't open after 10 minutes. When they're cooked, remove the meat from the shells and chop it finely. Set the meat and shells aside. Strain the cooking liquid through cheesecloth and set it aside.

Clean the clamshells and arrange them open side up on a baking sheet.

In a large skillet, melt the butter over medium-high heat and sauté the onion, pepper, and celery until the onion has softened, about 5 minutes. Add the garlic and sausage and cook for about 3 minutes. Stir in the clams and the bread crumbs. Add up to ¾ cup of the reserved cooking liquid, ¼ cup at a time, until the stuffing is moistened.

Spoon the stuffing into the shells, mounding it generously. Sprinkle the cheese over the stuffing. Bake for 15 to 20 minutes, until the stuffing starts to brown. Serve with lemon wedges and hot sauce.

MAKES 16 STUFFIES

8 quahog or other large clams, rinsed and scrubbed

3 tablespoons unsalted butter

1 onion, finely chopped

½ green bell pepper, finely chopped

1 stalk celery, finely chopped

2 cloves garlic, thinly sliced

8 ounces chourico or other dry, spicy sausage, finely diced

1½ cups fresh bread crumbs, toasted

2 tablespoons grated Parmigiano-Reggiano

Lemon wedges and hot sauce for serving

These little blini-like pancakes have become a trendy vehicle for hors d'oeuvres, but legend has it that they originated when Pilgrim women would cook them for men who were going on a journey. Regional dialects being what they are, "journey" became "johnny." The journeys must have been successful, though. Johnnycakes eventually became a staple throughout the South and Midwest. Definitely serve with butter. Serving with maple syrup or your favorite jam is either a moral imperative or heresy, depending on where you hail from.

JOHNNYCAKES

1 cup cornmeal, preferably white

1 teaspoon sugar

½ teaspoon kosher salt

6 tablespoons milk

1 piece of salt pork, rind removed (You can substitute with 1 tablespoon of either bacon fat or butter.)

In a small pot, boil 1 cup of water. (This is key—warm/hot water doesn't work—it must be boiling!)

Preheat a griddle over medium-high heat.

In a bowl, whisk together the cornmeal, sugar, salt, and the 1 cup boiling water until the mixture thickens. Let the batter rest 10 minutes, then whisk in the milk.

Place a fork into the piece of salt pork and drag it across the top of the hot griddle to grease it. Drop heaping tablespoonfuls of batter onto the griddle and cook for 3 to 4 minutes, until the edges set. Flip and cook on the other side for 4 to 5 minutes, until the cake is firm. Repeat with the remaining batter.

MAKES 12 JOHNNYCAKES

I might spread some room-temperature soft runny cheese like ripe brie or teleme on these, with a little Dijon or even horseradish, and serve them warm as an appetizer.

If you figure that we as a nation just kept Fish and Chips when we kicked the British out, your history is a little off. It hadn't been invented yet. The combination became popular here in the mid-1800s, about the same time the London working class was making it Britain's iconic dish.

FISH AND CHIPS

FOR THE FISH AND CHIPS

Canola or corn oil for deep-frying

2 cups all-purpose flour

1 teaspoon baking powder

1 teaspoon kosher salt plus more for seasoning

1 (16-ounce) bottle beer

1 large egg, lightly beaten

2 pounds russet potatoes (3 to 4 large potatoes), each cut lengthwise into 8 wedges, soaked in ice water for at least an hour

2 pounds cod fillets, cut into 8 pieces

Freshly ground black pepper

FOR THE TARTAR SAUCE

1 cup mayonnaise

½ cup sour cream

3 tablespoons chopped capers

3 tablespoons chopped pickles (gherkins preferred) plus 2 tablespoons of the brining liquid

1 tablespoon Dijon mustard

Juice of ½ lemon

Lemon wedges for serving

Malt vinegar for serving, optional

FOR THE FISH AND CHIPS: In a large, heavy pot or Dutch oven, heat 3 inches of oil to 300°F. Preheat the oven to 225°F.

In a large bowl, whisk together the flour, baking powder, salt, beer, and egg.

Line two baking sheets with newspaper and top with a wire rack. Remove the potatoes from the water and place on a clean kitchen towel, getting them as dry as possible.

Working in batches, carefully add the fries to the oil and cook for 5 to 8 minutes, until they are starting to cook but aren't browned. Remove the fries from the oil and scatter on the wire rack. Repeat to cook all the fries, then place them in the warm oven while you cook the fish. Increase the temperature of the oil to 360°F.

Dry the fish with a paper towel and season with salt and pepper. Working in batches, dip the fish in the beer batter, then carefully lower the pieces into the oil. Fry for about 6 minutes, turning halfway through. When they're golden brown, remove to the other baking sheet and keep warm in the oven while you fry the rest of the fish.

When all the fish is fried, bring the oil back up to 360°F, return the fries to the oil in batches, and fry until golden brown, just a minute or two. Remove to a paper towel–lined bowl to drain and season with salt immediately.

FOR THE TARTAR SAUCE: Combine the mayonnaise, sour cream, chopped capers, chopped pickles and juice, mustard, and lemon juice in a bowl. Stir to combine.

Serve the fish and chips on a plate, with the tartar sauce, lemon wedges, and malt vinegar, if using, on the side.

SERVES 6 TO 8

Before there was the United States or Canada, there was Tourtiere. While the meat pie is rightly thought of as indigenous to Quebec, the tradition is just as legit in the upper reaches of New Hampshire and Vermont. My French-Canadian grandfather made what I consider to be the definitive version of this around the Christmas holidays and I can still taste it to this day.

TOURTIERE

2 tablespoons extra-virgin olive oil

2 pounds ground pork

1 medium onion, finely chopped

3 green onions, thinly sliced, white and green parts separated

4 medium potatoes, about 1 pound, peeled and diced

1 teaspoon kosher salt

1 teaspoon cinnamon

Pinch allspice

Pinch ground cloves

1 tablespoon milk

Basic Pie Crust (page 481), one crust in 9-inch pan, the second crust rolled out

In a large skillet over medium-high heat, heat the oil and sauté the pork, onion, and the white parts of the green onions briefly. Add the potatoes, salt, and 1 cup water. Bring to a boil, then reduce the heat to medium and simmer gently, stirring often, until the liquid evaporates, about 1 hour.

Preheat the oven to 350°F.

Add the cinnamon, allspice, cloves, milk, and the green parts of the green onions to the pork mixture and stir to combine, mashing the potatoes as you stir. Spoon the pork mixture into the pie shell. Cover the pie with the top crust, crimping the edges to seal. With a sharp knife or fork, poke a few holes in the top crust to vent. Bake for 50 to 55 minutes, until the crust is golden. Let cool for at least 20 minutes before serving.

SERVES 6 TO 8

Perhaps the most succinctly named dish in culinary history, Boiled Dinner gets little culinary cred, but it might be the most-served dish in American history. It's not entirely original; the New England version certainly immigrated with the first settlers from the major European cultures.

NEW ENGLAND
BOILED DINNER

Place the corned beef in a large, heavy pot or Dutch oven, cover with water, and bring to a boil. Add the thyme and onions, cover the pot, and let the water return to a boil. Lower the heat to a high simmer, cover, and cook for about 3 hours. Add the cabbage, cover, and cook for 30 minutes. Add the potatoes, carrots, parsnips, and turnips, cover, and cook for 20 minutes, until the vegetables are tender.

Meanwhile, in a small bowl, mix the horseradish and sour cream and season with salt and pepper. Serve from the pot at the table, with the horseradish on the side.

SERVES 6 TO 8

1 (4-pound) corned beef

2 tablespoons chopped fresh thyme

2 large onions, quartered

1 head savoy cabbage, quartered

1 pound new potatoes, scrubbed

4 carrots, each peeled and cut into 3 pieces

4 parsnips, each peeled and cut into 3 pieces

4 turnips, peeled and halved

½ cup prepared horseradish

½ cup sour cream

Kosher salt and freshly ground black pepper

Lobster seems like such a luxury in most parts of the world that it may be hard to understand what it's like to have so much lobster that you make pot pies with it. In Maine, they understand. Some days I skip the crust and instead sprinkle ¼ cup crushed Ritz crackers evenly over the top of each pie (and bake for 6 to 8 minutes). You might want to give it a try. It is oddly luxurious.

LOBSTER POT PIES

1 medium potato, peeled and cut into ½-inch dice

1 large carrot, peeled and cut into ½-inch dice

6 tablespoons unsalted butter

6 tablespoons all-purpose flour

3 cups milk

2 tablespoons sherry, optional

½ teaspoon paprika

Kosher salt and freshly ground black pepper

Cooked meat from four 1-pound lobsters, steamed or boiled (about 4 cups total)

½ cup fresh or frozen peas

Basic Pie Crust (page 481)

In a medium saucepan over medium-high heat, bring some salted water to a boil. Add the potato and carrot and cook until slightly tender, about 8 minutes. Drain and reserve.

Preheat the oven to 400°F. Grease eight 8-ounce ramekins and arrange on a baking sheet.

In a large skillet, melt the butter over medium-high heat, whisk in the flour, and stir for about 2 minutes. Add the milk and sherry, if using, and whisk until it thickens. Remove from the heat, add the paprika, and season with salt and pepper. Add the lobster, peas, and cooked potato and carrot and toss to coat. Evenly divide the mixture among the ramekins.

Roll out the pie crust and cut pieces big enough to loosely cover each ramekin.

Bake for 12 to 14 minutes, until the crusts are browned. Serve hot.

MAKES 8 INDIVIDUAL POT PIES

There are two signs of spring in Connecticut: the shad running in the Connecticut River, and the fires set up, surrounded by wood racks to cook them on. In an official Shad Bake, the fish is strapped onto the cooking surface with strips of pork.

INDOOR
SHAD BAKE

3 slices smoky bacon

2 boneless shad fillets

Kosher salt and freshly ground black pepper, as desired

Lemon wedges

Preheat the oven to 350°F.

In a large, oven-safe skillet over medium-high heat, cook the bacon until crisp. Crumble and set aside. Pour off all but about 1 tablespoon of the bacon fat. Place the shad fillets in the pan, skin side down, and season with salt and pepper. Bake in the oven for 15 to 20 minutes. Serve with the crumbled bacon over the top of the fish and lemon wedges on the side.

SERVES 2 TO 4

The pot roast is one of those dishes that is practically a synonym for dinner. At its soul, it's a way to marry inexpensive ingredients so the dish becomes more than the sum of the parts. Chuck roast is the traditional centerpiece, but any tough cut of meat is an option: brisket, lamb shanks, or short ribs.

YANKEE
POT ROAST

Preheat the oven to 350°F.

Generously season the roast with salt and pepper. In a large, ovenproof heavy pot or Dutch oven, heat the oil over medium heat. Add the salt pork and cook until rendered, about 5 minutes. Remove the salt pork, but leave all the fat in the pot. Turn the heat to medium-high and brown each side of the roast, 8 to 10 minutes per side.

Return the rendered salt pork pieces to the pot, along with the carrots, onions, wine, 2 cups of the stock, and the rosemary and thyme. Bring to a boil, cover, and roast in the oven for 2 hours. Check occasionally to make sure there is plenty of liquid in the pot. If it gets low, add more stock or water. After 2 hours, add the potatoes, and bake, uncovered, for another 30 minutes.

Transfer the meat and vegetables to a platter. Put the pot over medium-high heat and bring the liquid to a boil. In a small bowl, whisk the flour into the remaining ½ cup of room-temperature stock. Pull the pot off the heat, whisk in the slurry, then return to the heat and continue whisking until the gravy thickens.

Serve the meat and vegetables with the gravy on the side.

SERVES 6 TO 8

1 chuck roast, 2 to 3 pounds

Kosher salt and freshly ground black pepper

1 tablespoon extra-virgin olive oil

4 ounces salt pork, cut into ¼-inch dice

2 large carrots, peeled and cut into 2-inch chunks

2 medium onions, quartered

2 cups red wine

2½ cups beef stock or broth

1 tablespoon chopped fresh rosemary

1 tablespoon chopped fresh thyme

1 pound small red-skin potatoes, halved

2 tablespoons all-purpose flour

Do you have an anodized, nonstick loaf pan that you paid a lot of money for at a fancy kitchen supply store? Leave it in the cabinet. This bread gets cooked in a coffee can, and the more times you make the bread in the same can, the better and more authentic it will taste. A slice or two is almost mandatory with a bowl of Boston Baked Beans (page 38).

BOSTON
BROWN BREAD

¾ cup rye flour

¾ cup cornmeal

¾ cup whole wheat flour

1 teaspoon baking soda

1 teaspoon kosher salt

1 cup buttermilk

¾ cup molasses

1 large egg, lightly beaten

Fill a large, deep pot about one-fourth full with water and bring to a boil over medium-high heat. Liberally spray the inside of a clean coffee can (one with a capacity of between 12 and 16 ounces) with cooking spray.

In a bowl, combine all the ingredients and mix well. Pour the mixture into the coffee can, leaving room for the bread to rise during cooking. Cover the can with foil and tie it in place with butcher's twine.

Place the can in the pot and cover the pot. Reduce the heat to medium-low and let the bread steam for 2 hours. Remove the bread from the can while it's still warm. If the bread doesn't easily slide out, use a can opener to remove the bottom of the can and gently nudge it out.

MAKES 10 TO 12 SLICES

It isn't unusual for dishes to be named after the city where they originated, but a dish goes to another level when it becomes part of the city's identity. "Bean Town" may be a nickname Boston embraces less these days, but it's one that was earned honestly and heroically. (Pictured on page 37.)

BOSTON
BAKED BEANS

1½ pounds dried white beans, about 3 cups

½ cup molasses

2 tablespoons tomato paste

1 tablespoon Colman's dry mustard

1 teaspoon kosher salt plus more for seasoning

½ teaspoon freshly ground black pepper plus more for seasoning

2 cloves

½ pound salt pork or bacon, cut into small pieces

1 medium onion, finely chopped

Soak the beans overnight. Drain. In a large, ovenproof heavy pot or Dutch oven, cover the beans with water and bring to a boil over high heat. Cover, reduce the heat to low, and simmer for 1 hour. Drain the beans and return them to the pot.

Preheat the oven to 325°F.

In a small bowl, mix the molasses, tomato paste, mustard, salt, pepper, and cloves.

Add the pork and onion to the beans and toss, then pour the molasses mixture over the beans.

Add 3 cups water and return the pot to a boil. Cover and bake in the oven for 4 hours. Check occasionally to see if the beans need more water. Season with salt and pepper and serve warm.

SERVES 8 TO 10

I just might take some thin slices of Boston Brown Bread (page 36) and lay them on top of the beans in the last hour of cooking in the oven, pushing them gently so they are almost submerged, where they will form a miraculous crust.

In New England, there is a major discussion as to whether a Lobster Roll is properly dressed with mayonnaise or simply with butter. In Maine, it's definitely mayonnaise; in Connecticut, it's definitely butter. There are clearly no losers here, but I prefer the Maine version.

LOBSTER ROLLS

¼ cup mayonnaise

1 tablespoon fresh lemon juice

1 stalk celery, finely chopped

Cooked meat from three
  1-pound lobsters, steamed
  or boiled, coarsely chopped
  (about 3 cups total)

1 tablespoon unsalted butter

4 hot dog buns, preferably
  split-top

Celery salt

In a bowl, stir together the mayonnaise, lemon juice, and celery. Add the lobster and gently toss to coat.

Heat a griddle or large skillet over medium heat. Lightly butter the cut sides of regular hot dog buns or the soft outer edges of split-top buns. Toast the buttered surfaces on the griddle until they slightly brown, turning as necessary.

Pile on the lobster, luxuriously overloading the buns. Shake some celery salt over the tops and serve.

SERVES 4

In New England, clams are whole-belly steamers, not the ubiquitous strips you might find in the freezer section. Whole-belly clams bring more flavor and a taste of the sea, making them the perfect choice for this clam roll, the focal point of commerce at beachside shacks across the region.

CLAM ROLLS

FOR THE CLAMS: In a bowl, combine the cornmeal, flour, salt, and paprika. In a large, heavy pot or Dutch oven over medium-high heat, bring about 2 inches of oil to 370°F.

Toss the clams in the cornmeal mixture to coat them. Working in batches if necessary, put the clams in a large spider or fry basket and shake off the excess dry mixture. Drop the clams into the oil and fry for about 3 minutes, until golden and crispy. Remove to a paper towel–lined platter and immediately season with a little more salt.

FOR THE ROLLS: Heat a griddle or large skillet over medium heat. Butter the cut sides of the hot dog rolls. Toast on the griddle, butter sides down, until nicely browned. Swipe a streak of tartar sauce on the bun. Pile fried clams up high and serve with lemon wedges and hot sauce for last-second personalization.

MAKES 4 GENEROUS CLAM ROLLS

FOR THE CLAMS

½ cup cornmeal

½ cup all-purpose flour

1 teaspoon kosher salt plus more for seasoning

½ teaspoon sweet paprika

Canola or corn oil for frying

1½ pounds shucked whole-belly steamer clams (18 to 20 clams)

FOR THE ROLLS

1 tablespoon unsalted butter

4 hot dog buns, preferably split-top

Tartar Sauce (page 24)

Lemon wedges and hot sauce for serving

I make a dusting salt (let's call it my Spiced Salt) with 3 tablespoons each kosher salt, cayenne, and celery seeds and 1 tablespoon lemon zest and grind it together in the food processor until it's dust. I sprinkle it instead of the salt over the hot clams—and often on anything I fry at home, and sometimes on my breakfast eggs! Mmmmmm.

Succotash has come to mean a lot of things throughout the country, and every region has a history with some concoction of vegetables they call succotash. But before there were any of those, there was *msickquatash*, the Narragansett word for a dish of boiled corn that was appropriated by European settlers.

NARRAGANSETT
SUCCOTASH

In a large saucepan, just cover the lima beans with water. Bring to a boil, then lower the heat and simmer until tender, about 2 minutes. Add the corn and cook to heat through, about 2 minutes more. Drain and toss with the melted butter, tomato, salt and pepper to taste, and nutmeg. Serve hot.

SERVES 6 TO 8

2 cups shelled lima beans, fresh, or thawed from frozen

2 cups corn kernels, from about 3 ears of corn

2 tablespoons unsalted butter, melted

1 large tomato, diced

Kosher salt and freshly ground black pepper

½ teaspoon freshly grated nutmeg

I might sprinkle this with a couple of tablespoons of fresh mint chiffonade; it would sure taste right.

Grape-Nuts cereal is a popular mix-in to desserts in two places: the New England seaboard (specifically Maine) and parts of the Caribbean. The connection is unclear, but they're both right. This ice cream tastes like it has a cone built in.

GRAPE-NUTS
ICE CREAM

6 large egg yolks

½ cup sugar

¼ teaspoon kosher salt

1½ cups heavy cream

½ cup malted milk powder

1½ cups whole milk

1 teaspoon vanilla extract

½ cup Grape-Nuts cereal plus more for optional garnish

In a bowl, whisk together the egg yolks, sugar, and salt. Add the cream and malted milk powder and whisk them in.

In a large saucepan over medium heat, warm the milk to 180°F. Whisk the cream mixture in and bring the temperature to 170°F, whisking constantly. Remove from the heat and strain through a fine-mesh sieve into a container. Cover and refrigerate for several hours, until completely chilled.

Whisk in the vanilla, then freeze the mixture in an ice cream maker according to the manufacturer's instructions.

Just before the ice cream is done turning, add the cereal and let the machine stir it into the ice cream. Freeze for at least 2 hours before serving.

MAKES ABOUT 1½ QUARTS

These cream-filled sandwich cakes are wildly popular in Maine and parts of Central Pennsylvania, where they're sometimes called Gobs. As sexy as the name sounds, the legend is that kids would shout "Whoopie!" when they got one, and the name stuck. I often tell my friends and associates to embrace their inner child more often...*Wheeeeeeeeeeeeeeeeee!*

WHOOPIE PIES

FOR THE CAKES

½ cup shortening

1 cup firmly packed brown sugar

2 large egg yolks

1 teaspoon vanilla extract

2 cups all-purpose flour

¼ cup unsweetened cocoa powder

1 teaspoon baking powder

1 teaspoon baking soda

1 teaspoon kosher salt

1 cup milk

FOR THE FILLING

2 large egg whites

1 cup shortening

2 cups confectioners' sugar

½ teaspoon kosher salt

1 teaspoon vanilla extract

FOR THE CAKES: Preheat the oven to 350°F. Line two baking sheets with silicone mats or parchment paper and lightly spray with cooking spray.

In a stand mixer with the paddle attachment, cream together the shortening, sugar, yolks, and vanilla. In another bowl, sift together the flour, cocoa, baking powder, baking soda, and salt.

Add half the dry ingredients to the shortening mixture, beating to incorporate. Add the milk, then the rest of the dry ingredients and mix until smooth.

Scoop ¼-cup portions of the batter—a large ice cream dasher works well—onto the prepared baking sheets to form 16 cakes, leaving about 2 inches between portions. Pat to form 2½-inch circles. I usually get 8 cakes on each baking sheet. Bake for 15 minutes, until the cakes are set. Let cool on a wire rack.

FOR THE FILLING: In a stand mixer with the paddle attachment, beat the egg whites to stiff peaks. Transfer to another bowl and set aside. Return the bowl and paddle attachment to the stand mixer—no need to clean them, it's all going to end up together anyway—and cream together the shortening and sugar, then add the salt and vanilla. Take the bowl off the stand mixer. Add the egg whites to the shortening mixture and use a whisk to mix them together. The goal is fluff. You might lose a little volume, but whisking will make it a lot easier to mix homogeneously.

TO ASSEMBLE: When the cakes are completely cool, spread the flat side of one chocolate cake with a generous amount of filling. Top with another cake, pressing down gently to distribute the filling evenly. Repeat with all the cakes.

Wrap the Whoopie Pies individually in plastic wrap, or place them in a single layer on a platter (do not stack them, as they'll stick together).

The wrapped pies can be frozen. Defrost them in the refrigerator before serving.

MAKES 8 PIES

The classic Maine-style blueberry pie may come out a little on the soupy side. That's how it's meant to be; ask anyone from Maine. Served with a scoop of ice cream, it doubles as a sauce! Wild Maine blueberries are smaller and a little more tannic and definitely worth the search.

WILD
BLUEBERRY PIE

Preheat the oven to 400°F.

Gently toss the berries with the flour and the ½ cup sugar. Sprinkle with lemon juice. Let stand 10 minutes.

Pour the berries into the pie shell. Scatter the butter over the berries. Place the second crust over the pie and crimp the edges to seal. With a sharp knife, cut a few slashes in the top crust to vent. (If you want to get fancy, feel free to cut strips of crust and weave a lattice top instead.) Brush the top crust with the egg and sprinkle with the 2 tablespoons sugar. Bake for 45 to 50 minutes, until the crust is brown and the filling bubbles up through the vents. Cool completely before serving.

SERVES 6 TO 8

5 cups wild blueberries, fresh or frozen, washed and stems removed

¼ cup all-purpose flour

½ cup sugar plus 2 tablespoons for the crust

1 teaspoon lemon juice

Basic Pie Crust (page 481), one crust in a 9-inch pan, second crust rolled out

1½ tablespoons cold unsalted butter, cut into small cubes

1 large egg, beaten

Through the vagaries of vernacular in the mid-1800s, this dessert, which was, is, and always will be a cake, took on the name of "pie." It was conceived by a chef at the Parker House Hotel and has since sensibly been named the official dessert of Massachusetts.

BOSTON CREAM PIE

FOR THE CAKE

1½ cups cake flour

1 tablespoon baking powder

½ teaspoon kosher salt

½ cup (1 stick) unsalted butter

¾ cup sugar

1 teaspoon vanilla extract

2 large eggs

½ cup milk

FOR THE FILLING

½ cup sugar

¼ cup cornstarch

½ teaspoon kosher salt

5 large egg yolks

1½ cups milk

2 tablespoons cold unsalted butter, cut into small cubes

1 teaspoon vanilla extract

FOR THE GLAZE

6 tablespoons heavy cream

5 ounces dark chocolate, chopped

FOR THE CAKE: Preheat the oven to 375°F. Spray two 8-inch round cake pans with cooking spray.

Sift together the flour, baking powder, and salt. In a stand mixer, cream together the butter, sugar, and vanilla. Add the eggs, one at a time. Add half the flour mixture, then the milk, then the remaining flour mixture. Divide the batter evenly between the two cake pans. Bake for 20 to 25 minutes; the cakes will not take on much color. Allow to cool completely.

FOR THE FILLING: In a medium saucepan, whisk together the sugar, cornstarch, salt, and egg yolks. Add the milk and whisk to combine. Put the pan over medium heat and stir constantly until the mixture thickens, about 8 minutes. (Do *not* walk away. It seems like it will never thicken, then it happens very fast. Keep whisking.) Remove from the heat and add the butter, a few pieces at a time. Whisk in the vanilla. Cover with plastic wrap to avoid forming a film and set aside to cool.

FOR THE GLAZE: Heat the cream in a small saucepan to a simmer. Put the chocolate in a bowl and pour the hot cream over the chocolate. Let this sit for 1 minute, then stir to incorporate.

TO ASSEMBLE: Remove the cakes from their pans. With a serrated knife, cut the domed top off one of the cakes, just enough to make it even. Place that cake on a plate or cake stand. Pour the filling on top and spread it with a spatula to within a half-inch of the edge. Put the other cake on top, domed side up. Cover that with the chocolate glaze.

SERVES 6 TO 8

Black & White Cookies, a symbol of New York, were my wife Susi's all-time favorite cookie long before Jerry Seinfeld turned them into a metaphor for cultural harmony. Any trip to a bakery or deli in the city should conclude with a few in the bag. Whether they make it home is optional. These will be much better than the deli-bought ones.

BLACK & WHITE
COOKIES

FOR THE COOKIES

5 cups all-purpose flour

1 teaspoon baking powder

1½ teaspoons kosher salt

1 cup (2 sticks) unsalted butter, softened

1½ cups granulated sugar

4 large eggs

¾ cup milk

2 teaspoons vanilla extract

FOR THE ICING

4 cups confectioners' sugar

2 tablespoons light corn syrup

1 teaspoon vanilla extract

½ cup unsweetened cocoa powder

FOR THE COOKIES: Preheat the oven to 350°F. Line two baking sheets with silicone mats or parchment paper. In a large bowl, whisk together the flour, baking powder, and salt.

In the bowl of a stand mixer with the paddle attachment, cream together the butter and granulated sugar until the color turns a pale yellow. Add the eggs, slowly, one at a time. On low speed, add half the flour mixture. When it's mixed in, add half the milk and all the vanilla. Add the rest of the flour, then the rest of the milk.

Using a 1½-inch ice cream scoop (a generous 2 tablespoons), scoop mounds of batter onto the baking sheets, about 2 inches apart. Using wet fingers, push the batter down to flatten into a round about 2½ inches wide. Repeat until the batter is gone or the sheets are full. Bake for about 16 minutes, until the edges look set and the cookies have a nice tan working. Cool completely on wire racks.

FOR THE ICING: In a large bowl, mix the confectioners' sugar with ¼ cup warm water. Add the syrup and vanilla and stir vigorously to form a smooth icing. Pour half the icing into a second bowl and add 2 to 3 tablespoons warm water and the cocoa. Mix to make the "black" icing.

Spread white icing on half of each cookie, then spread chocolate icing on the other half.

MAKES ABOUT 30 COOKIES

Purity is a hallmark of the New York Cheesecake. While others may mix cheeses and garnish with fruity toppings, the New York cake is made with one hundred percent cream cheese and unadorned. The most famous of New York's cakes, Junior's, eschews the typical graham cracker crust for a simple sponge base, putting further focus on the cheese. Although I love Junior's for many reasons, I am most decidedly a graham cracker crust guy.

NYC
CHEESECAKE

FOR THE GRAHAM CRACKER CRUST

1½ cups graham cracker crumbs (about 7 ounces of crackers)

2 tablespoons sugar

½ teaspoon kosher salt

¼ teaspoon freshly grated nutmeg

6 tablespoons unsalted butter, melted

FOR THE FILLING

2 pounds cream cheese, at room temperature

1½ cups sugar

3 tablespoons all-purpose flour

Zest and juice of 1 lemon

1 teaspoon vanilla extract

½ teaspoon kosher salt

4 large eggs plus 2 yolks

½ cup sour cream

FOR THE GRAHAM CRACKER CRUST: Preheat the oven to 350°F. Spray a 3-inch-deep, 9-inch round springform pan with cooking spray. Wrap the bottom and side of the pan with 2 layers of foil.

In a bowl, toss together the graham cracker crumbs, sugar, salt, and nutmeg. Slowly drizzle in the butter, tossing it through the crumbs until it looks like the consistency of wet sand.

Pour the graham cracker mixture into the pan and spread evenly over the bottom. With a flat-bottomed glass or measuring cup, firmly press the crumbs into the pan to form an even surface, making sure the crumbs reach the edge of the pan all the way around.

Bake the crust for 10 minutes. It won't look any different when it's done. Let cool for 10 minutes.

FOR THE FILLING: Reduce the oven temperature to 300°F. Boil some water and place a large roasting pan in the oven.

In the bowl of a stand mixer with the paddle attachment, cream together the cream cheese and sugar. Add the flour, lemon zest and juice, vanilla, and salt. With the mixer still running, add the eggs and yolks one or two at a time, then the sour cream. Pour the mixture over the crust.

Place the cake in the roasting pan and carefully add boiling water to come about 1 inch up the outside of the springform pan. Bake the cake for 60 to 70 minutes, until the cake is set but still a little jiggly in the middle. Turn off the oven and prop the door open slightly with a wooden spoon to let the oven and cake cool for about an hour. Refrigerate for several hours before serving.

SERVES 8 TO 10

Pie

My, my. American pie.

It's a great idea for a song, sure. But my version wouldn't be full of metaphors about ill-fated rock stars and the decline of Western civilization. And no one would drive out to the levee to check the water level.

We'd eat pie.

Can you finish off the berry pie?

'Cause I want the last piece of shoofly.

Is that apple with a piece of cheese?

Now I believe in sugar cream.

This Concord grape is just a dream.

Save me a Shaker lemon, if you please.

There are an endless number of ways to fill a 9-inch crust for dessert.

This is America, so you start with apple. It's everywhere, and it should be. But depending on where you are, and when you are, there are any number of fruits to turn into a pie.

And if there's no fruit, there's probably a nut. Pecans, peanuts, walnuts. All are fair game for a pie.

But before we fill the pie, there are decisions about the crust.

With rare exception, the crust in most sweet pies can be the same. How you embellish it can say a lot about you as a baker.

You can just use a single crust. This is easy. Simple. And it lets the filling be the star.

But maybe you really like crust. Or maybe your filling needs to be contained. You'll probably want to go with a double crust.

Are you a show-off? Nobody likes a show-off. Unless you show off by making a gorgeous lattice top for your pie. One that provides a little bit of structure, but also lets the filling bubble up and over. It looks like you spent a lot of time on it. And you probably did.

That isn't the end of it. There's still crimping to do. Single, double, or lattice top, you can meticulously pinch the edges of the pie to create a pattern. A high crimp, a low crimp, a deep crimp. They're all right. Or just use a fork to seal the edge. Or your thumb.

It would be fun to think there was a regional provenance to all those decisions, but really there isn't. You can find any—and all—of them in kitchens in any part of the country. Generally speaking, you probably crimp your pies the way your mom did, and she crimps them the way her mom did. And if you didn't learn to crimp a pie from your family's matriarchy, that's okay. Find a favorite and emulate it.

Just make sure you teach your kids how to do it, too.

… Singin' this'll be the day we eat pie.

There may be nothing more American than apple pie, but there are only certain corners of New England and the Upper Midwest where it's paired with Cheddar. In those places, though, it's regarded as nothing short of a natural combination. Sometimes it's as simple as a slice of cheese melted on top, which sounds nice, but here I bake the cheese into the crust. And I definitely add some more Cheddar over the top if I serve it still warm.

CHEDDAR CHEESE
APPLE PIE

FOR THE CRUST

3½ cups all-purpose flour plus extra for work surface

4 ounces sharp Cheddar cheese, finely shredded, plus additional slices to serve

1½ teaspoons kosher salt

½ teaspoon baking powder

1½ cups (3 sticks) very cold unsalted butter, cut into small cubes

1 large egg, lightly beaten

½ cup ice water plus more as needed

FOR THE FILLING

6 or 7 large apples, a combination of tart and sweet, such as Granny Smith and Gala (about 2 pounds), peeled, cored, and thinly sliced

½ cup sugar

3 tablespoons all-purpose flour

Zest and juice of 1 lemon

1 teaspoon cinnamon

¼ teaspoon freshly grated nutmeg

½ teaspoon kosher salt

FOR THE CRUST: In a food processor, combine the flour, cheese, salt, and baking powder. Add the butter and pulse until the mixture looks grainy. (Your food processor will be quite full; if it does not fit, then place the whole shebang in a large bowl and gently mix with hands for the next step.) Add the egg and 6 tablespoons ice water and pulse 4 or 5 times. Turn the dough onto a lightly floured surface and bring it together with your hands, drizzling extra water on it a tablespoon at a time until it comes together. Knead it as little as possible. Form the dough into 2 equal balls, wrap them separately in plastic wrap, and form them into discs. Refrigerate at least 1 hour before rolling out.

Roll one disc out to a round at least 12 inches wide and carefully line a 9-inch deep-dish pie pan. Refrigerate until ready to fill.

FOR THE FILLING: In a large bowl, toss together the apples, sugar, flour, lemon zest and juice, cinnamon, nutmeg, and salt. Let sit at room temperature for at least 20 minutes.

Preheat the oven to 400°F.

Roll out the second disc of dough to a round at least 11 inches wide.

Fill the crust with the apple mixture. Lay the second crust over the top and crimp the edges to seal. With a sharp knife, cut a few vents in the top of the pie. Bake for 15 minutes, then reduce the temperature to 350°F and bake for 45 minutes more, until the crust is golden. Serve warm or at room temperature, with a slice of Cheddar melted on top if you like.

SERVES 6 TO 8

It's hard to imagine a pie made largely of maple syrup, but it makes total sense that if one exists, it would be found in Vermont. The grading system for maple syrup used to refer to the dark, late-season batch that I prize as Grade B, a term that erroneously implied inferiority. Find the darkest and cloudiest syrup you can; it packs the most flavor and is the best choice for the cognoscenti.

MAPLE CREAM
PIE

Preheat the oven to 375°F.

In a large bowl, whisk together the eggs and flour, then add 1 cup of the cream, 2 cups of the syrup, and the salt. Mix well.

Pour the mixture into the prepared pie shell and bake for 50 to 60 minutes, until the custard is mostly set but still a little jiggly. Cool to room temperature.

With an electric mixer or stand mixer, beat the remaining 1 cup cream, gradually adding the remaining 2 tablespoons syrup. Whip to stiff peaks. Spread over the cooled pie.

SERVES 6 TO 8

3 large eggs, beaten

3 tablespoons all-purpose flour, sifted

2 cups heavy cream

2 cups plus 2 tablespoons real maple syrup; look for "dark and robust" on the label

½ teaspoon kosher salt

½ recipe Basic Pie Crust in 9-inch pan (page 481)

I might sprinkle the top of this with finely crumbled Saltines before adding the whipped cream, to add texture and salt.

Despite the name, this was a dish that British settlers brought to America, adapting their favored Hasty Pudding by replacing wheat flour with the cornmeal they found here. Traditionally it's a dessert flavored with molasses or maple syrup—or both, like in this example—and spices, but it can be adapted for savory dishes.

INDIAN PUDDING

3 cups milk

¼ cup molasses

¼ cup maple syrup

½ teaspoon ground ginger

½ teaspoon cinnamon

½ teaspoon kosher salt

¾ cup cornmeal

2 large eggs, beaten

Whipped cream or ice cream
    for serving

Preheat the oven to 300°F. Spray a 9-by-9-inch baking dish with cooking spray. Bring several cups of water to a boil.

In a large saucepan over medium heat, combine the milk, molasses, syrup, ginger, cinnamon, and salt and bring to a simmer. Whisk in the cornmeal and continue whisking until the mixture begins to thicken, 5 to 10 minutes. Whisk in the eggs.

Pour the pudding into the prepared baking dish and place it inside a larger baking dish. Pour the boiling water into the larger pan to come about halfway up the side of the baking dish. Carefully place in the oven and bake for 2 hours. Let cool for 15 minutes, then serve with whipped cream or ice cream.

SERVES 9

MID-ATLANTIC

Pennsylvania

New Jersey

99/LB

Delaware

D.C.

Maryland

West Virginia

Brunswick STEW

Virginia

SITTING AT A PICNIC TABLE at the edge of the Chesapeake Bay, eating a tray of oysters within view of the water where they were born, I can see why America's earliest settlers came here and never wanted to leave.

You can see it too, because if you're in the right spot, it still looks a lot like what those settlers saw all those years ago.

While most of the Mid-Atlantic doesn't resemble the unspoiled paradise of pre-Colonial times—some of our biggest cities and travel arteries run through it—parts of it still do. And you're never far from similarly unsullied environs.

From the gardens of New Jersey to the rolling hills of southern Virginia, the region is an alternating series of metropoli, national parks, and farmland.

For me, the tour starts in northern Jersey, just outside my Big Apple home, where Italian Americans make me feel right at home with a cuisine based on the homeland, but that they've redefined to make their own. I went to college at Rutgers in New Brunswick and quickly learned much about the accents, vocabulary, and vernacular.

In New Jersey, I saw the future of rock and roll, and tasted some of the best things in my life in homes and restaurants near the Jersey Shore and in magnificent towns like Nutley and Belleville, long before the Sopranos made it cool. What you're served looks like Italian food. It tastes like Italian food. But it isn't. It's Italian American, and it is beautiful for that specificity.

Roadside treasures of the Mid-Atlantic include **CHEESESTEAKS** and **STROMBOLI**, **SALTWATER TAFFY** and **SOFT PRETZELS** with deli mustard, **SCRAPPLE** and **PORK ROLL**, **DIRTY-WATER HOT DOGS**, and **PIZZA** by the slice.

Heading over to Pennsylvania gives us a chance to see the places where the ideal of America was born; then we can drive to a spot a few miles outside Philadelphia where most of the country's cultivated mushrooms are grown.

On to Maryland, where we can take in the scene that inspired the "Star-Spangled Banner" as we down steamed crabs, much like Francis Scott Key may have. So you, too, should be inspired to great works of patriotic poetry.

Through Virginia, we travel past historic battlefields that were once covered in blood. Some of these fields are now covered in grapevines that will become red wine. We'll pass homes of early presidents, then find a smokehouse producing hams that put a U.S. spin on my beloved prosciutto.

Along the way, we'll get to meet up with some of my favorite chefs, including Marc Vetri, Jeff Michaud, Brad Spence, and Michael Solomonov in Philadelphia, Spike Gjerde and Bryan Voltaggio in Baltimore, and *mi hermano* José Andrés in Washington.

But at the end of this drive, I really want to end up back on the banks of the bay for another tray of those oysters. That's the kind of history that should repeat itself. Over and over.

Scrapple used to frighten folks, as meat of unrecognized provenance (think face or hoof) often will. But after beef cheek or calves' brain ravioli, a mix of pork shoulder, pork liver, and cornmeal seems to fit right in again these days. And while it may seem to be owned by the great state of Pennsylvania, it's not nearly as geo-unique as we might think: In North Carolina, they have Liver Mush, which is the same thing, and in Eastern Kentucky, they have Goetta, which just subs out the cornmeal in favor of cross-cut oats. In any case, it is truly delicious and you can personalize it with the addition of mace, oregano, marjoram, coriander, paprika, sage; all of them are in play. Serve on toast with a fried egg. Or maple syrup. Or both!

SCRAPPLE

In a large saucepan, combine the pork shoulder and liver and chicken stock. Bring to a boil and cook for about 10 minutes. Add the cornmeal, thyme, and salt and stir. Bring the mixture to a boil, then reduce the heat to a low simmer and cook, stirring regularly, for 35 minutes, until the mixture is quite thick.

Line a 9-by-5-by-3-inch loaf pan with plastic wrap. Spoon the mixture into the pan, cover, and chill overnight.

Combine the flour and pepper in a shallow bowl. Unmold the scrapple and cut it into thick slices. Dredge the slices in the seasoned flour.

In a medium skillet over medium-high heat, heat the oil. In batches, add the sliced scrapple and cook until browned, 3 to 4 minutes. Turn over and brown the other side.

SERVES 6 TO 8

1 pound boneless pork shoulder, ground or finely chopped

1 pound pork liver, ground or finely chopped

1½ cups Brown Chicken Stock (page 480)

2½ cups cornmeal

½ teaspoon dried thyme

1 teaspoon kosher salt

½ cup all-purpose flour

½ teaspoon freshly ground black pepper

2 tablespoons extra-virgin olive oil, or more as needed

Country ham is America's often salty take on Italian prosciutto or Spanish *jamón*. The intense salinity makes it ideal as a component in any dish—here it becomes breakfast, with a gravy of melting pork fat combined with coffee along with biscuits to sop up every drop. Traditionally this is merely good, but with the not-so-traditional addition of cream, fresh thyme, and Worcestershire, it is excellent.

COUNTRY HAM AND
RED-EYE GRAVY

6 country ham slices with fat,
    ¼ inch thick

⅓ cup strong coffee

4 tablespoons unsalted butter

3 tablespoons cream

1 tablespoon Worcestershire
    sauce

1 teaspoon fresh thyme leaves

6 buttermilk biscuits (from
    Biscuits and Sausage Gravy,
    page 123)

Heat a large skillet, preferably cast iron, over medium-high heat. Working in batches, sear the ham slices until they begin to brown on each side, 3 to 4 minutes, then remove to a plate.

When all the slices are seared, pour the coffee into the skillet with ¼ cup water. Scrape the pan with a spatula to dislodge all the seared ham bits. Add the butter, cream, and Worcestershire and cook until the mixture reduces a bit, about 5 minutes. Add the ham back to the pan, swirl to cover, and stir in the thyme leaves. Serve the ham slices on biscuits with the gravy.

SERVES 6

Making your own sauerkraut isn't hard, and it is a key ingredient in many dishes throughout the country (see Sauerkraut Balls on page 281 and Runzas on page 353). You can buy a good alternative at the grocery store, but how cool is it to have your own kraut fermenting under the kitchen sink like your grandmother might have?

FERMENTED
SAUERKRAUT

1 large head green cabbage, about 4 pounds, thick core removed and discarded, remainder finely shredded

3 tablespoons kosher salt

Toss the cabbage and salt together to coat well. Pack the cabbage into a large, wide-mouth jar or ceramic crock. Place a small, flat, heavy plate on top, weighing it down to put pressure on the cabbage. The cabbage will begin to give up water, and you want to keep the kraut submerged in it. Cover the opening with a towel or cheesecloth. Let stand at room temperature for at least 6 weeks before using, skimming any scum that forms every 2 weeks or so. The kraut will last up to a year.

MAKES ABOUT 2 QUARTS

If you happen to be in Berkeley Springs, West Virginia, on Columbus Day weekend, don't miss the Apple Butter Festival. In fact, with the huge cauldrons hung over open fires on the sidewalks, if you're there that weekend, you *won't be able* to miss it. My family makes this preserve with apples, but also with just about any fruit that is going past perfect ripeness, including pears, peaches, plums, and even apricots. You can substitute directly by weight, 6 pounds, the world around. (Pictured on page 68.)

APPLE BUTTER

6 pounds apples, peeled, cored, and thinly sliced; a combination of tart and sweet apples works well

1½ cups packed light brown sugar

1 tablespoon lemon juice

1 tablespoon ground cinnamon

1 teaspoon ground cloves

In a large, heavy pot or Dutch oven over medium heat, combine all the ingredients. Stir until the sugar coats the apples, then stir every couple of minutes until the sugar melts. Turn the heat to low and cover the pot. Cook for 1 hour, stirring occasionally. After an hour, the apples should be brown and quite soft and should begin to fall apart when you stir vigorously. If stirring doesn't break down the apples, puree with a stick blender, then cover the pot and cook for another hour. The apple butter is done when it's thick and luscious.

The apple butter can be stored in the refrigerator for up to a month, frozen for up to a year, or canned according to the directions on page 9 and kept for up to a year.

MAKES 6 HALF-PINTS

Deviled Eggs had been around since before America was, but once they got here, they became the unofficial food of picnics and potlucks. Have you ever been to a good potluck without Deviled Eggs? I like them on the spicy side, but you can cut the cayenne out if it's too hot for you.

DEVILED
EGGS

Bring a large saucepan half-full of water to a boil over medium-high heat. Add the eggs, boil for 1 minute, then cover, turn the heat down to low, and simmer for 9 minutes. Discard the hot water and run cold water over the eggs until they're cool enough to handle. Carefully peel the eggs, cut them in half longways, and transfer the yolks to a bowl. Reserve the whites.

Mash the yolks with a fork a bit and add the mayonnaise, mustards, capers, hot sauce, vinegar, cayenne, salt, and pepper. Mix well. Arrange the egg whites on a platter. Using either a spoon or a piping bag with a fancy tip, fill the wells with the yolk mixture. Dust with paprika.

MAKES 24 DEVILED EGGS

1 dozen large eggs

½ cup mayonnaise

1 tablespoon Dijon mustard

1 teaspoon Colman's dry mustard

2 tablespoons capers, chopped

1 tablespoon chipotle hot sauce

1 teaspoon apple cider vinegar

1 teaspoon cayenne

½ teaspoon kosher salt

½ teaspoon freshly ground black pepper

Paprika (my favorite is the smoky pimentón from Spain)

I might add a squirt of Sriracha on half of these, just because.

The love Philadelphia has for the Soft Pretzel is nearly legendary. Some statistics put consumption of the doughy knots at ten times the national average. When you buy them there, you'll likely get a more compact knot than you would traditionally find elsewhere. That's a consequence of cooking so many of them at a time to keep up with demand. You can choose the shape you like.

SOFT
PRETZELS

1¾ cups warm water, about 110°F

1 envelope (2¼ teaspoons) active dry yeast

4½ cups all-purpose flour

2 teaspoons kosher salt

Extra-virgin olive oil for the bowl

¼ cup baking soda

Coarse sea salt

Mustard for serving

In the bowl of a stand mixer, mix ¼ cup of the warm water with the yeast and let stand about 10 minutes. With the dough-hook attachment, stir in the remaining 1½ cups warm water, 4 cups of the flour, and the salt. Add more flour ¼ cup at a time if necessary to make a stiff dough. Knead the dough for 10 minutes.

Lightly oil a large bowl. Form the dough into a ball, put it in the bowl, and cover with a towel. Allow to rise for 1 hour. It should about double in size.

Preheat the oven to 475°F. Spray a couple of baking sheets with cooking spray. Bring a large, heavy pot half-filled with water to a boil over medium-high heat, then add the baking soda.

Quarter the dough, and then cut each quarter into 3 equal pieces. Roll one piece out to about 18 inches long. Hold it up with one end in each hand, set the middle of the "U" on the counter, cross the two ends, and fold them back down onto the dough. If you've ever seen a pretzel, this should make more sense when you do it.

Drop the pretzels, one at a time, in the boiling water and cook for 15 seconds, then remove with tongs and place on the prepared baking sheet. Repeat with enough pretzels to fill the baking sheet. Sprinkle the pretzels with the coarse salt. Bake for 13 to 15 minutes, until dark brown. Serve with mustard.

MAKES 12 PRETZELS

The barrier islands of South Jersey are home to clam hatcheries, and many of those clams never leave the area, ending up steamed in the beer that they'll ultimately be consumed with.

CAPE MAY
STEAMERS

3 tablespoons extra-virgin olive oil

3 cloves garlic, thinly sliced

1 medium red onion, cut into ¼-inch dice

½ cup chopped fennel, fronds chopped and reserved

1 pound hot Italian sausage, removed from casing

Kosher salt and freshly ground black pepper

3 pounds fresh clams, scrubbed and rinsed

1½ cups beer (I like a light lager like Rolling Rock)

Toasted, crusty bread

In a large, heavy saucepan with a tight-fitting lid, heat the oil until hot but not smoking. Add the garlic, onion, chopped fennel bulb, and sausage, season with salt and pepper, and cook until the fennel softens and the sausage browns, about 7 minutes. Add the clams, pour in the beer, and cover the pan. Steam the clams until they open, about 8 minutes. Remove from the heat and discard any clams that did not open. Garnish with a sprinkle of chopped fennel fronds and serve immediately, with bread to soak up the broth.

SERVES 4

In the capital of New Jersey, there is a wrinkle on pizza that's worth exploring. All the ingredients look familiar, but there is a key difference: The cheese goes on before the tomato sauce. According to the fine citizenry of the great city of Trenton, this is no small distinction. Adding sugar to the sauce seems distinct to New Jersey Italian-American homes. My guess is that canned tomatoes in the '30s and '40s weren't as sweet as tomatoes from the ancestral gardens or pantries.

TRENTON
TOMATO PIE

6 Roma tomatoes, halved and cored

Kosher salt and freshly ground black pepper

Extra-virgin olive oil

2 cups Basic Tomato Sauce (page 480)

2 tablespoons sugar

Cornmeal for dusting

Basic Pizza Dough (page 481)

2 cups torn or shredded fresh mozzarella cheese

Preheat the oven to 350°F. Line a baking sheet with a silicone mat or parchment paper.

Place the tomato halves on the baking sheet, sprinkle with salt and pepper, and drizzle with olive oil. Roast for 30 minutes.

Turn the oven to 450°F.

Heat the tomato sauce in a large pot over medium heat. Cut the roasted tomatoes into chunks and toss them in the sauce, along with the sugar.

Spray a rimmed baking sheet, about 12 inches by 18 inches, with cooking spray and dust lightly with cornmeal.

Roll out the dough to a rough rectangle and fit into the baking sheet, pressing it out to fill. Spread the mozzarella over the dough, then top it with the tomato sauce.

Bake for 20 to 25 minutes, until the crust is golden and the center is cooked through. Slice and serve.

SERVES 6 TO 8

I might add 12 oil-packed anchovies to this, on the top in a parallel-lines pattern.

Peanut Soup is one of the many dishes introduced to the country via slaves' quarters and then co-opted to the main house. The early versions were made with ground nuts, but over time they have been largely replaced with the conveniently smooth option of peanut butter.

PEANUT SOUP

Melt the butter in a large saucepan over medium-high heat. Add the onion and celery, season with salt and pepper, and cook until the onion softens, about 5 minutes. Stir in the flour to form a roux. Cook for 2 minutes, without letting it take on any color.

Add the chicken stock and bring to a boil, whisking constantly to incorporate the roux. Reduce the heat to medium and cook for about 20 minutes, until the soup has thickened a bit. Reduce the heat to low, then whisk in the peanut butter, cream, and red pepper flakes. When the peanut butter is thoroughly mixed in, cook for an additional 10 minutes, whisking occasionally to be sure everything is smooth. Add lemon juice and serve warm, garnished with the chopped peanuts and green onions.

MAKES 2 QUARTS, SERVING 6 TO 8

4 tablespoons unsalted butter

1 medium onion, finely chopped

2 stalks celery, finely chopped

Kosher salt and freshly ground black pepper

¼ cup all-purpose flour

4 cups Brown Chicken Stock (page 480)

1 cup creamy peanut butter

1 cup cream

1 teaspoon crushed red pepper flakes

Juice of 1 lemon

½ cup peanuts, chopped

2 green onions, thinly sliced

I prefer this soup jacked up with chopped raw jalapeños and fresh lime served on the side; go where you can.

Spoon Bread seems more likely to have evolved than originated anywhere. When settlers arrived, they came upon the corn pudding of Native Americans, while likely missing the steamed puddings, like Yorkshire, they had left behind. Someone would have then applied the process of making savory puddings they knew and loved to the ingredients they found, just like the origin stories of many of the best dishes.

SPOON BREAD
WITH CORN

Preheat the oven to 400°F. Spray a 9-by-9-inch casserole with cooking spray.

In a large pot, heat the milk and salt until the milk nearly boils. Slowly whisk in the cornmeal. Continue to stir until smooth, then reduce the heat to low and simmer, uncovered and stirring often, for about 15 minutes, until the mixture is quite thick.

Remove the pan from the heat and stir in the butter to incorporate. Beat in the egg yolks one at a time, then stir in the corn kernels.

Beat the egg whites to stiff peaks. Gently fold the egg whites into the corn mixture and pour into the prepared casserole. Bake uncovered for 25 to 30 minutes, until the top is golden brown and the center is almost set.

SERVES 4 TO 6

3 cups milk

2 teaspoons kosher salt

1 cup white cornmeal

4 tablespoons unsalted butter, cut into pieces and softened

3 large eggs, separated

3 ears of corn, kernels removed from cobs, about 2½ cups

I might stir in 1 teaspoon cayenne or 1 tablespoon brown sugar or several gratings of fresh nutmeg before baking. Any or all...in fact, I would definitely add them all.

On the Eastern Shore of the Chesapeake, Oyster Fritters are a festival favorite, sort of a cross between a fried oyster and a pancake. On a cool November morning, I could eat these for breakfast.

CHESAPEAKE BAY
OYSTER FRITTERS

1 cup all-purpose flour

¼ cup cornmeal

1 teaspoon baking powder

1 teaspoon kosher salt

½ teaspoon ground fennel seed

2 large eggs

½ cup milk

20 oysters, shucked, liquor reserved

½ cup extra-virgin olive oil

Coarse sea salt

Into a large bowl, sift together the flour, cornmeal, baking powder, salt, and fennel seed. In a separate bowl, beat the eggs and milk together. Add the milk mixture and the reserved oyster liquor to the dry ingredients and mix to form a batter. Gently fold in the oysters.

Heat the oil in a large skillet over medium-high heat. Drop large spoonfuls of the batter into the oil, making sure each one has at least one oyster in it—two if it's for you. Cook until the fritters are golden on one side, 2 to 3 minutes. Turn and cook until golden on the second side, 2 or 3 more minutes. Repeat to use the rest of the batter. Sprinkle with sea salt and serve warm.

MAKES 10 TO 15 FRITTERS

For these, I would make a dipping sauce with equal parts soy sauce, lemon juice, and Sriracha.

On the north end of Delaware, you're likely to find people picking whole steamed crabs, but down at the southern end, these little fritters are the approved delivery device for crab. I like the texture I get with the not-so-traditional addition of panko, but a lot of people love crumbs from the mighty Ritz cracker as a binder. Go with what you like.

CRAB PUFFS

4 tablespoons unsalted butter

1 small onion, finely diced

½ red bell pepper, chopped into ¼-inch dice

¼ cup all-purpose flour

1 cup milk

8 ounces crabmeat

2 large eggs, well beaten

1 cup panko bread crumbs

1 teaspoon Colman's dry mustard

½ teaspoon celery salt

½ teaspoon kosher salt plus more for seasoning

½ teaspoon freshly ground black pepper

Canola or corn oil for frying

Tartar Sauce (page 24) for serving

1 lemon, cut into 8 wedges, for serving

Melt the butter in a large skillet over medium-high heat. Add the onion and bell pepper and sauté until beginning to soften, 1 to 2 minutes. Add the flour and stir to form a roux. Reduce the heat to medium and cook, stirring, for about 4 minutes, without allowing the roux to take on color. Add the milk and whisk to incorporate. Continue to cook, whisking, until the mixture thickens, about 5 minutes. Fold in the crab, then pour the mixture into a bowl. Add the eggs, panko, mustard, celery salt, salt, and pepper and stir to combine.

In a large pot or Dutch oven, heat 2 inches of oil over medium-high heat to 375°F.

Using two spoons, form the dough into small nuggets and carefully drop them into the oil 7 or 8 at a time. Fry for about 2 minutes, until they've barely started to turn brown. Remove to a paper towel–lined plate and season with salt. Repeat to use the rest of the batter. Serve with tartar sauce and lemon wedges.

MAKES 20 TO 24 PUFFS

LIME GIN RICKEY

MAKES 1 COCKTAIL

Lore says this drink was invented in Washington, D.C., in the 1880s with bourbon as the star, then took off when someone swapped in gin.

Ice
1 ounce freshly squeezed lime juice
2 ounces gin
2 ounces club soda
Lime wedge or wheel

Fill a rocks glass halfway with ice. Add the lime juice and gin and stir. Top with the club soda and garnish with the lime.

I can totally get behind the bipartisan effort that keeps Senate White Bean Soup on the menu at the Senate restaurant every day. But I'm sure that the congressional policy of orchestrating trumped-up sound bites while avoiding action on actual problems facing the country will ultimately result in a special subcommittee hearing to find out who knew what about this soup's origins and when. If called to testify, I'll take the fifth… bowl of soup. And then maybe a sixth.

SENATE
WHITE BEAN SOUP

Put the beans, ham hock, and 1 tablespoon of the thyme in a large, heavy pot or Dutch oven and cover with 2 quarts water. Bring to a boil over medium-high heat and boil for 15 minutes. Cover, reduce the heat to medium-low, and simmer for 2 to 3 hours, until the beans are tender.

When the beans are almost ready, pull out the ham hock and allow to cool.

Melt the butter in a large skillet over medium-high heat. Add the onion, carrots, celery, and remaining 1 tablespoon thyme and sauté until the vegetables begin to soften, about 5 minutes. Add the vegetables to the soup. Pull the meat off the ham hock, discarding the fat and bone. Chop the meat and add it to the soup.

With a potato masher or immersion blender, crush some of the beans and stir until it reaches the consistency you like. Season with salt and pepper to taste and serve.

MAKES 2 QUARTS, SERVING 6 TO 8

1 pound dried white beans, such as navy or Great Northern, rinsed

1 smoked ham hock

2 tablespoons chopped fresh thyme

2 tablespoons unsalted butter

1 medium onion, chopped

2 carrots, finely diced

3 stalks celery, finely diced

Kosher salt and freshly ground black pepper

I would drizzle each bowl with a teaspoon of good balsamic vinegar.

The cheesesteak is one of those terrific American foods that grow in legend because of the competing passions that swell among its devotees. Who invented it and who makes it best may be in dispute, but in truth they're debates best never solved, as they're ultimately integral to Philadelphia's identity. The pedal hits the metal when you begin the discussion of the proper bakery or bread maker. And then there's the cheese choice of "whiz" or provolone. I am on the provolone side at home and the whiz side at the shop.

PHILLY
CHEESESTEAK

3 tablespoons extra-virgin olive oil

1 large onion, sliced

1 green bell pepper, chopped

4 ounces mushrooms, thinly sliced

Kosher salt and freshly ground black pepper

2 pounds rib eye or round steak, thinly sliced (⅛ inch or less)

1 teaspoon red wine vinegar

16 slices provolone

4 sub rolls, split and toasted

Preheat the broiler in the oven.

Heat the oil in a large skillet, preferably cast iron, over medium-high heat. Add the onion and sauté until it begins to soften, about 5 minutes. Add the bell pepper, mushrooms, and salt to taste and sauté until they're softened and the mushrooms begin to brown. Remove from the pan and set aside.

Turn the heat under the skillet up to high.

Season the meat aggressively with salt and pepper. Working in batches if necessary, add meat to the hot pan and cook, without turning, until dark brown on the first side, 1 to 2 minutes. Turn the meat, cook briefly, and push to the side of the pan to give you room to cook more of the meat. Repeat until all the meat is cooked, then splash the vinegar in the pan, and cook until the vinegar is gone, probably another 30 seconds.

Divide the cheese among the sub rolls, then top with the meat and the onion mixture. Place the sandwiches under the broiler to melt the cheese. Serve hot.

MAKES 4 SANDWICHES

In Philly, they always offer chopped hot cherry peppers in the little condiment trolley outside. I slather them on with the same abandon as Roman Gabriel's long bombs.

George Washington knew his way around a good Pepper Pot, and while it probably came to Philly from the West Indies, the thrifty use of meat made it a staple during the time of the Revolution. Today, a walk through the city's Italian Market district will net you any of the unusual cuts in the many original versions of this—but if you don't get tripe, it isn't Pepper Pot.

1½ pounds honeycomb tripe

2 tablespoons extra-virgin olive oil

1 leek, cleaned and thinly sliced, white and light green parts

3 stalks celery, finely chopped

1 large carrot, finely chopped

Kosher salt and freshly ground black pepper

5 cups Brown Chicken Stock (page 480)

1 pound beef bones

1 veal knuckle

1 teaspoon ground cloves

1 small green bell pepper, finely diced

1 small yellow bell pepper, finely diced

2 large potatoes, cut into ½-inch dice

1 tablespoon chopped fresh marjoram

¼ cup chopped fresh parsley

PHILADELPHIA
PEPPER POT

Put the tripe in a large, heavy pot or Dutch oven and cover with water. Bring the water to a boil, then reduce to low and simmer for 15 minutes. Allow to cool in the water.

In another large pot, heat the oil over medium-high heat and add the leek. Sauté for 5 minutes, then add the celery and carrot, season with salt and pepper, and cook for an additional 3 minutes. Add the stock, beef bones, veal knuckle, and cloves.

When the tripe is cool enough to handle, remove it from the water, cut it into bite-size pieces, and add it to the pot. Bring the stock to a boil, reduce to low, cover, and simmer for 90 minutes. Remove the beef bones and knuckle and pick any meat off them. Discard the bones and return the meat to the pot. Add the bell peppers, potatoes, and marjoram and simmer for 30 minutes, or until you're ready to eat. Season with salt and serve in bowls, garnished with fresh parsley.

SERVES 6 TO 8

I would finish this with finely chopped red onions.

Think of Bott Boi as a nice chicken noodle soup. In its purest form, it's a pot pie with pasta instead of a crust. The two names are interesting, too: "Slippery" is a word used for the fresh pasta that's made for the dish. "Bott Boi" is a little cloudier, but could be a reverse translation, with German immigrants becoming accustomed to the term "pot pie," and adapting it.

SLIPPERY POT PIE

OR BOTT BOI

FOR THE POT PIE

2 tablespoons extra-virgin olive oil

1 onion, chopped

2 cloves garlic, thinly sliced

2 stalks celery, chopped

2 carrots, diced

1 chicken, about 4 pounds

1 tablespoon fresh thyme

1 teaspoon kosher salt

1 teaspoon freshly ground black pepper

4 small potatoes, diced

FOR THE PASTA

1½ cups all-purpose flour

½ teaspoon kosher salt

2 large eggs

FOR THE POT PIE: Heat the oil in a large, heavy pot or Dutch oven over medium-high heat. Add the onion, garlic, celery, and carrots and sauté until the onion begins to soften, about 5 minutes. Add the chicken, thyme, salt, and pepper and cover with water. Bring to a boil, cover, reduce to a simmer, and cook for 50 to 60 minutes, until the chicken is cooked through.

FOR THE PASTA: Mix the flour, salt, and eggs. Add up to 3 tablespoons of water, a tablespoon at a time, to form a dough. Knead for 2 or 3 minutes, then form into a ball, cover, and let rest in the refrigerator for 20 minutes.

Roll the pasta out on a floured work surface until very thin, then cut into 1½-inch squares.

Remove the chicken from the pot and allow to cool. Add the potatoes to the pot, return it to a boil, and cook uncovered for 15 minutes, until the potatoes are tender.

When the chicken is cooled, pull the meat from the bones, and discard the skin and bones. Chop the meat into bite-size chunks. Add the chicken to the pot and drop the pasta squares into the boiling soup. The pasta will cook in 3 to 4 minutes, and the dish is ready to serve.

SERVES 6 TO 8

I would put this under the broiler for 4 or 5 minutes to set the pasta "crust."

This particular piece of Italian-Americana is particularly close to my heart. Its roots are in Italy, but it was born in the U.S.A., and I know it best from my days as a member of the furiously fast and hilarious Boli Makers Club, led by Billy Calzone and Bill Boli at Stuff Yer Face in New Brunswick, New Jersey. Stromboli filling variations are infinite. Finely chopped fresh raw vegetables like broccoli and cauliflower are great, as is anything left over from a party, like chili, shredded osso buco...Go wild!! We did!

STROMBOLI

Preheat the oven to 450°F. Line a baking sheet with parchment paper and spray with cooking spray.

Heat the olive oil in a large skillet over medium-high heat, add the onion, garlic, and bell pepper, and season with salt and red pepper flakes. Sauté until softened and fragrant, then remove from the heat.

Roll out the pizza dough and stretch into about a 16-inch square. Evenly spread the tomato sauce, meats, sautéed vegetables, and mozzarella over the dough, leaving about an inch uncovered on all four sides.

Carefully roll up the stromboli, tucking the ends until it looks like a big burrito and pinching to seal the edge, and move it onto the prepared baking sheet, seam side down. Brush it with olive oil, then sprinkle red pepper flakes and Parmigiano over the top. Bake until golden brown, 10 to 15 minutes. Let rest for 10 minutes before slicing to serve. Serve with additional tomato sauce.

MAKES 1 LARGE STROMBOLI, SERVING 4 TO 6

2 tablespoons extra-virgin olive oil plus more for brushing

1 small onion, finely diced

2 cloves garlic, thinly sliced

1 green bell pepper, finely diced

Kosher salt

Crushed red pepper flakes

Basic Pizza Dough (page 481)

2 cups Basic Tomato Sauce (page 480) plus more for serving

4 ounces salami, thinly sliced

4 ounces capicola, thinly sliced

1 pound mozzarella cheese, cut into small cubes

Grated Parmigiano-Reggiano

I would probably make two and eat one cold from the fridge the next day...wheeeee!

In traditional Sunday Supper Gravy, the meat lends its unctuousness to the tomato sauce, then comes out. The tomato sauce becomes the star of a pasta course, and the meat moves on to be featured on its own.

The dispute as to the proper English term for *sugo* goes on. It is either "gravy" or "sauce," and the topic is hotly debated to this day. I believe the two schools of thought are based in Nutley and Belleville, both in the great state of New Jersey. In the end, trust the name of the dish to whoever makes it for you. She will always be correct.

SUNDAY SUPPER
GRAVY

Season the meats with lots of salt and pepper. Heat the oil in a large, heavy pot or Dutch oven over medium-high heat and brown the veal and beef, about 10 minutes. Add the wine and stir constantly until it evaporates, about 5 minutes.

Add the tomato sauce, stir, then add the sausage, neck bones, 1 teaspoon salt, and red pepper flakes to taste. Reduce the heat to simmer, cover halfway, and cook, stirring occasionally and skimming fat as necessary, for about 3 hours.

Cook the pasta according to the package directions.

Remove the gravy from the heat and adjust the seasoning with salt and pepper. Transfer the meat to a platter. On a separate platter, pile the pasta, dress it with the gravy, and serve as your first course. Then serve the meat as a main course.

Some people save the neck bones for their dogs, but I like to pick at them cold from the fridge, hot sauce in hand, late, late at night…alone.

SERVES 4 TO 6

1 pound veal shoulder, cut into 1-inch chunks

1 pound beef chuck, cut into 1-inch chunks

Kosher salt and freshly ground black pepper

¼ cup extra-virgin olive oil

¾ cup red wine

8 cups Basic Tomato Sauce (page 480)

1 pound sweet Italian sausage, cut into 1-inch pieces

1 pound pork neck bones

Pinch crushed red pepper flakes

1 pound dry spaghetti

My grandma would also put in a pound of spare ribs cut into 1-inch lengths.

In Baltimore, Pit Beef is its own sort of open-fire cookery: a hybrid somewhere between barbecue and grilling. Think of it as a roast beef sandwich with a more interesting backstory. The coffee is the secret of the rub; an old cook gave the recipe to me, right before he expired.

Please don't skimp on the Tiger Sauce.

PIT BEEF
SANDWICHES

FOR THE BEEF

2 tablespoons kosher salt

1 tablespoon freshly ground black pepper

1 teaspoon garlic powder

1 teaspoon dried oregano

1 teaspoon ancho chile powder

1 teaspoon instant coffee

1 top round or eye of round roast, about 3 pounds

FOR THE TIGER SAUCE

½ cup mayonnaise

½ cup sour cream

½ cup prepared horseradish

Zest and juice of 1 lemon

8 hamburger buns, lightly toasted

1 medium sweet or red onion, thinly sliced

FOR THE BEEF: Mix together the salt, pepper, garlic powder, oregano, ancho chile powder, and instant coffee. Sprinkle it all over the roast, cover with plastic wrap, and refrigerate overnight.

FOR THE TIGER SAUCE: Combine all the ingredients in a small bowl. Mix well, cover, and refrigerate until the beef is ready.

Prepare a gas or charcoal grill for indirect cooking. Sear the meat over the fire for 7 to 8 minutes per side, until there's a nice char around the outside of the roast. Then move the roast over to the unlit side, cover the grill, and cook until the interior of the meat reaches about 120°F on an instant-read thermometer, about 1 hour.

Let the roast rest for about 10 minutes, then slice it against the grain as thinly as possible. Stack the meat on the buns, adding onion slices and Tiger Sauce to taste.

MAKES 8 BIG SANDWICHES

There's a short window for soft-shell crabs, and when that window is open, frying them up and serving them as part of an already perfect BLT is a favorite strategy at seafood shacks and fancy restaurants alike.

SOFT-SHELL CRAB
BLT

Canola or corn oil for frying

1 cup all-purpose flour

1 tablespoon Old Bay seasoning

1 teaspoon kosher salt plus more for seasoning

1 teaspoon freshly ground black pepper

4 soft-shell crabs, cleaned and rinsed in cold water

Mayonnaise

4 hamburger buns, lightly toasted

8 slices bacon, cooked

1 small head of Romaine lettuce, shredded

1 tomato, sliced ¼ inch thick

In a large, straight-sided skillet, heat an inch of oil to 360°F.

Place the flour, Old Bay, salt, and pepper in a shallow dish. Dredge the crabs in the seasoned flour.

Working 2 crabs at a time, carefully place them in the oil—the crabs will splatter as they cook. Fry until crispy and golden brown, 2 to 3 minutes per side. Drain on a paper towel–lined plate. Season immediately with salt.

Spread mayonnaise on the bottom half of each bun and top with the bacon, dividing it evenly among the sandwiches. Add a crab to each bun and top with shredded lettuce, a couple tomato slices, and the top of the bun.

MAKES 4 SANDWICHES

I am a big fan of lots of black pepper on a tomato sandwich, so I suggest adding 2 tablespoons freshly ground black pepper with the Old Bay in the dredging mix. It's a lot, but it's awesome.

A lot of places like to brag about the size of their crab cakes, but I advise keeping them small. In my recipe, there's no filler, and smaller cakes hold together better. The little bit of bread is on the outside of the cakes, giving them a nice crunchy texture.

CRAB CAKES

In a medium bowl, combine the egg, mayo, mustard, Worcestershire, Old Bay, and parsley. Gently toss in the crab, taking care to not break the lumps.

Heat about ½ inch of oil in a large skillet over medium-high heat.

Place the panko in a shallow bowl. Portion one crab cake by scooping some of the mixture with an ice cream scoop, then drop it into the panko and roll quickly with your hands. Then carefully drop the cake into the hot oil. Repeat to use all the crab mixture, working in batches to not crowd the pan. Allow the cakes to fry without disturbing them until they're golden brown on one side, 2 to 3 minutes. Flip and brown the other side, another 2 to 3 minutes. Drain on paper towel–lined plates and serve with lemon wedges.

MAKES 24 SMALL CRAB CAKES

1 large egg, beaten

2 tablespoons mayonnaise

1 tablespoon Colman's dry mustard

2 teaspoons Worcestershire sauce

2 teaspoons Old Bay seasoning

2 teaspoons chopped fresh parsley

1 pound picked crabmeat, any combination of jumbo lump, lump, claw, and back fin

Canola or corn oil for frying

1 cup panko bread crumbs

Lemon wedges for serving

There's a (mostly) friendly disagreement as to which Brunswick has proper claim to this stew. Is it the county in southern Virginia? Or is it the town in coastal Georgia? And how is it different from Kentucky's Burgoo? Whichever, the original premise of it was to feed a lot of people with inexpensive—or free—meat. The dish has evolved to generally star chicken or pork, but if you have a good source for rabbit, squirrel, or 'possum, please use it—if only for complete authenticity. The hot sauce quantity is often adjusted up for wilder, more gamey meat.

3 tablespoons extra-virgin olive oil

1 chicken, 3½ to 4 pounds, cut into 8 pieces

1 onion, coarsely chopped

2 medium potatoes, cut into ½-inch cubes

2 ears corn, kernels cut from cob, preferably white, cobs reserved (may sub 1 cup frozen corn and omit cobs)

3 stalks celery, finely diced

1 teaspoon kosher salt

1 teaspoon freshly cracked black pepper

1 cup lima beans, raw or frozen

1 (6-ounce) can tomato paste

2 tablespoons apple cider vinegar

1 tablespoon honey

2 teaspoons hot sauce

1 teaspoon chopped fresh marjoram

Brown Chicken Stock (page 480), optional

BRUNSWICK

STEW

In a large, heavy pot or Dutch oven, heat the oil over medium-high heat and brown the chicken pieces, working in batches if necessary, and transfer the browned pieces to a plate. Return all the chicken to the pot and add the onion, potatoes, cobs, celery, salt, and pepper. Cover all the ingredients with water, bring to a boil, and cook at a low boil until the chicken is easily pulled from the bone, about 45 minutes. Remove the chicken and allow to cool. Remove the corn cobs and discard.

To the pot, add the corn kernels, lima beans, tomato paste, vinegar, and honey. Reduce the heat to medium-low and cook, uncovered, for about 10 minutes.

Remove the chicken from the bones and shred. Return the meat to the stew and stir in with the hot sauce and marjoram.

The stew should be thick and full of meat and vegetables. Lore suggests Brunswick, Georgia, prefers it thicker than Brunswick, Virginia, does. If you prefer to thin yours, add chicken stock until it's where you like it.

SERVES 4 TO 6

My mom made these a lot when I was a kid and we always thought of it as a self-contained, single-serving apple pie that we didn't have to share. Of all the dishes the Pennsylvania Dutch have made famous, the Apple Dumpling may be the most prevalent across the country.

APPLE DUMPLINGS

Basic Pie Crust (page 481)

6 medium cooking apples, such as Granny Smith or Braeburn, peeled and cored, but left whole

¾ cup packed light brown sugar

1 teaspoon ground cinnamon

1 teaspoon freshly grated nutmeg

½ teaspoon kosher salt

½ cup raisins

3 tablespoons unsalted butter, cut into pieces

½ cup cream

Preheat the oven to 375°F. Spray a 9-by-13-inch baking pan with cooking spray.

Roll the pie dough out to about ¼ inch thick and cut into six 6-inch squares. Place one apple in the center of each square.

In a small bowl, combine the sugar, cinnamon, nutmeg, and salt. Divide the sugar mixture, raisins, and butter among the apples, stuffing them into the core of the apple and allowing it to generously overflow. Bring the corners of the dough to the top of each apple and pinch the edges together. Place the apples in the pan, at least 1 inch apart. Bake for 30 to 35 minutes, until the crust is golden. Serve warm with cream.

MAKES 6 DUMPLINGS

Filled with molasses and brown sugar, Shoofly Pie is the go-to if you've got a serious sweet tooth. The name may or may not have been derived from the fact that the pie is so sweet that it attracted insects that had to be shoo'd away. For me, the real decision is whether you want a wet bottom or dry bottom. I like it wet; if you like it dry, bake for an additional 12 minutes.

SHOOFLY
PIE

1½ cups all-purpose flour

¼ cup granulated sugar

¼ cup packed light brown sugar

½ cup cold unsalted butter, cut into small pieces

¾ cup warm water

½ cup unsulfured molasses

½ teaspoon ground mace

1 large egg

1 teaspoon baking soda

½ recipe Basic Pie Crust in 9-inch pan (page 481)

Preheat the oven to 375°F.

In a medium bowl, combine the flour and sugars. Cut in the butter with a fork or a pastry blender to make a coarse crumb mixture.

Combine the warm water, molasses, and mace in the bowl of an electric mixer. Add the egg and baking soda and mix at low speed for about 3 minutes. Add half the crumb mixture and beat until smooth.

Pour the molasses mixture into the pie shell and sprinkle the remaining crumb mixture over the top. Bake for 40 minutes, until the topping begins to brown. Cool completely before serving.

SERVES 6 TO 8

How did a tiny island near the southern tip of Maryland become known for a cake? The cake is made up of an inordinate number of slim layers of cake separated by thin layers of frosting. A lot of flavor combinations are available, but this yellow cake with chocolate icing is the one that became the state's official dessert.

SMITH ISLAND
CAKE

FOR THE CAKES: Preheat the oven to 350°F. Spray as many 9-inch round cake pans as you have with cooking spray.

In a stand mixer with the paddle attachment, cream together the sugar and butter. Add the eggs, one at a time, and beat until smooth. Sift together the flour, baking powder, and salt and gradually add to the egg mixture. With the mixer running, slowly pour in the milk and vanilla and mix until smooth.

Pour ½ cup batter into each pan and spread evenly using an offset spatula. Bake for 10 to 12 minutes, until set (the cake will not take on much color). Turn the cakes out onto a cooling rack and cool. Repeat until you use all the batter to make 10 cakes.

FOR THE FROSTING: While the cakes are baking, warm the cream in a medium saucepan over medium heat. Add the chocolate and butter and stir until melted. Then cook for about 5 minutes, whisking regularly, until smooth. Remove from the heat and stir in the vanilla. Allow to cool, then stir in the sour cream.

When the cakes are cooled, put one on a serving platter. Top with ¼ cup of the frosting and spread evenly over the top. Refrigerate for 10 minutes. Remove from the fridge, top with another cake, frost, and refrigerate. Repeat until all the cakes are stacked. Frost the top and the sides, then refrigerate for at least 1 hour before serving.

SERVES 8 TO 10

FOR THE CAKES

1½ cups sugar

1 cup (2 sticks) unsalted butter, cut into chunks

5 large eggs

4 cups all-purpose flour

2 teaspoons baking powder

1 teaspoon kosher salt

1½ cups milk

2 teaspoons vanilla

FOR THE FROSTING

1 cup cream

24 ounces semisweet chocolate chips

13 tablespoons unsalted butter, cut into chunks

2 teaspoons vanilla extract

½ cup sour cream

Mountain people are resourceful. With only a handful of ingredients, most of which hold up well in the pantry, this cake has been a favorite all along the Appalachian range. A tale that may be taller than the cake says that this was a wedding cake made when a collection of thin cakes were gifted to the bride and assembled for the event, a tall cake being the mark of a popular bride. Make it a day or two in advance so the filling soaks into the cake.

APPLE STACK CAKE

FOR THE DRIED APPLE FILLING: In a large saucepan, combine the apples, brown sugar, cinnamon, ginger, and enough water to cover. Bring to a boil over medium-high heat, then reduce the heat to low and cover. Simmer, stirring frequently, until the apples are tender and the filling is very thick, about 1 hour, adding more water if necessary. It should look like a thick apple sauce. Transfer the mixture to a food processor and pulse 8 to 10 times to make a chunky sauce. Set aside.

FOR THE CAKE LAYERS: Preheat the oven to 350°F. Grease and flour two 9-inch round cake pans. In a bowl, whisk together the flour, baking soda, baking powder, and salt. In another bowl, beat the shortening with the brown sugar and molasses with an electric mixer until smooth. Add the eggs and beat until smooth.

Add one-third of the flour mixture and incorporate. Then add half the buttermilk, and alternate until all the flour and buttermilk are mixed in. The dough should be thick.

Divide the dough into 6 equal pieces, each about 10 ounces or a heaping cup. Wrap four of the pieces in plastic wrap. Pat each piece of the unwrapped dough into the cake pans, making it about ½ inch thick. Bake until the cake is set, about 15 minutes. Remove from the oven and allow to cool for 10 minutes.

Remove one cake from the pan and put it on a cake platter. Spread one-fifth of the apple filling, about 1 cup, evenly over the cake. Add the second cake and repeat.

Repeat the baking and layering steps with the remaining four pieces of dough, being sure to grease and flour the cake pans before putting the dough in. Leave the top layer of cake bare. Let the cake sit for several hours. Dust with sifted confectioners' sugar before serving.

SERVES 8 TO 10

FOR THE DRIED APPLE FILLING

½ pound (4 to 5 packed cups) unsulfured dried apples

½ cup firmly packed light brown sugar

½ teaspoon ground cinnamon

½ teaspoon ground ginger

FOR THE CAKE LAYERS

5 cups all-purpose flour plus more as needed

1 teaspoon baking soda

1 teaspoon baking powder

1 teaspoon kosher salt

¾ cup vegetable shortening

1 cup firmly packed light brown sugar

1 cup molasses, preferably sorghum

2 large eggs, lightly beaten

1 cup buttermilk

Confectioners' sugar for dusting

Deep South

Kentucky

North Carolina

BBQ

Tennessee

South Carolina

Mississippi

Alabama

Georgia

-XXX- moon shine

XXX

IN MY OPINION, the strongest culinary connection from the past to the present exists in the Deep South. It is the place where there are traditional, super-delicious dishes served everywhere from a roadside deli to a funky juke joint on the outskirts of town and on through to the fanciest places downtown, like those run by chef pals like Frank Stitt, Hugh Acheson, Kelly English, Sean Brock, Andrea Reusing, John Currence, and a whole mess more.

Following the early settlers, immigration to the South started with the brutal chapter of slave trade from western Africa. Africans brought rice, black-eyed peas, okra, sorghum, watermelon, sesame, peanuts (originally brought to Africa by Portuguese sailors from South America), and a whole list of other ingredients that seem to define American eating and cooking to this day.

Recently touted as "fancy," the delicious Low Country cuisine of South Carolina and Georgia is based magnificently on the influence of western African dishes reinterpreted through the prism of the American melting pot.

And let's not overlook the significance of bourbon in American gastronomy. The New World whiskey is great with food, both sweet and savory, easy to enjoy in a dozen different ways, and most significantly speaks of a cultural beverage tradition as close as we have to European wine culture. We hold the producers of our favorite acclaimed bourbons—which have to be selectively allocated due to high demand and short supply—to be something like royalty. It certainly feels good to have an American bottled product venerated as world-class, and also to know that a lot of the good stuff stays right where it should, in and around Kentucky.

Country and bluegrass music were born here and, along with jazz, are part of America's most profound and influential gift to the world. It's natural to enjoy the Southern food and the music together, particularly at celebratory events.

The Deep South has a real lead in culinary historical perspective, the gastronomic goods are easy to find, and because of the natural law of Southern hospitality, a true Southerner is always eager to share. So let's hit the road!

The roadside treasure in the Southern kingdom is **BBQ**, and BBQ is in the very same line of reverence as bourbon and music. We all know that the road best traveled is not the interstate. Cooks, chefs, and pit masters in tiny towns and hamlets all over the Deep South, particularly the Carolinas, celebrate their take on the smoke, the timing, the sauce—mustard or vinegar based—and the condiments of the low-and-slow cooking of divine porcine royalty. As you travel, you will know you are in the right place if there is a sign with an animated portrait of a smiling pig, rear end on display. In this chapter, I lay out some simple ways to approximate excellent BBQ at home; let me know how these recipes work out for you!

Back when breakfast was the fuel for a true hard day's physical labor, a hefty meal of carbs, protein, and fat wasn't a luxury; it was a necessity. Today, it's certainly worth budgeting extra time on the treadmill in exchange for an occasional indulgence. Don't skimp on the black pepper; it's the defining touch.

BISCUITS AND
SAUSAGE GRAVY

FOR THE BUTTERMILK BISCUITS: Preheat the oven to 400°F. Line a baking sheet with parchment paper.

In a large bowl, combine the flour, baking powder, baking soda, and salt. Using the back of a fork or a pastry cutter, cut in the lard and cold butter until the mixture resembles a coarse meal with small, pea-size bits of butter and lard. Add the buttermilk and mix only enough to bring everything together. On a floured surface, knead the dough 2 or 3 times. Gently roll out, or pat gently with your hands, to an even ¾-inch thickness. Cut out rounds with a 2½-inch biscuit cutter, and put the biscuits on the baking sheet. Gently bring together the scraps and cut a few more biscuits. Brush the biscuits with melted butter. Bake for 15 to 17 minutes, until the tops are golden and irresistible.

FOR THE GRAVY: In a large skillet, preferably cast iron, cook the sausage over medium-high heat, breaking it up with a spatula. Cook until well browned and starting to sizzle. Transfer the sausage to a bowl, but leave behind the fat. Add the flour to the skillet and stir to incorporate with the fat, about 1 minute. Slowly add the milk, whisking constantly to smooth the mixture. Reduce the heat to medium-low. Add the sausage to the gravy and season heavily with black pepper. Taste and add salt and more pepper if necessary.

Serve the gravy over split biscuits, with plenty of hot sauce on the side.

MAKES 10 TO 12 BISCUITS, WITH PLENTY OF GRAVY

FOR THE BUTTERMILK BISCUITS

4 cups all-purpose flour

1 tablespoon baking powder

1 teaspoon baking soda

2 teaspoons kosher salt

6 tablespoons lard (you could sub vegetable shortening, but why?)

6 tablespoons cold unsalted butter, cut into small cubes; plus 2 tablespoons butter, melted

2 cups buttermilk

FOR THE GRAVY

2 pounds sweet Italian sausage, removed from casings

¼ cup all-purpose flour

3 cups milk

1 to 2 tablespoons freshly ground black pepper

Kosher salt

Hot sauce for serving

The "waste not, want not" concept behind Chow-Chow is once again hip. This table staple is a relish that combines anything and everything that's ripe, or even almost ripe, in the garden at the time. It's as perfect on a hot dog as on a warm bowl of beans. The base is usually green tomatoes, cabbage, or both. Then it is all about frugality, the mother of creativity. Feel free to add 1 to 2 teaspoons of other pickling spices to make this relish your own. I like coriander seeds, allspice, cloves, and dill seeds. (Pictured on page 137.)

CHOW-CHOW

12 medium green tomatoes, cored and chopped into ¼-inch dice

2 green bell peppers, stemmed, seeded, and chopped into ¼-inch dice

2 red bell peppers, stemmed, seeded, and chopped into ¼-inch dice

1 small head green cabbage, grated or shredded

4 medium onions, chopped into ¼-inch dice

2 tablespoons kosher salt

2 tablespoons mustard seed

1 tablespoon celery seed

2 teaspoons turmeric

1 teaspoon coriander seeds

6 cloves

1 cup water

1½ cups apple cider vinegar (may sub red or white wine vinegar)

1 cup sugar

Place a large, heavy non-reactive pot over medium-high heat, and add all the ingredients. Bring to a boil, stirring often, and reduce the heat to medium-low. Simmer uncovered for 1 hour, or until the mixture has thickened.

Ladle the chow-chow into sterilized pint canning jars. Seal and process for 10 minutes according to the directions on page 9. The processed chow-chow can be stored for up to a year.

MAKES ABOUT 8 PINTS

I like it spicy, so I might add 3 chopped jalapeños with seeds.

The adage is that "if it grows together, it goes together." Sure, you don't actually "grow" bourbon, but wherever you find a distillery, you're likely to find a peach grove nearby. Slather this on a warm biscuit with butter and just *try* to stop smiling. (Pictured on page 122.)

BOURBON-PEACH
JAM

Set up an ice bath in a large bowl.

Bring a large pot of water to a boil over medium-high heat. With a sharp paring knife, score the bottom of each peach with an X. Drop the peaches in the boiling water for 30 seconds. Remove them with a slotted spoon and drop in the ice water. When cool, slip off the skins, then chop the fruit into small dice, discarding the pits.

In a large pot over medium-high heat, combine the sugar and peaches. Bring to a boil and cook for 30 minutes. Stir in the bourbon and lemon juice. When the mixture returns to a boil, stir in the pectin and boil for 1 minute. Skim any foam off the top and ladle the jam into sterilized half-pint canning jars. Seal and process for 10 minutes according to the directions on page 9. The preserved jam can be stored for up to a year.

MAKES 6 HALF-PINTS

3 pounds ripe peaches

6 cups sugar

½ cup bourbon

3 tablespoons lemon juice

6 ounces liquid fruit pectin

Remember the Corn Muffins (page 18) in New England? This is nothing like those. True Southerners would scoff at the notion of putting sugar anywhere near their cornbread. I have double-checked with Carla Hall several times, and although I may prefer a little sugar, it ain't right in the South. Beyond that, the cast-iron pan is a key here. Preheating the pan helps form the crust on the cornbread, and that's the whole game.

SOUTHERN
CORNBREAD

1 cup all-purpose flour

1 cup yellow cornmeal

1 teaspoon baking powder

1 teaspoon baking soda

1 teaspoon kosher salt

1 cup buttermilk

2 large eggs, beaten

4 tablespoons unsalted butter, melted; plus 2 tablespoons cold butter

Preheat the oven to 400°F. Place a 9-inch cast-iron skillet in the oven to heat.

In a bowl, combine the flour, cornmeal, baking powder, baking soda, and salt. Add the buttermilk, eggs, and melted butter and stir.

Carefully remove the heated pan from the oven. Add the cold butter and let it sizzle until it browns and the noise subsides, then pour the batter into the pan. Return the pan to the oven and bake for 15 to 17 minutes, until the craggy ridges on top of the cornbread start turning brown. Serve warm.

MAKES 8 WEDGES

I might toss in a large handful of chopped green onions right before pouring the batter into the cast-iron pan.

PIMENTO CHEESE

MAKES ABOUT 4 CUPS

I stole this from Carla Hall and jacked it up a bit. In addition to using it to top the Fried Green Tomatoes, you can serve Pimento Cheese on wheat or rye as a sandwich.

1½ pounds extra-sharp Cheddar cheese, shredded

1 (7-ounce) jar sliced pimentos, with juice

6 tablespoons mayonnaise

¼ cup sweet pickle relish, drained in colander 5 minutes

¼ cup grated sweet white onion
    (Vidalia or Walla Walla sweet are the best)

1 teaspoon sugar

Freshly ground black pepper

Mix all the ingredients together in a large bowl. Keep it in an airtight container in the fridge for up to a week.

If you go to the namesake cafe in Irondale, Alabama, and order the dish that inspired the movie, you'll get the traditional condiment of remoulade sauce, and it will be delicious. But my preference has always been to pair fried green tomatoes with another favorite of the Deep South, Pimento Cheese.

IRONDALE CAFE
FRIED GREEN TOMATOES

Pour the buttermilk into a wide, shallow bowl. In another wide, shallow bowl, mix together the cornmeal, salt, and pepper.

In a large, heavy skillet over medium-high heat, heat about ¼ inch of bacon fat.

Dip the tomato slices in the buttermilk, then dredge them in the cornmeal, coating both sides. Working in batches, carefully fry the tomatoes in the hot bacon fat until golden brown, about 3 minutes per side. Remove the tomatoes, drain on a paper towel–lined plate, and season with salt. Repeat to fry all the tomato slices.

Serve the slices topped with Pimento Cheese.

SERVES 4 TO 6, WITH PLENTY OF PIMENTO CHEESE LEFT OVER FOR SANDWICHES ALL WEEK

1 cup buttermilk

1½ cups cornmeal

½ teaspoon kosher salt plus more for seasoning

1 teaspoon freshly ground black pepper

Bacon fat for frying, or sub canola oil

4 large, firm green tomatoes, cut into ¼-inch slices

Pimento Cheese (page 128) for serving

This dip became popular because it comes together quick with pantry staples. The dried beef makes it feel substantial and luxurious. It's perfect for last-minute entertaining. Serve with crackers.

CHIPPED BEEF
PECAN DIP

1 (8-ounce) package cream cheese, at room temperature

½ cup sour cream

1 (2.5-ounce) jar dried beef, julienned

1 small onion, grated

½ green bell pepper, finely diced

1 clove garlic, minced

½ teaspoon freshly ground black pepper

¾ cup chopped pecans

Preheat the oven to 350°F. Spray an 8-by-8-inch baking dish or oven-safe skillet with cooking spray.

In a bowl, stir together the cream cheese, sour cream, dried beef, onion, bell pepper, garlic, and black pepper. Pour into the baking dish and top with the pecans. Bake for 20 to 25 minutes, until bubbling.

SERVES 8 AS AN APPETIZER

I might use the Alpine Italian air-dried beef called bresaola instead of the jarred American dried beef. It's less dry and more supple, and easier to find in delicatessens in cities outside the South, or you can always order it online.

There's something about the soil in a couple of places that produces onions that are nearly sweet enough to eat out of hand. Vidalia, Georgia, is one of those lucky places, and Walla Walla, Washington, is another. As many wonderful kinds of onion as there are, for this kind of dish there really is no substitute for Vidalias.

STUFFED VIDALIA ONIONS

6 large Vidalia onions, tops cut off and root ends trimmed to form a flat base

8 ounces ham, finely chopped

1 cup fresh bread crumbs

6 tablespoons unsalted butter, melted

2 tablespoons sherry vinegar

2 teaspoons chopped fresh sage

½ cup grated Parmigiano-Reggiano

Preheat the oven to 325°F. Spray a 9-by-13-inch baking dish with cooking spray.

With a spoon or melon baller, scoop out the middle of each onion, leaving a shell that's 2 or 3 layers of onion thick. Finely dice the scooped-out onion and set aside.

Bring a large saucepan of water to a boil. Working in batches if necessary, carefully drop the onion shells into the water and blanch for about 5 minutes. Drain.

Line up the onions in the baking dish. In a medium bowl, combine the diced onion, ham, ¾ cup of the bread crumbs, the butter, vinegar, and sage. Toss to moisten the bread crumbs, then divide the filling evenly among the onions. Bake for 45 minutes. Toss the cheese and the remaining ¼ cup bread crumbs together, then evenly divide the mixture over the onions and bake for 10 minutes longer, until the onions are tender. Turn on the broiler and broil for 3 to 4 minutes, until the tops are deep golden brown. Serve hot.

SERVES 6

I like draping a paper-thin slice of country ham or prosciutto over the top of each onion just before serving, and let it kind of melt in.

Charleston is a city with a lot of signature dishes, and She-Crab Soup is among them. Locals insist that the meat of the female crabs is sweeter—an easy notion to believe—but the definitive element of this soup isn't the meat; it's the roe. The roe is extremely seasonal and sometimes hard to come by even in season, so responsible and creative cooks have taken to grating a boiled egg yolk over the soup when necessary. I like to make this soup a day before and let it rest in the fridge overnight. It seems to make it crabbier.

SHE-CRAB
SOUP

In a large saucepan over medium heat, melt the butter. Add the onion and celery and sauté until softened, about 5 minutes. Season with the salt and pepper. Add the flour, whisk to create a roux, and cook for 4 minutes (the roux should not brown). Add the stock and Worcestershire and whisk, then add the milk and continue to whisk. Reduce the heat to low, add 1½ cups of the crabmeat, and simmer for 20 minutes. Stir in the sherry and simmer for 5 minutes longer. Serve in wide, shallow bowls. Garnish with the remaining crabmeat and the roe or egg yolk, and dust with paprika.

MAKES ABOUT 6 CUPS, SERVING 4 TO 6

4 tablespoons unsalted butter

1 small onion, finely chopped

2 stalks celery, finely chopped

1 teaspoon kosher salt

½ teaspoon freshly ground black pepper

¼ cup all-purpose flour

1 cup Brown Chicken Stock (page 480)

2 tablespoons Worcestershire sauce

3 cups milk

2 cups picked crabmeat (about 1 pound), any mix of lump, jumbo lump, or back fin

3 tablespoons dry sherry

2 tablespoons crab roe, or 2 hard-boiled egg yolks, grated, for garnish

Paprika for garnish

The origin of much of the cuisine of the Low Country is easily traced back to Africa, and the notion that eating Hoppin' John on New Year's Day will attract good luck probably started in Africa as well. Serve with Chow-Chow (page 124) to add a hint of sweetness.

HOPPIN' JOHN

¼ cup canola or corn oil

1 smoked ham hock (may sub mild or hot sausage, salt pork, or bacon)

1 medium onion, chopped

10 cups water

1 pound dry black-eyed peas or field peas, rinsed

2 teaspoons kosher salt

3 sprigs parsley

3 sprigs thyme

2 cups long-grain white rice

In a large pot, heat the oil over medium heat. Add the ham hock and onion and cook, stirring, until the onion browns, about 8 minutes. Add 8 cups of the water, the peas, salt, parsley, and thyme. Bring to a boil, then reduce to a simmer. Cover and simmer for 2½ hours, until the peas are tender. Remove the hock and let cool, then pull the meat from the bone. Shred the meat and return it to the pot.

Add the remaining 2 cups water and bring to a boil. Stir in the rice and reduce the heat. Cover and simmer for 20 minutes, until the rice is tender, adding more water if necessary. Serve hot.

SERVES 8

Beer Cheese started off as a complimentary appetizer with crackers, radishes, and celery in the Winchester, Kentucky, restaurant of John Allman in the 1940s. The Allman family still makes the recipe, and now the city has embraced the snack, throwing an annual festival in its honor.

WINCHESTER
BEER CHEESE

In a food processor, pulse the cheese, garlic, Worcestershire, mustard, and cayenne until the cheese is finely chopped and the seasonings incorporated. With the processor running, slowly add the beer and process until all the beer is added and the dip is smooth. Let sit overnight in the refrigerator before serving with crackers or crudités.

MAKES ABOUT 2 QUARTS

1 pound sharp Cheddar cheese, shredded

1 pound mild Cheddar cheese, shredded

2 cloves garlic, thinly sliced

3 tablespoons Worcestershire sauce

1 teaspoon Colman's dry mustard

½ teaspoon cayenne

8 ounces beer (I like a simple lager)

Crackers for serving

PEPPER VINEGAR

MAKES 2 CUPS

2 cups white wine vinegar

6 ounces small chile peppers, such as serrano,
    Thai bird, or Tabasco

1 teaspoon kosher salt

In a medium saucepan over medium heat, warm the
vinegar but do not boil. Meanwhile, with a sharp knife,
poke a slit through each pepper and drop them, one
by one, into an empty wine bottle, preferably a clear
bottle from the white wine you finished off with dinner
last night. Whisk the salt into the warm vinegar. With a
funnel, pour the vinegar into the bottle and top with a
pour-spout. It should sit at least a day but will be better
after a week.

As you use the vinegar, you can replenish with more
white wine vinegar.

With Hoppin' John (page 136) and Southern Cornbread (page 126), Collard Greens are part of the generally accepted lucky New Year's meal, representing success and money. The collards' potlikker—the braising liquid—is a critical element. You'll want plenty of Cornbread to sop it up.

COLLARD GREENS AND
POTLIKKER

In a large, heavy pot or Dutch oven, heat the oil over medium-high heat.

Lightly score the skin on the ham hock or turkey wing (if you use necks, you won't need to score) and place in the pot. Add the onion and garlic and sauté until the onion softens, about 5 minutes. Add 8 cups water and the salt. Bring the water to a boil, then cover the pot, reduce the heat, and simmer for about an hour.

Add the collards, vinegar, sugar, and hot sauce. Stir until the collards are wilted into the liquid, then cover and simmer for 1½ to 2 hours. Check occasionally for tenderness, and replenish with a cup or two of water if it seems dry. The greens are ready when they're tender but still have some texture. Remove the hock, wing, or neck. Pick any meat from the bones, chop it, and stir it into the pot. Discard the bones. Season with salt and pepper to taste—I like a lot of both. Serve with Pepper Vinegar (and Southern Cornbread for sopping up the likker).

SERVES 8 TO 10

2 tablespoons extra-virgin olive oil

2 pounds smoked meat (ham hocks, turkey wings, or neck bones)

1 medium onion, chopped

4 cloves garlic, thinly sliced

2 teaspoons kosher salt plus more for seasoning

3 large bunches collard greens (about 3 pounds), stems removed and discarded, leaves rinsed and cut into inch-wide ribbons

¼ cup apple cider vinegar

2 tablespoons sugar

2 teaspoons hot sauce

Freshly ground black pepper

Pepper Vinegar (page 140) for serving

When Chef Paul Prudhomme started blackening redfish in New Orleans in the mid-'80s, the technique became so popular that limits had to be placed on catching redfish to protect the species. That led to cooks blackening other firm, white-fleshed fish. Catfish, both wild and farmed, is a sustainable option. And if you don't feel like making the spice blend, my late, great pal Paul has some for you in almost every supermarket spice aisle in America.

BLACKENED CATFISH

1 tablespoon dried thyme

1 teaspoon garlic powder

1 teaspoon paprika

1 teaspoon sugar

1 teaspoon freshly ground black pepper

½ teaspoon cayenne

½ teaspoon kosher salt

3 tablespoons unsalted butter

4 (6-ounce) catfish fillets, skinned

Open a window and turn on a fan. It's about to get smoky.

In a shallow bowl, combine the thyme, garlic powder, paprika, sugar, black pepper, cayenne, and salt.

In a large skillet, preferably cast iron, over medium-high heat, melt the butter. Dredge each fillet in the spice mixture on both sides, lay the fillets skin side down in the hot pan, and cook for 4 minutes. Be patient and let it go until literally "blackened." Flip the fish and cook just until cooked through, probably just 1 minute, then serve hot and now!

SERVES 4

This dish will look familiar to curry fans, and it comes by the similarities honestly. Country Captain Chicken is popular in—and nearly limited to—the neighboring Southern port cities of Charleston and Savannah and is thought to have been introduced by a British captain who had traveled to India before coming to the Low Country.

COUNTRY CAPTAIN
CHICKEN

Preheat the oven to 350°F.

Heat the oil in a large, deep, straight-sided ovenproof skillet over medium-high heat. In a small bowl, combine the salt, pepper, and paprika. Season the chicken with the mix and brown the pieces well in the skillet. It should take about 10 minutes, then flip the chicken and brown the other side for about 6 minutes. Remove the chicken to a platter.

Reduce the heat to medium and add the onion, garlic, bell pepper, curry powder, thyme, and ½ cup of the currants to the skillet. Sauté for about 5 minutes, then add the tomatoes and stock. Bring to a boil and stir well, then nestle the chicken pieces on top of the sauce and cover. Put the skillet in the oven and bake for 1 hour, until the chicken is cooked through.

Carefully remove the skillet from the oven and arrange the chicken on a platter. Stir the parsley into the sauce, season with salt and pepper, then spoon over the chicken. Garnish with the nuts and remaining currants. Serve with white rice.

SERVES 6 TO 8

At my house, we add 1 tablespoon of almond butter right before spooning the sauce over the chicken for a deeper nut flavor, but that isn't traditional.

¼ cup extra-virgin olive oil

1 teaspoon kosher salt plus more for seasoning

1 teaspoon freshly ground black pepper plus more for seasoning

1 teaspoon paprika

1 chicken, 3½ to 4 pounds, cut into 8 pieces

1 large onion, finely chopped

3 cloves garlic, thinly sliced

1 medium green bell pepper, finely chopped

1 tablespoon curry powder

1 tablespoon fresh thyme leaves, or 1 teaspoon dried

¾ cup dried currants or golden raisins

1 (14½-ounce) can whole tomatoes, crushed, with juices

1 cup Brown Chicken Stock (page 480)

¼ cup chopped fresh parsley

½ cup chopped peanuts or sliced almonds

Cooked white rice for serving

BBQ

Cooking meat over fire dates back to the dawn of true carnivorism, of course, but the art of barbecue—exposing whole beasts to regulated flame for hours and hours, allowing time, heat, and smoke to transform or even preserve them—is seen as an American original. The first recorded barbecue was by European settlers, or possibly pirates, in the Caribbean, but it's likely that Native Americans had been doing it for a long time before that.

With that established, in modern America barbecue means something just a little bit different depending on who's stoking the fire, and in what part of the country.

THE CAROLINAS: A drive down a rural road is likely to feature several businesses sporting signs with a cartoonish neon pig improbably inviting you to eat it. Stop at one. If you get really lucky, you might see a piece of plywood with "BBQ" spray-painted on it and an arrow pointing toward the side of a gas station. Follow it. It's whole hog here, and most closely related to the very origin of barbecue (see page 148).

TEXAS: It's cattle country, and barbecue is all about beef. Namely, brisket (see page 399). When asked whether you prefer wet or dry, your tolerance for fat is being assessed. There's no judgment. Texas barbecue is also unique in that, while side dishes of beans or potato salad might be available, the proper accompaniment to your brisket is a smoked sausage, the scent of which will leave with you, attached to your clothing, whether you eat one or not.

KANSAS CITY / ST. LOUIS / MEMPHIS: The Midwest is very inclusive of all kinds of meat to barbecue, but it is defined by pork ribs. Kansas City (see page 348) and Memphis (see page 165) are known for their BBQ styles, and St. Louis is the name for the butcher's cut of the rack that's most often used. In Kansas City, ribs are normally anointed with sauce while Memphis prefers a dry seasoning rub.

ALABAMA: You probably won't find White Barbecue Sauce anywhere outside northern Alabama, where it was first concocted by the legendary Bob Gibson. No problem: Just mix a cup of mayo, ½ cup of white vinegar, 2 tablespoons of sugar, the juice of a lemon, and a teaspoon each of horseradish, salt, and pepper, then drape it over your grilled chicken.

MARYLAND: When in Baltimore, it's tempting to eat crab cakes at every meal, I know. But Pit Beef Sandwiches (page 104) are the Charm City's signature meaty option. It's decidedly more of a grilling exercise than barbecuing (the terms are not synonymous). But we're giving credit here for anything with fire.

CALIFORNIA COAST: Just up the 101 from Los Angeles is the little town of Santa Maria, which has a grilling style all to itself (see page 450). The meat of choice is a specific cut of the sirloin called tri-tip, and the grill is a brilliant contraption that has a cooking surface that can be raised and lowered depending on how much heat is needed.

PACIFIC NORTHWEST: A salmon bake is nothing short of an art installation featuring sticks, fish, and fire. And when the tilting and spinning start, it becomes performance art. At home, you can approximate it with Cedar-Planked Salmon (page 467).

HAWAII: In paradise, a proper luau will include Kalua Pork (page 463), which will have been cooked for the better part of the day buried in a hole in the ground surrounded by aromatic leaves, burning embers, and hot rocks.

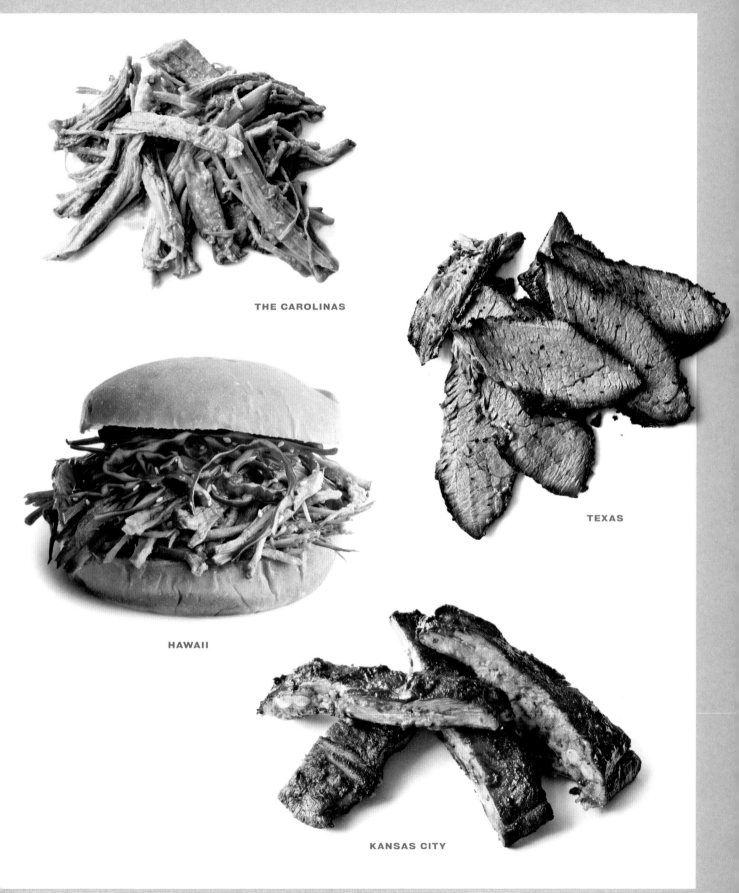

THE CAROLINAS

TEXAS

HAWAII

KANSAS CITY

In the Carolinas, a pork barbecue would start with a whole pig cooked over an open pit for hours and hours, until the flesh is easily pulled from the bones by hand. By limiting this recipe to a shoulder, you can get it done with only about 5 hours on the smoke. Depending on which Carolina you're in, the sauce of choice will be based on either vinegar (North) or mustard (South). The pork can be served on a platter or a sandwich, but either way, it should be paired with the vinegary slaw.

CAROLINA SMOKED
PORK BBQ

2 tablespoons paprika

1 tablespoon kosher salt

1 tablespoon freshly ground black pepper

1 bone-in Boston butt or pork shoulder, about 5 pounds, but any size is fine

North Carolina Red Vinegar Sauce or South Carolina Mustard Sauce for serving

Chopped Carolina Coleslaw for serving

Hamburger buns for serving, optional

Soak 3 cups of hickory wood chips in water for 30 minutes. Set up a charcoal or gas grill for indirect cooking.

Mix together the paprika, salt, and pepper. Liberally season the pork with the mix.

If smoking on charcoal, spread about half the chips over the coals. If smoking on gas, wrap some of the chips in foil and poke holes in the packet. Place the packet on one of the burner elements, under the grate.

Put the pork on the grill, over the unlit side. Close the grill and let the pork cook for 4 to 5 hours, until the internal temperature reaches about 200°F. Turn the pork around every 90 minutes to ensure even cooking and avoid scorching. Replenish the charcoal as necessary, and replenish the wood chips once or twice during the cooking.

Let the pork rest for 15 to 20 minutes. Cut large slabs of meat off the bone and use two forks to shred the meat. Discard any large pockets of fat. If any meat remains on the bone, pull that off with a fork or your fingers. It should fall right off.

Toss the pork in some North Carolina Red Vinegar Sauce, or dress it with some South Carolina Mustard Sauce. Serve with Chopped Carolina Coleslaw, as part of a platter, or on a hamburger bun.

SERVES 8 TO 10

NORTH CAROLINA RED VINEGAR SAUCE

MAKES ABOUT 2¼ CUPS

1½ cups cider vinegar

½ cup hot water

3 tablespoons brown sugar

2 tablespoons ketchup

1 tablespoon kosher salt

1 teaspoon freshly ground black pepper

1 teaspoon cayenne

Mix together all the ingredients and serve in a squeeze bottle.

SOUTH CAROLINA MUSTARD SAUCE

MAKES ABOUT 2¼ CUPS

1 cup prepared yellow mustard

¾ cup apple cider vinegar

2 tablespoons water

½ cup packed light brown sugar

1 tablespoon lemon juice

1 tablespoon kosher salt

1 teaspoon cayenne

1 teaspoon freshly ground black pepper

Mix together all the ingredients and serve in a squeeze bottle.

CHOPPED CAROLINA COLESLAW

SERVES 8 TO 10 AS A SIDE

Serve as a side for BBQ pork or as a topping on a pulled-pork sandwich.

1 medium head green cabbage, about 1 pound, shredded, grated, or finely chopped

1 small red onion, grated

½ cup North Carolina Red Vinegar Sauce

Kosher salt

Combine the cabbage and onion in a bowl. Dress with the vinegar sauce and toss. Refrigerate for at least 2 hours. Taste and season with salt when ready to serve.

Okay, so you like barbecue pork, but you don't want to tend the grill or the smoker for half the day? Here's a hack that will require only about 15 minutes of prep work followed by 10 or so hours of complete and utter neglect. No one on the competitive barbecue circuit will endorse this method, but for dinner on a random weeknight, almost nothing could be better. Slow cookers are very, very hip!

SLOW-COOKER
CAROLINA BBQ PORK

¼ cup packed brown sugar

6 cloves garlic, thinly sliced

1 tablespoon kosher salt

1 teaspoon freshly ground
    black pepper

1 teaspoon smoked paprika

2 tablespoons extra-virgin olive
    oil

1 boneless pork shoulder, 3 to
    4 pounds, cut into 3-inch
    chunks

1 (6-ounce) can tomato paste

¼ cup cider vinegar

1 tablespoon tamarind paste

1 tablespoon Worcestershire
    sauce

Hamburger buns for serving

Chopped Carolina Coleslaw
    (page 149) for serving

In a large bowl, combine the brown sugar, garlic, salt, pepper, and paprika. Add the oil to form a paste. Toss the pork in the mixture, cover, and refrigerate for an hour. Remove from the fridge and pat the pork dry with paper towels.

In a large skillet over medium-high heat, brown the pork on two or three sides. Move the pork to a slow cooker. With the skillet still over the heat, add 1½ cups water to the pan and scrape the bottom with a wooden spoon to dislodge any pork or spices. Add the tomato paste, vinegar, tamarind paste, and Worcestershire and bring to a boil. Pour that over the pork, cover, and set the slow cooker on low to cook for 8 to 10 hours.

When the pork is cooked, pull the chunks out and shred with two forks.

Transfer the cooking liquid to a saucepan over medium-high heat. (Or just remove the insert on your slow cooker and put it on your cooktop if yours is so equipped.) Bring to a boil and reduce the heat to medium. Cook for 15 minutes, or until the liquid has reduced by one-third and thickened. Add the shredded meat to the pot and toss.

Serve on hamburger buns with the coleslaw.

SERVES 6 TO 8

To make this dish truly authentic, your cast-iron pan would be sitting over an open fire and under the clear-blue sky, and the catfish would be fresh from the stream next to the tent you spent the night in. The Doobie Brothers would be camping next to you and playing a set after they poured you a cold beer. This is camping food, and in its best iteration, it's breakfast. I usually fry the hushpuppies after the fish because I like them with a bit of fresh-catch flavor!

FRIED CATFISH
AND HUSHPUPPIES

FOR THE CATFISH: In a large bowl, cover the catfish with the buttermilk. Lift the fillets to reposition them and make sure they're all making full contact with the buttermilk.

In a large skillet, preferably cast iron, over medium-high heat, heat about ½ inch of oil to 360°F.

Mix the cornmeal, flour, salt, pepper, and onion powder in a paper or plastic zip-top bag. Add the fish pieces, 3 or 4 at a time, and shake the bag to coat the fish.

Carefully add the fish to the hot oil by holding each fillet by one end and lowering it to let the other end hit the bottom of the pan, then gently laying the fillet down away from you. Work in batches of 2 or 3 fillets and cook for 5 minutes on each side, until they turn golden brown. Drain on paper towels and immediately season with salt.

FOR THE HUSHPUPPIES: In a large bowl, mix together the cornmeal, flour, baking powder, and salt. Add the egg, buttermilk, and onion and mix well.

After the fish is cooked, bring the oil back to 360°F. Drop the hushpuppy batter by the tablespoonful in the hot oil and fry for about 2 minutes, then flip over and fry for 2 more minutes. They're done when they're gorgeous.

Remove from the oil, drain on a plate lined with paper towels, and season with salt to taste.

Serve the catfish and hushpuppies with lemon wedges.

SERVES 6

FOR THE CATFISH

2 pounds catfish fillets, 4 to 6 ounces each, boneless

1 cup buttermilk

Canola or corn oil for frying

1 cup cornmeal

½ cup all-purpose flour

1 teaspoon kosher salt plus more for seasoning

1 teaspoon freshly ground black pepper

½ teaspoon onion powder

FOR THE HUSHPUPPIES

1½ cups cornmeal

½ cup all-purpose flour

1 teaspoon baking powder

1 teaspoon kosher salt plus more for seasoning

1 large egg, lightly beaten

1 cup buttermilk

1 onion, grated

Lemon wedges for serving

There might not be any other dish as immediately identifiable as "Southern" as grits. Until the '80s, the dish was virtually unknown above the Mason-Dixon Line, unless you were in Italy and called it "polenta." And while their traditional role may be as a side dish at breakfast, grits shine as the co-star of Shrimp and Grits, the warm base for a saucy stew of shrimp. Splurge for American-grown Gulf shrimp if you can. It's good for the country.

SHRIMP AND GRITS

FOR THE GRITS

2 cups Brown Chicken Stock (page 480)

2 cups milk

1 cup stone-ground white grits

1 teaspoon kosher salt

2 cups finely shredded sharp white Cheddar cheese

FOR THE SHRIMP

2 slices thick-cut bacon, cut into small strips

½ teaspoon kosher salt

½ teaspoon freshly ground black pepper

½ teaspoon cayenne

1½ pounds medium shrimp, peeled and deveined

6 green onions, thinly sliced, white and green parts separated

2 cloves garlic, thinly sliced

1 cup Brown Chicken Stock (page 480)

1 teaspoon hot sauce, or more to taste

4 tablespoons unsalted butter, softened

2 tablespoons all-purpose flour

2 tablespoons fresh lemon juice

FOR THE GRITS: In a large saucepan, combine the stock and milk and bring to a boil. In a steady, gradual stream, add the grits, stirring constantly. Add the salt and continue stirring until the liquid returns to a boil. Reduce the heat to low and cook, stirring regularly but not constantly, for 20 to 25 minutes. When the grits start to thicken, they'll gurgle, and they'll be molten hot, so make sure you're using a long-handled spoon. Remove from the heat and cool a spoonful to take a taste. If the grit is gone, you're ready to gradually stir in the cheese, then cover and set aside in a warm place.

FOR THE SHRIMP: Cook the bacon in a large skillet over medium heat until crisp. Remove with a slotted spoon to a paper towel–lined plate, leaving the grease in the pan.

Mix together the salt, pepper, and cayenne and use it to season the shrimp. Add the shrimp to the pan and sauté for about 1 minute, then flip and sauté for another minute, until opaque. Remove to a plate. Add the green onion whites and the garlic to the pan and cook for a minute. Add the stock and hot sauce and bring to a boil.

Meanwhile, in a small bowl, mix together the butter and flour. When the stock comes to a boil, take the pan off the heat, add the butter/flour mixture, and whisk to incorporate. Put the pan back over the heat and stir until the sauce thickens. Add the shrimp to the pan and simmer for 2 minutes, then add the lemon juice. Stir through and remove from the heat.

Serve the shrimp over the grits, garnishing with the crisped bacon and onion greens.

SERVES 6

OYSTER
ROAST

A traditional Charleston Oyster Roast is less a recipe and more an event. You'll need a fire. A big steel plate. A shovel. Some wet burlap. A bushel of oysters. Beer. A bunch of friends.

Can you re-create the experience on a smaller scale? You can try!

Fire up a grill and cover the grates with an old baking sheet or two. Close the grill and let them get blistering hot. Get an old towel and soak it in hot water.

When the baking sheets are hot, dump on a pile of oysters. You can have more than one layer, but spread them out a bit. Cover them with the towel, but keep the towel over the pan(s) so it isn't exposed to the fire. Close the grill and let the oysters cook for 4 or 5 minutes.

Remove the towel with tongs and remove the oysters to a waiting table lined with butcher paper or newspaper. Arm everyone with an oyster knife and open them from the hinge end. Eat straight from the shell, with a little lemon, butter, or Pepper Vinegar (page 140). You will eat many more than you thought you could.

MAKES AS MANY AS YOU CAN GET.

Rice is big in the Carolinas. Red rice is a specific kind of pilau that comes from the Gullah, a community of people in the rural, isolated coastal area between Charleston and Savannah who have retained much of their African culture for more than 300 years. This dish is traced back to an African dish called Jollof rice, and can be a side, or add chicken or shrimp to make it a main course.

CHARLESTON
RED RICE

Preheat the oven to 350°F.

In a large ovenproof skillet over medium-high heat, cook the bacon until crisp. Remove the bacon from the pan with a slotted spoon.

In the bacon drippings still in the pan, cook the onion until soft, about 8 minutes. Add the rice, water, tomato paste, salt, pepper, hot sauce, and bacon pieces and cook for 10 minutes. Cover the skillet and place it in the oven. If it looks dry, add up to ½ cup warm water. Bake for 1 hour, until the liquid has been soaked up and the rice is tender.

SERVES 8 AS A SIDE

6 ounces thick-cut bacon, cut into small pieces

1 medium onion, chopped

2 cups long-grain rice

3 cups water, or more as necessary

1 (6-ounce) can tomato paste

1 teaspoon kosher salt

1 teaspoon freshly ground black pepper

1 teaspoon hot sauce, or more to taste

In the 1920s, Louisville's Brown Hotel was the place to go for dancing on the weekend. A long night of rug-cutting tended to result in a hungry crowd, which was good news for the kitchen crew at the hotel. This open-faced sandwich was created to fill up the dancers, and it has ever since. It simply has to be on white bread; that's all I have to say.

KENTUCKY
HOT BROWNS

4 slices bacon, diced

2 tablespoons unsalted butter

1 small onion, chopped

¼ cup all-purpose flour

2 cups milk

Kosher salt and white pepper

½ cup shredded Cheddar cheese

2 tablespoons grated Parmigiano-Reggiano

4 slices soft white bread, toasted

12 ounces roasted turkey breast, thinly sliced

1 large red tomato, sliced

In a medium skillet over medium heat, cook the bacon until crisp. Remove with a slotted spoon and drain on a paper towel–lined plate.

Add the butter to the bacon drippings, then the onion and sauté until soft, about 5 minutes. Whisk in the flour and cook for a minute or two, until a smooth roux forms. Slowly add the milk, continuing to whisk, until the sauce begins to thicken. Add about ½ teaspoon each salt and white pepper, then add the cheeses and continue whisking until they're melted and the sauce is smooth. Set aside.

Preheat the broiler.

On each of four heatproof dishes, put one piece of toast. Top with 3 ounces of turkey, then tomato slices, and drape the cheese sauce over. Place the dish under the broiler, at least 5 inches from the flame—it needs to get hot inside too—until the sauce browns. Remove, garnish with the crisp bacon, and serve hot.

SERVES 4

In Memphis, they have a thing about not putting sauce on their ribs. No one will stop you from doing it, but it isn't encouraged. That's because they work hard on the rub that seasons the meat in the first place, and once you have eaten a Memphis dry-rub rib, you understand. Other than the paprika and salt, virtually every rub ingredient is in play (try adding ground coffee sometime). I limited the ingredients to nine here, but fifteen to twenty is not unusual.

MEMPHIS DRY-RUB
PORK RIBS

Mix all the spices together in a small bowl.

If your ribs have a silver skin on the bone side, remove it with a knife. Generously coat the ribs with the spice mix and rub it in. (You might not use it all, but I always do.) Wrap the ribs in plastic wrap and refrigerate for at least 2 hours, or overnight.

Prepare a gas or charcoal grill for indirect cooking.

Unwrap the ribs and place them over the unlit part of the grill. Cover and cook for 3 hours for spareribs, or 2½ hours for baby backs. The bone ends will be exposed when the ribs are ready, but the meat should not be "fall-off-the-bone tender." That's overcooked. The meat should require a gentle tug to come away from the bone. If using a charcoal grill, you'll need to replenish the charcoal once or twice during the cooking. Serve hot.

SERVES 6 TO 8

¼ cup paprika

¼ cup kosher salt

¼ cup dark brown sugar

1 teaspoon cayenne

1 teaspoon Colman's dry mustard

1 teaspoon freshly ground black pepper

1 teaspoon garlic powder

1 teaspoon celery seed

1 teaspoon dried thyme

2 racks pork spareribs or baby backs, 5 to 7 pounds total

Fried Chicken

With the possible exception of bacon, almost nothing gets our collective juices flowing faster than the prospect of a fried chicken dinner. And one of the best things about fried chicken in America is that it isn't really just one thing.

We can start defining it with the Colonel—though I've never seen a dish that actually benefits from eleven herbs and spices. Focus, Colonel!

Better to take a look in the kitchen of your grandmother, where Sunday supper might have featured a fried bird that had spent a couple hours in buttermilk before being swathed in flour—two, maybe three times—then fried in lard in a cast-iron skillet.

Maybe if you went to your aunt's house, it was batter-dipped and deep-fried, and it tasted a little like…lemon? She might have wanted to know if you liked it just a little bit better than your grandma's. At that moment, maybe you did. But the story could change by the next time you were at Grandma's house. In fact, it better have, if you wanted more chicken.

Maybe you had dinner at a friend's house and it wasn't even fried. It came out of the oven and got its crunch from bread crumbs that were attached by…magic?

The options are endless, and none are wrong!

On pages 168 and 169, I've included my recipes for two of my favorite kinds of fried chicken: the classic buttermilk Southern Fried Chicken that will bring back memories, and an incendiary version called Nashville Hot Chicken that folklore says was developed to punish a philanderer. Now it's a local industry.

Fried chicken is at the same time universal and highly personal. Follow these recipes, then think about what you like. Maybe you'd like a lemon-herb brine instead of buttermilk. Or pickle-juice brine. Maybe you'd like a tablespoon of your favorite herb in the flour. Try it. If you want, you could even add a little bit of bacon fat to the oil.

Before long, you'll have a new favorite fried chicken.

Yours.

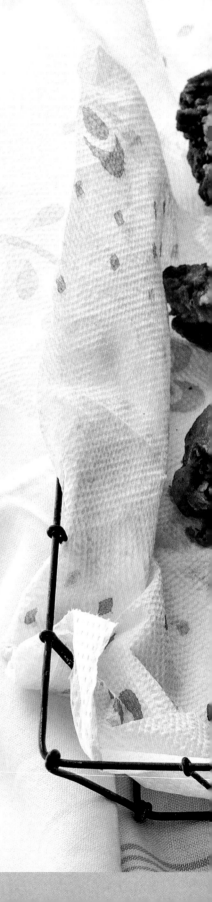

NASHVILLE
HOT
CHICKEN

2 chickens, 3½ to 4 pounds
   each, each cut into 8 pieces
8 tablespoons cayenne plus
   more for seasoning
2 tablespoons kosher salt
Canola or corn oil for frying
1 tablespoon dark brown sugar
1 tablespoon paprika
1 teaspoon garlic powder
2 cups buttermilk
¼ cup hot sauce (such as
   Tabasco or Texas Pete)
3 cups all-purpose flour
White bread and sweet pickles
   for serving

Lay the chicken pieces out on a rack over a baking sheet and pat dry with paper towels.

Combine 2 tablespoons of the cayenne and 1 tablespoon of the salt and season the chicken on all sides. Refrigerate for at least 4 hours.

In a deep, heavy pot or Dutch oven over medium-high heat, heat 2 inches of oil to 350°F. Preheat the oven to 200°F.

In a small bowl, combine the remaining 6 tablespoons cayenne, the brown sugar, paprika, and garlic powder. Divide this mixture in half.

In a shallow bowl, combine the buttermilk and hot sauce. In another shallow bowl, combine the flour, remaining 1 tablespoon salt, and half the cayenne mixture.

Dip each piece of chicken into the buttermilk, dredge through the flour mixture, then back in the buttermilk, and once more through the flour. Set aside.

In batches, carefully drop the chicken into the oil and fry, turning once, for 14 to 16 minutes. Insert an instant-read thermometer into the thickest part of a breast; it's done at 160°F. Remove the chicken to a clean baking sheet and hold in the warm oven while frying the rest of the chicken.

When all the chicken is fried, carefully ladle ½ cup of the frying oil into a heat-safe bowl containing the rest of the cayenne mixture. Stir to combine and spoon with abandon over the fried chicken. Season with more cayenne to taste.

Serve with white bread and sweet pickles in an attempt to calm your taste buds.

SERVES 6 TO 8

SOUTHERN
FRIED
CHICKEN

Lay the chicken pieces out on a rack over a baking sheet and pat dry with paper towels.

Put 2 cups of the buttermilk in a large bowl and add 1 tablespoon of the thyme and 1 tablespoon of the salt. Add the chicken to the bowl, making sure to coat each piece, then cover the bowl and refrigerate for 4 to 8 hours.

In a large cast-iron skillet or Dutch oven, heat 2 inches of oil to 350°F. Preheat the oven to 200°F.

In a wide, shallow bowl, combine the flour, remaining 1 tablespoon salt and 1 tablespoon thyme, along with the paprika, pepper, and garlic powder. In another wide, shallow bowl put the remaining 2 cups buttermilk. Line two baking sheets with paper towels and put a wire rack over each.

Working with 2 or 3 pieces at a time, remove the chicken from the buttermilk and dredge in the flour. Then dip in the fresh buttermilk and dredge in flour again. If you run short of buttermilk, it's OK to use the buttermilk marinade. Place the chicken on one of the wire racks while coating the rest of the chicken.

In batches, use tongs to put the chicken in the hot oil. Fry, turning occasionally, for 14 to 16 minutes. Insert an instant-read thermometer into the thickest part of a breast; it's done at 160°F. Remove the chicken to the clean wire rack and hold in the warm oven while frying the rest of the chicken.

Serve hot, though it will be good cold the next day, too.

SERVES 6 TO 8

2 chickens, 3½ to 4 pounds each, each cut into 8 pieces
4 cups buttermilk
2 tablespoons fresh thyme
2 tablespoons kosher salt
Canola or corn oil for frying, or lard if you're serious about it
3 cups all-purpose flour
2 tablespoons paprika
1 tablespoon freshly ground black pepper
2 teaspoons garlic powder

MINT JULEP

MAKES 1 COCKTAIL

The drink forever associated with the Kentucky Derby probably made its way there from the farms of Virginia, where a similar drink was a favorite way for farmers to start the day. But ever since bourbon and mint met a silver cup, a Mint Julep has been an integral part of a day at the races.

FOR THE SYRUP

1 cup water

1 cup sugar

1 cup mint leaves

FOR THE JULEP

2 ounces bourbon

1 ounce mint simple syrup

10 mint leaves plus one sprig

Crushed ice

FOR THE SYRUP: Bring the water and sugar to a boil in a medium saucepan. Add the mint and stir. Remove from the heat and steep for 20 minutes. Strain and cool completely before using.

FOR THE JULEP: In a shaker, muddle the bourbon, syrup, and mint leaves. Add crushed ice and shake. Fill a rocks glass with more crushed ice and strain the liquid into the glass. Garnish with the mint sprig.

If you see a Sweet Potato Pie sporting a marshmallow top, you're probably looking at one made by a Northerner. Some people put marshmallows on their sweet potato side dish at Thanksgiving, but true Southerners don't put them on Sweet Potato Pie.

SWEET POTATO

PIE

2 pounds sweet potatoes
   (3 to 4 large)

½ recipe Basic Pie Crust in
   9-inch pan (page 481)

3 large eggs

4 tablespoons unsalted butter,
   melted

1 cup packed light brown sugar

½ cup half-and-half

2 tablespoons bourbon,
   optional

2 tablespoons molasses plus
   more for serving, optional

1 teaspoon vanilla extract

1 teaspoon freshly grated
   nutmeg

Whipped cream for serving

Preheat the oven to 400°F.

Line a baking sheet with foil or a silicone mat. Prick each potato several times with the tip of a small, sharp knife. Place on the baking sheet and roast for 60 minutes, turning them over halfway through, until soft. When cool enough to handle, remove the skins, put the flesh in a large bowl, and mash with a fork.

Prebake the prepared pie crust for 12 minutes, until just tan. (You can put it in the oven during the last 12 minutes the potatoes are roasting.) Reduce the oven temperature to 350°F.

In the bowl of a stand mixer with the paddle attachment, combine the eggs, butter, sugar, half-and-half, bourbon (if you like), molasses, vanilla, and nutmeg until smooth. Add the roasted sweet potato and mix to form a smooth filling.

Pour the filling into the pie crust and bake for 45 minutes, until the filling begins to set. Allow to cool to room temperature. Serve with softly whipped cream and a drizzle of molasses, if you like.

SERVES 6 TO 8

The South is covered in beautiful, lattice-topped peach pies, but the most famous variation in the Atlanta area is the Fried Peach Pie from the Varsity restaurants. *Waddaya have?! Waddaya have?!*

FRIED
PEACH PIES

4 peaches, just ripe but not overripe

¼ cup sugar

½ teaspoon freshly grated nutmeg

1 tablespoon water

1 tablespoon all-purpose flour

1 teaspoon almond extract or bourbon

Basic Pie Crust (page 481)

2 tablespoons brown sugar

½ cup sliced almonds, toasted

Canola or corn oil for frying

Bring a pot of water to a boil and have a bowl of ice water waiting nearby. With a sharp knife, cut an X in the bottom of each peach. Submerge them in the boiling water for 15 seconds, then move them to the ice water. Pull the skin away with a paring knife. Chop the peaches into small dice, discarding the pits.

In a medium saucepan, cook the diced peaches, sugar, and nutmeg over medium heat until the sugar has melted and the peaches have softened, about 3 minutes. In a small bowl, whisk together the water and flour and add to the peaches. Stir and heat until thickened. Set aside to cool completely, then stir in the extract.

Working in batches, roll out the dough to about ⅛ inch thick and cut out fourteen to sixteen 5-inch rounds. Place about 1½ tablespoons of the cooled filling on each round, a little off-center. Fold the dough over to encase the filling and crimp the edges closed. Repeat to use all the filling and crust. Reroll crust scraps and cut out more circles until you are done.

In a food processor, combine the brown sugar and almonds. Chop them together to form a coarse dust. Set aside.

In a large, straight-sided skillet, heat about an inch of oil to 365°F. In batches of 3 or 4, fry the pies until golden brown and crisp, about 4 minutes. Remove to a paper towel–lined platter and dust with the almond-sugar mixture.

MAKES 14 TO 16 INDIVIDUAL PIES

In my own home version, I love the addition of 1 teaspoon ground cardamom to the peach mixture, but it is far from traditional, bordering on heretic.

Peaches

Peaches are grown in forty-seven of the United States, and if you ask someone where the best peaches in the country are grown, they're likely to have the same answer: "Right here." It's a compelling argument. The best peach will be one that was allowed to ripen on the tree, so all the sugars can develop. A peach that will be shipped has to be picked before it's really ripe, and degradation occurs during shipping, making the fruit softer but not a bit sweeter. So it's true. The best peach comes from the tree you are currently closest to.

CALIFORNIA: Like so many crops, more peaches come from the Golden State than any other. Almost three-quarters of the nation's peaches grow in California, including almost all the peaches that are processed for canning.

GEORGIA: The Peach State has undergone a bit of an identity crisis over the years. Georgia earned the nickname because it is likely one of the entry points for the first trees that came to the continent, via monks on St. Simons Island in the late 1500s. Despite its historic connection, neighbor South Carolina long ago surpassed Georgia in production, and it's something no one in Georgia really wants to talk about.

SOUTH CAROLINA: Just to rub it in a little bit, South Carolina likes to refer to itself as the "tastier peach state." Quality is subjective, but quantity isn't arguable. South Carolina ships more peaches than Georgia, but the two states feud over which has sweeter peaches. They agree on one thing, though: They don't like California's.

COLORADO: It may not seem terribly impressive that the state is in the top ten peach producers in the country, but it is notable that most of its orchards are in one county: Mesa. If not for the town of Palisades on the Western Slope of the Rockies, there wouldn't be a fresh peach season at all in a huge swath of the West.

NEW JERSEY / PENNSYLVANIA: The area of South Jersey and southeastern Pennsylvania is an important area for peach growers, and peaches hold a surprising footnote in Civil War history here: Some of the most intense fighting of the Battle of Gettysburg happened in a peach orchard.

There was a time when refined sugar was an expensive luxury. Molasses was an accessible and inexpensive substitute and makes for a funky favorite that now has a tradition all its own.

MOLASSES COOKIES

½ cup (1 stick) unsalted butter, softened

¼ cup sugar plus more for rolling

½ cup molasses

1 large egg

2 cups all-purpose flour

2 teaspoons baking soda

1 teaspoon ground ginger

1 teaspoon ground cinnamon

½ teaspoon freshly grated nutmeg

½ teaspoon ground allspice

1 teaspoon kosher salt

In the bowl of a stand mixer with the paddle attachment, cream together the butter and sugar until fluffy. Add the molasses and egg and mix them in.

In another bowl, combine the flour, baking soda, ginger, cinnamon, nutmeg, allspice, and salt. Slowly add the dry ingredients to the butter mixture and mix to combine. Let the dough rest in the refrigerator for at least an hour, or up to overnight.

Preheat the oven to 350°F. Line two baking sheets with silicone liners or parchment paper.

Pour some sugar into a small bowl. Form the dough into balls about the size of Ping-Pong balls and roll in the sugar. Place on the baking sheets about 2 inches apart. Bake for 10 to 12 minutes. Remove to wire racks to cool.

MAKES ABOUT 36 COOKIES

The state itself isn't the inspiration behind the name of the Mississippi Mud Pie. The thinking is that the dark, sludgy pie bears a striking resemblance to the murky bed of the mighty river. The similarities likely end there, unless the waterway is lined with delicious chocolate cake and pudding on a stretch I have not yet seen. In some versions, this is like a cake, in some, it is wetter, like a pie. In this recipe, it's definitely a combination. You can make it more cakey by baking it 5 to 10 minutes longer.

MISSISSIPPI
MUD PIE

FOR THE PUDDING: In a medium saucepan, combine the half-and-half, sugar, and espresso over medium heat. Whisk until the sugar dissolves, then add the chocolate and whisk until it melts.

In a small bowl, whisk together the yolks and cornstarch. Add ¼ cup of the warmed half-and-half mixture to the bowl and whisk, then pour it into the pan, whisking vigorously to combine. Gently raise the heat and cook until the pudding begins to thicken, about 10 minutes. Cover the surface with plastic wrap and refrigerate for at least an hour.

FOR THE CAKE: Preheat the oven to 350°F. Spray a 9-by-13-inch baking pan with cooking spray.

In a medium saucepan over medium heat, melt the butter and add 1 cup of the chocolate chips. Stir until the chocolate melts. Remove from the heat. With a whisk in a large bowl, or in the bowl of a stand mixer with the paddle attachment, combine the butter/chocolate mixture with the sugar and vanilla. Add the eggs one at a time, whisking or beating and letting each incorporate before adding the next. Sift together the flour and cocoa and carefully stir that into the mixture. Fold in the remaining 1 cup chocolate chips. Pour the batter into the baking pan. Bake for 20 to 25 minutes. It will be a moist cake. Let cool to room temperature.

Preheat the oven's broiler.

TO ASSEMBLE: Spread the pudding over the cake, top with the pecans first and then the marshmallows. Place under the broiler until the marshmallows begin to brown. Watch closely, because it will only take about a minute, and it will quickly go from delicious to incinerated if you aren't paying attention.

SERVES 15

FOR THE PUDDING

2 cups half-and-half

½ cup sugar

2 tablespoons instant espresso powder

4 ounces bittersweet dark chocolate, finely chopped

3 large egg yolks

3 tablespoons cornstarch

FOR THE CAKE

1 cup (2 sticks) unsalted butter

2 cups chocolate chips

1 cup sugar

1 teaspoon vanilla extract

4 large eggs

1½ cups all-purpose flour

1 tablespoon unsweetened cocoa powder

1½ cups pecans, chopped

3 cups mini marshmallows

Cobbler is the classic dessert in the South and peaches are omnipresent throughout South Carolina for about four glorious months of the summer. It's a simple dessert that only gets better when served warm with a scoop of ice cream.

PEACH COBBLER

3 large fresh peaches, peeled, pitted, and sliced (about 3 cups)

¾ cup sugar

7 tablespoons unsalted butter

1 cup milk

1½ cups all-purpose flour

1 teaspoon baking powder

1 teaspoon ground cinnamon

1 teaspoon kosher salt

Vanilla ice cream for serving

Preheat the oven to 375°F.

In a bowl, toss the peaches with ¼ cup of the sugar. Set aside for about 15 minutes.

Melt the butter by putting it in a 9-by-9-inch baking pan in the oven for a few minutes. In a bowl, whisk to combine the remaining ½ cup sugar, the milk, flour, baking powder, cinnamon, and salt.

Without stirring—Southerners are adamant on that point—pour the batter into the pan, then put the peaches, including any juices, on top. Use a fork to poke the peaches down a bit, until they are nearly submerged. Bake for 50 to 60 minutes, until the cobbler is golden. Let rest for at least 20 minutes before serving with a little warm cream or ice cream.

SERVES 9

The Coconut Cake is the iconic dish of Charleston, with the skyscraping twelve-layer version of the Peninsula Grill the benchmark. Here we go for eight layers, but the more layers you can do, the more icing you get! The cake is traditionally served around the holidays. Which holiday? Any of them! If you have this cake, you have reason to celebrate. It's a lot of work, but plan on making the coconut cream and the filling one day, then make the cakes and frosting and assemble it the next. It's worth the effort. If there is one cake in this book that will change your life, this is it.

COCONUT
CAKE

FOR THE COCONUT CREAM

2 pints heavy cream

2 cups coconut flakes,
    preferably unsweetened

FOR THE FILLING

½ cup granulated sugar

½ cup (1 stick) unsalted butter

2 tablespoons cornstarch

½ cup sour cream

1 teaspoon vanilla extract

FOR THE CAKE LAYERS

4 cups all-purpose flour

1 tablespoon baking powder

1 teaspoon kosher salt

2 cups granulated sugar

1½ cups (3 sticks) unsalted
    butter, softened

5 large eggs

1 tablespoon vanilla extract

FOR THE COCONUT CREAM: Combine 1 pint of the cream and all of the coconut in a blender and puree. Pour the mixture in a bowl, add the remaining cream, and stir well. Cover and refrigerate for at least 2 hours, or overnight. Strain through a fine sieve, pushing the solids to extract as much liquid as possible. Discard the solids and reserve the cream, refrigerating until needed. Makes about 3 cups.

FOR THE FILLING: In a medium saucepan over medium heat, warm 1½ cups of the coconut cream, the granulated sugar, and butter. In a small bowl, whisk together the cornstarch and sour cream. Raise the heat to bring the cream to a slight boil and whisk in the sour cream, whisking constantly until thickened. Take off the heat, whisk in the vanilla, and refrigerate overnight.

FOR THE CAKE LAYERS: Preheat the oven to 325°F. Spray four 9-inch round cake pans with cooking spray. (Or prepare two pans and plan to repeat the baking step.)

Sift together the flour, baking powder, and salt. In the bowl of a stand mixer with the paddle attachment, beat the granulated sugar and butter. Add the eggs one at a time, waiting until each is incorporated before adding the next. Beat in the remaining 1½ cups coconut cream and the vanilla. Gradually add the flour mixture to the butter mixture, beating until incorporated. Divide the batter among the 4 pans and bake for 25 to 30 minutes. The cakes should not take on much color. Remove the cakes by inverting onto a wire rack and allow them to cool completely.

FOR THE FROSTING: With an electric or stand mixer, combine the cream cheese and confectioners' sugar and mix until smooth, then add the sour cream and mix again until smooth.

TO ASSEMBLE: If the cakes formed domes on top, take a serrated knife and slice parallel to the work surface to mostly even them up. Now, cutting parallel to the work surface, cut each cake in half horizontally to make eight thin rounds. Very carefully move one round to a cake platter. If you have coconut cream left over, brush it onto the surface of the cake. Spread ¼ cup of the filling evenly on the top. Add another layer of cake and repeat until all the cake layers are filled and stacked, leaving the top layer uncovered.

Beat the frosting to loosen it up and spread it over the top and side of the cake. Press the coconut flakes into the top and side.

Present the cake proudly before serving.

SERVES 10 TO 12

FOR THE FROSTING

8 ounces cream cheese, room temperature

1 cup confectioners' sugar

1 cup sour cream

3 cups coconut flakes, preferably unsweetened

Woodford County, Kentucky, is known for two things. There's the bourbon distillery, and there's Woodford Pudding. The two aren't necessarily related, but the gooey, cake-like treat is traditionally enrobed with a buttery caramel sauce that often benefits from a shot or two. Most Woodford Pudding recipes call for blackberry jam, but I am such a fan of fresh blackberries that I changed it up a bit. When it comes to blackberries, that's just how I roll.

WOODFORD
PUDDING

FOR THE PUDDING

2 pints fresh blackberries

1½ cups granulated sugar

½ cup (1 stick) unsalted butter, softened

3 large eggs

½ cup sour cream

1 cup all-purpose flour

1 teaspoon ground cinnamon

1 teaspoon baking soda

FOR THE SAUCE

1 cup packed dark brown sugar

4 tablespoons unsalted butter

¼ cup bourbon or sherry

2 tablespoons cream

FOR THE PUDDING: In a bowl, toss the blackberries with ½ cup of the granulated sugar. Set aside for 1 hour.

Preheat the oven to 350°F. Spray a 9-by-9-inch baking dish with cooking spray.

In a stand mixer with the paddle attachment, cream together the remaining 1 cup sugar and the butter. Add the eggs, one at a time, then the sour cream. Sift together the flour, cinnamon, and baking soda. Still beating, gradually mix that into the butter mixture until well incorporated.

Fold the berries and their juice into the batter and pour the batter into the baking dish. Bake for 30 to 35 minutes.

FOR THE SAUCE: In a medium saucepan over medium-high heat, combine the brown sugar and butter and cook until the sugar melts, then until it starts to caramelize, about 8 minutes total. Off the heat, add the bourbon and cream. Return to the heat and whisk until smooth.

Serve the pudding warm with the sauce on top.

SERVES 9

You're familiar with the big horse race in Louisville in May, right? The Kentucky Derby? Well, there's a famous pie from Kentucky that's popular right around the time of the Derby. The chocolate-and-nut pie originated in the 1950s and has become synonymous with the race. Eponymous, even. The family that claims to have invented it owns a trademark to the commonly used name of the pie, as smart Southerners are wont to do. So I won't say it here. But I'll say Derby. And Pie. Separately.

FAMOUS KENTUCKY
HORSE RACE PIE

3 large eggs

½ cup granulated sugar

½ cup packed dark brown sugar

¼ cup all-purpose flour

½ cup (1 stick) unsalted butter, melted and cooled

2 tablespoons bourbon (may sub 1 teaspoon vanilla extract)

½ recipe Basic Pie Crust in 9-inch pan (page 481)

1 cup chocolate chips

1½ cups pecans, coarsely ground

Whipped cream for serving

Preheat the oven to 350°F.

In a bowl, whisk together the eggs, sugars, and flour. Mix in the butter, then the bourbon.

In the pie shell, scatter the chocolate and pecans. Pour in the egg mixture. Bake for 50 to 60 minutes, until the filling is set. Serve warm with whipped cream.

SERVES 6 TO 8

I might spike the whipped cream, stirring in an ounce of my best bourbon just after whipping.

Frankfort, Kentucky, is the home of the Buffalo Trace distillery, makers of Pappy Van Winkle bourbon. Coincidentally, it was also the home of Ruth Booe, a candymaker who in 1938 took the challenge of combining her confection with the local distillate. What she created has been a gift-giving favorite ever since. When it comes to cookies, we go all brand-name at our house, so let's just say it—they're Nilla Wafers.

BOURBON BALLS

In a food processor, combine the cookies and pecans and grind together into a fine meal. Pour into a large bowl and add ¾ cup of the confectioners' sugar, the bourbon, corn syrup, and cocoa. Form into 36 to 40 balls. Put the remaining ¼ cup confectioners' sugar in a shallow bowl and roll the balls in the sugar.

MAKES ABOUT 3 DOZEN

1 (11-ounce) box vanilla wafer cookies

1 cup pecans, toasted in a 350°F oven for 6 to 8 minutes

1 cup confectioners' sugar

½ cup bourbon

2 tablespoons light corn syrup

2 tablespoons unsweetened cocoa powder

Instead of rolling them in confectioners' sugar, I like to roll them in a shallow bowl of Demerara sugar for added crunch and subtle complexity.

The origin of the name is in doubt, but the likelihood is that it involves a mispronunciation that stuck. Whatever it was called, Chess Pie has probably been made in America since before it was America, and modest variations can be found in other parts of the country. Maple Cream Pie (page 63) is similar but with syrup instead of sugar; Hoosier Sugar Cream Pie (page 307) thickens with cornstarch instead of eggs.

CHESS
PIE

½ cup (1 stick) unsalted butter

2 cups sugar

6 large eggs

¾ cup milk

2 teaspoons white vinegar

1 teaspoon vanilla extract

½ teaspoon kosher salt

½ recipe Basic Pie Crust in 9-inch deep-dish pan (page 481)

Preheat the oven to 350°F. In a stand mixer with the paddle attachment, cream together the butter and sugar. Add the eggs, one at a time, beating to incorporate each before adding the next. Add the milk, vinegar, vanilla, and salt. Pour into the pie shell. Bake on the low rack in the oven for 15 minutes. Reduce the heat to 325°F and bake for 50 to 60 minutes longer, until the filling is set.

SERVES 6 TO 8

GULF COAST

Louisiana

Mississippi

FISH FRY

Alabama

Florida

IF THERE IS ONE PLACE in the whole U S of A that is defined by a kick-back-and-relax mind-set, it is the Gulf Coast. This is where fun comes to have a good time. This is where Jimmy Buffett's Parrotheads were born and continue to thrive in the joyous recognition of simple, natural beauty. Forrest Gump might be considered the mayor here, always in pursuit of perfect shrimp, where the sweet breezes off the gulf bring everyone dreams of oysters, po' boys, and gumbo. There is a simplicity of culture and a pursuit of happiness that is unique. Half of it is because of the remarkable climate and landscape, and the other half is because of the people who boat, fish, dance, sing, cook, and reflect on their good fortune to live in paradise.

In Louisiana, the Cajun and Creole cultures brim with the music and the delicious cooking redolent of the bayou and the city: the trinity of the sofrito and the mystery of the voodoo queen all wrapped into one undeniably magnetic culture. I can think of no other town in the entire U.S. that has as much unique and region-specific flavor packed into one place as New Orleans. My chef pals there include my brother Emeril Lagasse, Donald Link and Stephen Stryjewski, John Besh, Susan Spicer, Tory McPhail, Alon Shaya, John Folse, and Sue Zemanick—they all practice the culinary arts like alchemists and wizards, at once playing the music of respect for the ancient traditions of gumbo and jambalaya and crawfish etouffee while pushing the edge of innovation. Chefs and home cooks alike know the importance of their roots and suffer no loss of street cred when they do not reinvent the wheel every day just for reinvention's sake.

Roadside treasures in the Gulf Coast include **PO' BOYS, FISH-FRY SHACKS** for sandwiches and baskets, **BOUDIN TO GO,** and oddly enough, **DRIVE-THRU DAIQUIRI STANDS!**

The undeniable wealth of traditional ingredients like Apalachicola oysters, gulf shrimp, sassafras, andouille sausage, tasso ham, catfish, crawfish, redfish, kumquats, persimmons, and boudin make it easy as pie to write and cook a menu that celebrates just about everything good in life on the Gulf Coast.

Traveling around the coast of Florida starts in Miami, through the Keys and then up to Tampa and St. Pete. I go from stone crab claws for breakfast in Miami, into fried grouper sandwiches on St. Pete Beach for lunch and key lime pie for dessert, then head up the coast on my way to oysters Rockefeller and bread pudding in the panhandle.

The entire Gulf Coast seems to enjoy a high level of culinary technique. Just about every "Bubba" or "Moon Doggie" or "Gopher" I have ever met can filet a fish, fry a hushpuppy, and make a damn good gumbo with what looks like very little effort. It may be a natural gift, but it's also because cooking here has always been for fun and pleasure, and almost never out of duty. Get-togethers are as much about the making of stuff as about the eating and drinking of it, so I suggest just joining in and cooking!

The French brought the fried dough concept to New Orleans in the 1700s, and doughnuts, as the rest of the country knows them, evolved later. You're going to want a nice, strong cup of cafe au lait with this, and they'll taste even more delicious if you sit outside at an ornate, cast-iron bistro table with a Dixieland jazz soundtrack, sometime after 3 a.m.

BEIGNETS

1 envelope (2¼ teaspoons) active dry yeast

½ cup warm water, about 110°F

1 large egg, beaten

1 cup milk

4 tablespoons unsalted butter, melted

¼ cup granulated sugar

½ teaspoon freshly grated nutmeg

½ teaspoon kosher salt

4 cups all-purpose flour

Canola or corn oil for frying

Copious amounts of confectioners' sugar

In a large bowl, dissolve the yeast in the warm water. When it begins to foam, add the egg, milk, melted butter, granulated sugar, nutmeg, and salt and stir to combine. Mix in the flour until a dough forms. Cover with a towel and let rise for an hour or 2, or refrigerate overnight.

In a large, heavy pot or Dutch oven, heat about 2 inches of oil to 375°F.

Dust a work surface with flour and roll out the dough to about ½ inch thick. Cut into about 2 dozen 2-inch squares. Working in batches, fry the beignets for 1 to 2 minutes per side, until just golden brown. Drain on paper towels. While they're still warm, put 2 or 3 on a plate, shake confectioners' sugar on them, and watch them disappear.

MAKES 24 TO 30 BEIGNETS

The most famous item at the All Steak Restaurant in Cullman, Alabama, isn't steak, and it isn't even on the menu. It's the orange roll that comes with your meal. You should probably make a double batch ...

HOT
ORANGE ROLLS

FOR THE DOUGH: In the bowl of a stand mixer with a dough-hook attachment, combine the yeast, 1 teaspoon of the sugar, and the warm water. When it begins to foam, add the remaining ¼ cup sugar, milk, melted butter, egg, and salt. Mix to combine. Add the flour and slowly mix until damp, then mix on high speed for 6 to 7 minutes, until the dough comes together. Continue to knead the dough for a few minutes, then put in a large, greased bowl, cover with a towel, and set in a warm place to rise for about an hour, or until doubled in size.

FOR THE FILLING: In a small saucepan, heat the orange juice and raisins. Bring nearly to a boil, remove from the heat, and soak for 15 minutes. Drain the raisins, reserving ½ cup of the juice for the glaze. In a bowl, combine the orange zest and soaked raisins with the cream cheese, brown sugar, and cinnamon.

TO ASSEMBLE: Butter a 9-by-13-inch baking pan. On a floured work surface, roll out the dough into about a 12-by-18-inch rectangle. Spread the raisin filling over the dough, leaving a 1-inch bare border along one long side. Starting on the long side opposite the bare border, roll up the dough like a jelly roll. Seal the seam with a little water.

Cut the log into twelve 1½-inch-thick slices and place in the prepared pan. Cover with a towel and let rise in a warm place for 45 minutes.

Preheat the oven to 350°F.

Bake the rolls for 30 minutes, until the rolls are golden.

FOR THE GLAZE: In a bowl, whisk the confectioners' sugar and reserved ½ cup orange juice to form a glaze. Spread over the warm rolls and serve.

MAKES 12 ROLLS

FOR THE DOUGH

1 envelope (2¼ teaspoons) active dry yeast

¼ cup plus 1 teaspoon granulated sugar

¼ cup warm water, about 110°F

1 cup milk

4 tablespoons unsalted butter, melted

1 large egg, beaten

½ teaspoon kosher salt

3½ cups all-purpose flour

FOR THE FILLING

Zest and juice of 2 oranges

½ cup golden raisins

8 ounces cream cheese

1 cup packed light brown sugar

1 teaspoon ground cinnamon (or nutmeg or cloves)

FOR THE GLAZE

2 cups confectioners' sugar

½ cup orange juice, reserved from filling

One of the ways people in warm climates combat the heat is by eating fiery food, and anything can become a fiery food with a couple shakes of hot sauce. Most famous is Tabasco sauce, from near New Orleans. But if you can't find Tabasco peppers to make your own, Scotch Bonnet peppers are readily available, and hot sauce made from them is popular in the Caribbean communities of South Florida. Scotch Bonnet heat is punishing, but the peppers are fruity, a trait accentuated by the sweetness of carrot and cane syrup. (Pictured on page 210 and 221.)

SCOTCH BONNET

HOT SAUCE

½ pound ripe Scotch Bonnet or habanero chile peppers

½ cup kosher salt

1 cup cider vinegar plus more if necessary

1 medium carrot, shredded

1 small red onion, finely chopped

4 cloves garlic, smashed

3 tablespoons cane syrup or honey

Put on a pair of latex gloves to handle the peppers. Do *not* skip this step.

Stem and chop the peppers. In a large bowl and using a large spoon, toss the peppers with the salt. Cover with a lid or plastic wrap and let sit at room temperature for 3 to 5 days.

After the peppers have fermented, put on another pair of gloves, and goggles aren't a bad idea if you have them. Rinse the peppers under cool water. Add them to a saucepan with the vinegar, carrot, onion, garlic, and syrup. Heat until the mixture boils, then cook, stirring, for 5 minutes. Reduce the heat to low and simmer for 30 minutes. Allow to cool to room temperature, then puree in blender until smooth. Add more vinegar if the hot sauce seems too thick.

Stored in small, glass bottles, the sauce will last indefinitely, but you'll use it faster than you can determine its true shelf life.

MAKES ABOUT 2 CUPS

When you drive into Florida and stop at the Welcome Center, the first thing they do is hand you a cup of orange juice. Citrus is that much a part of the state's identity. When you drive out, there will likely be a jar or two of preserved sunshine in your car, picked up as a souvenir.

ORANGE
MARMALADE

Place 2 small plates in the freezer.

Cut each orange in half, then cut each half into four pieces, removing any seeds as you go. Thinly slice each piece of orange and put the fruit in a bowl. Quarter the lemons, removing and discarding the seeds. Thinly slice the lemons and add them to the oranges.

Weigh the citrus. You want a little less sugar than you have citrus. If you have about 2½ pounds of citrus, figure on 2 pounds of sugar.

In a large saucepan, combine the citrus, sugar, and water. Cook, stirring regularly, until the mixture reaches 220°F, 30 to 45 minutes. Test the consistency by doing the frozen-plate test as described on page 9. When the marmalade is ready, skim any foam off the top and ladle it into half-pint or 4-ounce canning jars. Can according to the directions on page 9.

MAKES 6 HALF-PINTS

5 oranges, washed in warm water

2 lemons, washed in warm water

About 2 pounds sugar

2 cups water

One of the greatest aspects of American sports culture is tailgating. It's easy to forget there's a game at all if the food is good enough. Football fans in Louisiana and Mississippi prep for their big games with spreads that often start with these gems. You can pretty much do whatever you want to do with the spices: make it sweet, savory, spicy, hot. If you choose to personalize the recipe, start with a little spice and add more in the inevitable second batch.

CAJUN SPICED
PECANS

4 tablespoons unsalted butter, melted

2 tablespoons sugar

1 teaspoon cayenne

½ teaspoon ground cinnamon

½ teaspoon paprika

3 cups (12 ounces) pecan halves

1 teaspoon kosher salt

Preheat the oven to 300°F.

In a bowl, whisk together the melted butter, sugar, cayenne, cinnamon, and paprika. Toss the pecans in the mixture, then spread them out in a single layer on a baking sheet. Sprinkle salt over the nuts, then bake for 30 minutes. Store in an airtight container.

MAKES 3 CUPS

SAZERAC

MAKES 1 COCKTAIL

The concept of the cocktail was born in America, and New Orleans claims to be where it all started. So the city's signature drink, the Sazerac, may have been the original. The reason the recipe specifically calls for Peychaud's bitters is because the drink is credited to Antoine Peychaud, who mixed up the first Sazerac in 1838.

FOR THE SIMPLE SYRUP

½ cup water

½ cup sugar

FOR THE COCKTAIL

2 ounces rye

3 dashes Peychaud's bitters

Ice

½ ounce anisette, such as Pernod or Herbsaint

1 lemon twist

FOR THE SIMPLE SYRUP: Bring the water and sugar to a boil in a medium saucepan. When the sugar has dissolved, remove from the heat and cool completely before using.

FOR THE COCKTAIL: In a cocktail shaker, combine the rye, 1 ounce simple syrup, bitters, and ice. Cover and shake.

In a rocks glass, pour in the anisette and tilt the glass to coat the entire interior with a film of it, then pour out any excess (into the next glass). Add a couple of ice cubes to the glass, then strain the cocktail into the glass and add the lemon twist.

Dixie Crossroads is a restaurant in Titusville, Florida, that made rock shrimp famous; it was founded by the guy who figured out how to split the previously inedible creatures open. Broiled rock shrimp is a signature of theirs, but I made up the spice butter and added the cocktail sauce. You can buy cleaned and ready-to-cook rock shrimp all over the country almost year-round, but they are at the peak from July to November.

BROILED ROCK SHRIMP
COCKTAIL

1 cup ketchup

3 tablespoons freshly grated horseradish (may sub prepared horseradish)

Zest and juice of 1 lime

2 teaspoons hot sauce, or more to taste

½ cup (1 stick) unsalted butter, melted

1 teaspoon sweet paprika

1 teaspoon celery salt

1 teaspoon freshly ground black pepper

½ teaspoon kosher salt

2 pounds rock shrimp, shells split and shrimp cleaned (you can usually buy them shelled and cleaned)

In a bowl, make the cocktail sauce: Stir together the ketchup, horseradish, lime zest and juice, and hot sauce. Refrigerate.

Preheat the broiler and set a rack in the top position.

In a large bowl, whisk together the melted butter, paprika, celery salt, pepper, and salt. Reserve half the butter sauce in a ramekin. Add the shrimp to the remaining butter mixture in the bowl and toss to coat. Pour the shrimp out onto a baking sheet and spread out into a single layer. Put the sheet under the broiler and broil for 2 to 4 minutes, until the shrimp become opaque and begin to curl.

Serve warm with the cocktail sauce and reserved butter sauce.

SERVES 4

In bygone days on the streets of Tampa's Ybor City neighborhood, vendors would hawk these handheld crabby croquettes. The best part: The dough employs the old childhood trick of deflating spongy commercial white bread into a dough of sorts. Go ahead, be ten years old again!

DEVIL CRAB

In a food processor, grind one of the loaves of bread into bread crumbs. You should get about 5 cups crumbs.

Remove and discard the crust from the other loaf. Tear the bread into large pieces, place in a large bowl, and add water to cover. Pour out into a large sieve and drain. Wrap the saturated dough in a clean tea towel, twist it closed, and squeeze as much water as possible out. You won't get it all, and that's fine.

Put the soaked white-bread "dough" in a large bowl and add the paprika and about a teaspoon each salt and pepper. Add 3 cups of the bread crumbs and stir to incorporate. Wrap the dough in plastic wrap and refrigerate for at least an hour while you make the filling.

In a medium skillet over medium heat, melt the butter, then add the bell peppers and onion and sauté until softened, about 5 minutes. Add the parsley, Worcestershire, mustard, and hot sauce and mix to heat through and incorporate. Remove from the heat, add the crab, and stir carefully to incorporate, but try to avoid breaking the meat. Let the filling cool completely.

When ready to assemble, divide the dough into 8 to 10 uniform balls. Dust your work surface with some bread crumbs, reserving the rest. Working one at a time, roll each ball of the dough in the reserved bread crumbs. Flatten the ball on the work surface and use a rolling pin to form a 6-inch disc, about ¼ inch thick. Add ¼ cup of the crab filling, carefully fold the dough around the filling, and pinch the sides together to make a croquette that is roughly football-shaped…or crab-shaped, if your mind is open. Sprinkle some more of the crumbs on top and set on a parchment-lined tray while you repeat to use all the dough and crab.

In a large, straight-sided skillet, heat about 1 inch of oil to 350°F.

Working in batches to avoid crowding, carefully add the croquettes to the oil and fry until golden brown, about 2 minutes, then flip and fry the other side another minute or 2. Drain on paper towels and season with salt immediately. Serve with lemon wedges.

MAKES 8 TO 10

2 loaves sliced white bread

1 teaspoon paprika

Kosher salt and freshly ground black pepper

2 tablespoons unsalted butter

½ green bell pepper, finely diced (about ¼ cup)

½ red bell pepper, finely diced (about ¼ cup)

½ small onion, finely diced (about ½ cup)

2 tablespoons chopped fresh parsley

2 teaspoons Worcestershire sauce

1 teaspoon Colman's dry mustard

1 teaspoon hot sauce

8 ounces crabmeat, any mix of lump, claw, and back fin

Canola or corn oil for frying

Lemon wedges for serving

Mullet was once practically currency on the Gulf Coast of Florida, and shacks that smoked them were everywhere. There are fewer now, but you can still find places such as Ted Peters in St. Petersburg that specialize in the fish. Any oily smoked fish will work in a good dip. Serve with Saltines.

SMOKED FISH DIP

1 pound smoked fish, such as mullet, whitefish, mackerel, salmon, or sable, skin and bones removed

8 ounces cream cheese, at room temperature

Zest and juice of 1 lemon

1 tablespoon chopped chives, optional

2 cloves garlic, minced

1 teaspoon kosher salt

Smoked paprika

In a medium bowl, break up the fish into small pieces. Add the cream cheese, lemon zest and juice, chives (if you like), garlic, and salt and mix with a fork, using the back of it to break up the fish against the side of the bowl. Put in a serving bowl and dust with paprika.

MAKES 1 QUART, SERVING 8 TO 10

When you're driving through southern Louisiana on Highway 90, deep in the heart of Cajun country, find a little gas station somewhere and stop whether you need gas or not. Because you definitely need a paper bag full of fresh-boiled boudin, the rice-and-pig-parts sausage that fuels that part of the country.

BOUDIN

OR CAJUN WHITE SAUSAGE

1½ pounds pork shoulder

8 ounces pork liver

8 ounces pork kidney or heart (may sub more shoulder or liver)

1 small onion, finely chopped

1 poblano chile pepper, stemmed, seeded, and finely chopped

3 tablespoons kosher salt

1 tablespoon freshly ground black pepper

1 tablespoon cayenne

2 teaspoons ground cumin

6 cups cooked rice

1 cup chopped green onions, green parts only

½ cup finely chopped fresh parsley

Sausage casings, optional

Cut all the meats into strips or cubes that will go through your meat grinder and grind them together on your grinder's most coarse setting. (You can have your butcher grind the meats. He or she will probably ask what you're making and will be impressed when you answer.)

In a large bowl, toss together the combined ground meats with the onion, poblano, salt, black pepper, cayenne, and cumin. Cover and refrigerate for 2 to 4 hours, then mix in the rice, green onions, and parsley.

For authenticity, stuff the sausage into casings and boil them for 15 to 20 minutes, until the meat is cooked through.

The sausage is just as delicious formed into patties and pan-fried, or formed into balls and deep-fried.

MAKES ABOUT 12 LINKS OR 10 TO 12 PATTIES

Calas are rice fritters that are traditionally prepared and served like beignets, coated in powdered sugar. They are also sometimes rethought as a savory vehicle with andouille but can go in many directions. Most recipes are linked to families, not towns. My personal version adds another definitive and intuitive Big Easy ingredient: crawfish.

SAVORY CALAS

1 tablespoon unsalted butter

1 stalk celery, finely chopped

½ green bell pepper, finely chopped

8 ounces peeled, cooked or fresh crawfish tails (may sub shrimp), coarsely chopped

Kosher salt and freshly ground black pepper

1 envelope (2¼ teaspoons) active dry yeast

2 tablespoons warm water, about 110°F

1½ cups cooked rice

3 large eggs

1 cup all-purpose flour

1 teaspoon kosher salt

Canola or corn oil for frying

Cayenne for seasoning

2 green onions, finely chopped

In a large skillet over medium-high heat, heat the butter and sauté the celery and bell pepper until softened, about 4 minutes. Add the crawfish and season with salt and black pepper. If the crawfish was precooked, just heat through. If it was fresh, sauté until cooked through, 4 to 5 minutes. Place in a bowl to cool and set aside.

In the bowl of a stand mixer with the paddle attachment, dissolve the yeast in the warm water. Add the rice, eggs, flour, and salt and mix. Stir in the crawfish mixture, cover with a towel, and let rise for 1 hour.

In a large, deep pot or Dutch oven, heat 2 inches of oil to 370°F. In batches, using two spoons, make round balls of the batter and drop by heaping spoonfuls into the oil. Fry until golden brown, turning to brown both sides, 3 to 4 minutes total. Drain on paper towels and dust with cayenne. Stack on a platter and scatter the green onion over the top.

MAKES 16 TO 18

In 1899, when a restaurant wanted to get everyone's attention, it didn't gild an omelet with gold leaf and charge $1,000. It made a dish that evoked richness and gave it a bold name that people would immediately associate with luxury. That was the year that the proprietor of Antoine's in New Orleans introduced Oysters Rockefeller and put the restaurant on the culinary map forever.

OYSTERS
ROCKEFELLER

Preheat the broiler.

In a large skillet over medium-high heat, melt the butter and sauté the minced celery, green onions, and garlic for a couple of minutes, just until softened. Add the spinach and celery leaves and sauté until wilted, 2 or 3 minutes. Mix in the bread crumbs, hot sauce, and anisette, if using.

Arrange the oysters in their shells on a baking sheet. Top each one with a teaspoonful of the spinach mixture. Broil long enough to brown the topping and get the edges of the oysters starting to curl, about 5 minutes. Serve immediately.

MAKES 24 PIECES, SERVING 4 TO 6

4 tablespoons unsalted butter

1 stalk celery, finely minced, plus any leaves

2 green onions, finely minced

2 cloves garlic, thinly sliced

5 ounces baby spinach, julienned

½ cup panko bread crumbs

1 teaspoon hot sauce

2 tablespoons anisette, such as Pernod or Herbsaint, optional

24 oysters, shucked, on the half shell

Sitting on Clearwater Beach. Facing west. Toes in sand. Sun quickly descending into the far reaches of the Gulf of Mexico. A plastic cup covered in condensation from its frosty contents. If this scene does not also include a Fried Grouper Sandwich, the picture is incomplete and I am unhappy. Be happy. Choose joy. I'll gladly eat these for breakfast any day I can see the magnificent Gulf of Mexico.

FRIED GROUPER
SANDWICH

Canola or corn oil for
    deep-frying

1 (16-ounce) bottle beer

1 large egg, lightly beaten

1½ cups all-purpose flour

½ cup cornmeal

1 teaspoon baking powder

Kosher salt

2 pounds grouper fillets,
    cut into 4 pieces

Freshly ground black pepper

4 hamburger buns, toasted

½ cup Tartar Sauce
    (page 24)

1 medium tomato, thinly sliced

Shredded iceberg lettuce

Dill pickle chips

Hot sauce for serving

In a large, heavy pot or Dutch oven, heat 3 inches of oil to 370°F. Preheat the oven to 225°F.

In a large bowl, whisk together the beer, egg, flour, cornmeal, baking powder, and 1 teaspoon salt.

Dry the fish with a paper towel and season with salt and pepper. Working in batches, dip the fillets in the batter, then carefully lower into the oil. Fry for about 6 minutes, turning as necessary. When they're golden brown, remove to a paper towel–lined baking sheet and keep warm in the oven while the rest of the fish fries.

Open the toasted buns and slather the bottoms with tartar sauce. Add a fish fillet to each sandwich and top with tomato, lettuce, and pickles. Have a bottle of hot sauce handy and serve with fries and a sunset. Experience American happiness.

MAKES 4 SANDWICHES

In Florida, October 15 is something of a holiday, because that's the start of stone crab season. If you're not diving for your own, you can get the claws from vendors all along the coastline, steamed, cracked, and ready to eat. Among the various crabs in American waters, the stone crab is unique. We eat only the claws, and only one is harvested from a crab at a time. The crab is returned to its habitat and regenerates the claw.

STONE CRAB CLAWS
WITH MUSTARD SAUCE

In a small bowl, whisk together the mayo, cream, mustard, Worcestershire, salt, and lemon juice. Serve in dipping bowls with the cold crab claws.

SERVES 4 TO 6

1 cup mayo, I prefer Hellmann's (it's called Best Foods west of the Mississippi)

2 tablespoons cream

2 tablespoons Colman's dry mustard

2 teaspoons Worcestershire sauce

½ teaspoon kosher salt

Juice of 1 lemon

12 jumbo stone crab claws, steamed, cracked, and chilled

I would make the sauce spicier with the addition of 2 chopped serrano chiles and a tablespoon of green Tabasco.

In essence—(*whassssup* brother Emeril!)—a Crawfish Pie is an etouffee wrapped up in a pie crust. It's so beloved that it's part of the chorus in the Hank Williams song, "Jambalaya." *Son of a gun, we'll have big fun on the bayou!*

CRAWFISH PIE

2 tablespoons unsalted butter

1 medium onion, finely chopped

1 green bell pepper, finely chopped

3 stalks celery, finely chopped

3 cloves garlic, thinly sliced

1½ pounds fresh or thawed frozen cooked crawfish tails, peeled

Kosher salt and freshly ground black pepper

2 teaspoons cayenne, or more to taste

1 cup Brown Chicken Stock (page 480)

¼ cup all-purpose flour

3 green onions, finely chopped

1 teaspoon hot sauce, or more to taste

½ recipe Basic Pie Crust in 9-inch deep-dish pan (page 481)

Preheat the oven to 325°F.

In a large skillet over medium-high heat, melt the butter and sauté the onion, bell pepper, celery, and garlic until the onion is softened, about 5 minutes. Add the crawfish tails, season with salt, black pepper, and the cayenne, and sauté for 5 minutes.

In a bowl, whisk together the stock and flour. Pour into the skillet and cook, stirring until the mixture begins to thicken. Add the green onions, hot sauce, and salt to taste.

Pour into prepared pie shell and bake for 30 minutes. Serve hot, in bowls.

SERVES 8 TO 10

Seafood Boils and Bakes

If you follow the perimeter of the country, you'll find people taking the seafood that's most available to them and turning it into a party.

In Maine, it's lobster. Down the coast of New England, it's clams, possibly with some lobster thrown in.

In Maryland, it's blue crabs. From the Carolinas and along most of the Florida coastline, it's shrimp. And in New Orleans, it's crawfish. Or shrimp. Or crabs.

Head west and the Dungeness crab is the star all the way up the coast. At some point, king crab legs might enter the picture.

A lobster bake or a clambake involves a fire on the beach with seaweed and burlap creating steam. A crab boil, shrimp boil, or crawfish boil requires only a large pot and propane burner. But re-creating any iteration at home is a similar process.

First, you get a huge pot, preferably one with a perforated insert. If you have a turkey fryer with a propane burner that you used only one time, it just became a multitasker. Get a couple of days' worth of newspaper and spread them on a picnic table.

The number of people you're hosting—and the size of your pot—will determine the amount of each ingredient to buy, but you're going to find a familiar cast of characters in each pot:

- The star, whether it's lobster, clams, crab, shrimp, or crawfish. Figure a pound or so per person. But you know who you're inviting. You might want more.
- Corn on the cob. About an ear per person. Each ear shucked and cut in half.
- Some parts of the country add a couple of whole artichokes. This is an excellent idea.
- Small new or red-skin potatoes. Three or four per person.
- A few onions, cut in half.
- Smoked sausage, cut in 1-inch lengths.
- A couple boxes of boil seasoning. Popular brands are Old Bay in the Mid-Atlantic area and Zatarain's on the Gulf Coast.
- A couple of lemons.
- Plenty of melted butter.

The pot gets filled halfway with water and brought to a boil. Drop in the perforated basket that came with the pot. The seasoning mix goes in. Cut the lemons in half, squeeze in the juice, and throw the rest in. Add the potatoes, the onions, the corn, artichokes if you have them, and the sausage. Boil for about 10 minutes.

The time everything cooks after this depends on who the star is, which goes in next. Lobsters, clams, crawfish, and crabs need 15 to 20 minutes. Shrimp need only about 5 minutes.

To remove the basket, don some heavy, heatproof gloves, then lift the basket slowly to allow it to drain, and dump the basket on the newspaper. Have melted butter and lemon wedges on hand, and mallets if you're having crabs.

Creole is the fancy city cooking of the Gulf Coast region, as opposed to the more rustic offerings of the Cajuns. The name of these stuffed peppers may be derived more from the tomato-cayenne-thyme sauce than from the overall provenance of the dish. I usually make three times this recipe because I love them cold from the fridge for lunch two days later. Ground pork is my choice, but you can use the Boudin recipe (page 214) to make this a little more elaborate and *yumbangwheee*!

CREOLE STUFFED
BELL PEPPERS

4 large bell peppers, any color

2 tablespoons extra-virgin olive oil

1 pound ground pork

1 small onion, finely chopped

2 stalks celery, finely chopped

2 cloves garlic, thinly sliced

1 cup cooked rice

2 cups Basic Tomato Sauce (page 480)

Kosher salt and freshly ground black pepper

1 teaspoon cayenne

1 tablespoon fresh thyme leaves

1 cup shredded Cheddar cheese

½ cup fresh bread crumbs

¼ cup chopped fresh parsley

Fill a large saucepan halfway with water and bring to a boil over medium-high heat. Preheat the oven to 350°F.

Cut the top ½ inch off one pepper and pull the stem and seedpod out. Trim the pepper flesh from around the stem, finely chop, and reserve; discard the stem and pod. Pull the veins out of the pepper and discard. Repeat with the remaining peppers. Drop the peppers in the boiling water and cook for 4 to 5 minutes, until they start to soften. Remove, drain, and set aside.

In a large skillet, heat the olive oil over medium-high heat and sauté the pork until it is browned. Remove the pork with a slotted spoon and leave the grease behind. In it, sauté the chopped bell pepper, onion, celery, and garlic until the onion softens, about 5 minutes. Return the pork to the pan and add the rice. Stir to incorporate. Add the tomato sauce and cook for 10 minutes, stirring regularly. Season with salt and pepper to taste and add the cayenne and thyme.

Stand the peppers upright in a baking dish just large enough to hold them.

Stuff them to overflowing with the pork and rice mixture. Bake for 30 minutes. Meanwhile mix the cheese, bread crumbs, and parsley together. Top each pepper with one-fourth of the cheese mixture and bake for 10 minutes more, to melt the cheese. Serve hot.

MAKES 4 PEPPERS, SERVING 8 IF YOU CUT THEM IN HALF

Po' Boys famously originated as a symbol of solidarity during a streetcar strike in New Orleans in 1929. Today, there are purveyors on every street, and there really is no definitive kind of Po' Boy. The key is the soft French bread. What fills it is the cook's imagination. A favorite is the Roast Beef Debris version. The "debris" in this hero comes from the gravy made with all the delicious bits that fall off in the cooking and carving of the roast.

THE PO' BOY

FOR THE ROAST BEEF: Liberally season the beef with salt and pepper on all sides. Preheat the oven to 350°F.

In a large, deep ovenproof pot or Dutch oven, heat the olive oil over medium-high heat. Sear each side of the beef, about 5 minutes per side. Drop the onion in the pot around the beef, and add the thyme. Add enough water to come about an inch up the side of the beef. Cover the pot and put it in the oven. Cook for about 3 hours, checking each hour to maintain the water level and adding more if necessary.

Carefully transfer the roast to a cutting board and let rest for 15 to 20 minutes.

Remove and discard the thyme stems. Put the pot over medium-high heat. In a bowl, whisk together the flour and water. When the broth is boiling, whisk in the flour mixture and continue to whisk until the gravy thickens. Scrape any bits off the bottom of the pot. That's the "debris." Taste and adjust the seasoning if necessary. Take the gravy off the heat and set aside.

Slice the beef against the grain into ¼-inch slices. It may fall apart. That's fine. That's more debris.

FOR THE SANDWICHES: Spread one half of each piece of bread with mayo. Dip slices of beef in the gravy and add them to the sandwiches. Top the meat with tomato, lettuce, and pickle chips, then add the top piece of bread and serve.

MAKES 6 SANDWICHES

FOR THE ROAST BEEF

1 top round or chuck roast, 3 to 4 pounds

Kosher salt and freshly ground black pepper

3 tablespoons extra-virgin olive oil

1 onion, thinly sliced

½ bunch thyme

¼ cup all-purpose flour

½ cup water

FOR THE SANDWICHES

6 (6-inch) lengths soft French bread, cut open and toasted

Mayonnaise

3 large tomatoes, thinly sliced

Shredded iceberg lettuce

Dill pickle chips

Remember, a Po' Boy isn't one thing. There are many variations. My fave versions are made with fried shrimp or fried oysters: Take a pound of peeled shrimp or shucked oysters, dredge them in flour, dip them in beaten egg, then coat them in panko bread crumbs. Fry in shallow oil in a large skillet over medium-high heat until they're crispy, then season with salt, pepper, and cayenne and pile them on the bread until they start falling out.

Natchitoches Meat Pies are a street food that may predate streets. They've been popular in the Cane River area of Louisiana's Natchitoches Parish since the time of the Louisiana Purchase. The operative theory is that Native Americans in the area were making a meat pie and shared it with Spanish explorers, who noted its similarities to their beloved empanada.

NATCHITOCHES
MEAT PIES

2 tablespoons extra-virgin
   olive oil

1 pound ground beef

1 pound ground pork

6 green onions, chopped

2 teaspoons kosher salt plus
   more for seasoning

2 teaspoons freshly ground
   black pepper

2 teaspoons crushed red
   pepper flakes

1 teaspoon hot sauce

½ cup all-purpose flour

Basic Pie Crust (page 481)

Canola or corn oil for
   deep-frying

In a large skillet over medium-high heat, heat the olive oil and add the beef, pork, green onions, salt, black pepper, pepper flakes, and hot sauce. Cook, stirring, until the meat is cooked through, 8 to 10 minutes. Dust the meat mixture with the flour, a little at a time, stirring in between additions. Allow the mixture to cool, then drain any remaining liquid.

Dust a large work surface with flour. Working with about a quarter of the dough at a time, roll the dough out ⅛ inch thick. With a 5-inch round cookie cutter, cut out 14 to 16 circles. As you make the rounds, place about 2 tablespoons of the meat mixture off-center on each piece of dough. Dampen an edge of the dough, and fold it over to encase the meat. Crimp the edge to close. Repeat until all the dough and filling are used.

In a large, deep pot, heat about 3 inches of oil to 350°F. In batches of 2 or 3, fry the pies, swirling them around a bit so they don't stick to the bottom of the pan, until golden brown, about 5 minutes. Drain on paper towels, sprinkle with salt while the pies are still hot, and serve.

MAKES 14 TO 16 PIES

The origin of the word jambalaya is in question, but one theory is that it's a mash-up of *jamón*, the French word for ham, and a West African word for rice. That may or may not be true, but it bears resemblance to the Spanish paella and is a favorite when there's a big crowd to feed.

SHRIMP

JAMBALAYA

In a large, heavy pot, heat the oil over medium-high heat. Add the onions, bell pepper, and celery and sauté until the onion softens, about 5 minutes. Add the sausage and sauté for 5 minutes. Add the tomato sauce and stock, reduce the heat to medium-low, and simmer for 30 minutes.

Bring the liquid to a boil, add the rice, 2 teaspoons salt, and cayenne and stir. Reduce to a simmer, cover, and cook for 18 to 20 minutes, until the rice has soaked up most of the liquid. Add the shrimp and half of the green onions and cook for 5 minutes, until the shrimp have turned opaque. Season with salt and black pepper. Serve with hot sauce and the rest of the green onions on the side.

SERVES 10 TO 12

¼ cup extra-virgin olive oil

2 large onions, diced

1 green bell pepper, diced

2 stalks celery, diced

1 pound smoked sausage, such as andouille or kielbasa, cut into ½-inch slices

3 cups Basic Tomato Sauce (page 480)

4 cups Brown Chicken Stock (page 480) or water

2 cups uncooked long-grain white rice

2 teaspoons kosher salt plus more for seasoning

1 teaspoon cayenne

1½ pounds shrimp, peeled and deveined

6 green onions, thinly sliced

Freshly ground black pepper

Hot sauce for serving

There are lots of rules, and no rules, with gumbo. The only one I have is to start with a dark, musky roux. I like to feature a fish and a fowl; you can use almost any to make it your own. Swap in duck and crawfish for the chicken and shrimp and you'll be the hero of the potluck. Okra is a controversial vegetable and was originally used as a thickener, but I do not love the slime. If you want okra, garnish with Crispy Cornmeal Okra (page 323).

CHICKEN AND SHRIMP
GUMBO

2 tablespoons plus 1 cup canola or corn oil

1 chicken, 3½ to 4 pounds, cut into 10 pieces

1 cup all-purpose flour

1 large onion, diced

1 green bell pepper, diced

2 stalks celery, diced

1 pound andouille sausage (may sub kielbasa), sliced into ½-inch rounds

8 cups Brown Chicken Stock (page 480) or water

2 teaspoons kosher salt, or more to taste

1 teaspoon cayenne, or more to taste

6 green onions, thinly sliced

1 pound shrimp, preferably head-on

1 teaspoon gumbo filé powder, optional

Cooked white rice for serving

Hot sauce for serving

In a large, deep pot or Dutch oven, heat 2 tablespoons oil over medium-high heat, and working in batches, brown the chicken pieces, turning the pieces to evenly brown, about 7 minutes. Remove the chicken to a platter and set aside.

Reduce the heat to medium. In the same pot, mix 1 cup oil and the flour and cook, stirring, for about 15 minutes to make a peanut butter–colored roux. Add the onion and continue to cook for about 30 minutes, until the roux is a dark, brick red. Add the chicken, bell pepper, celery, sausage, and stock. Bring to a boil, add the salt and cayenne, and reduce the heat to medium-low. Simmer, stirring occasionally, for about 3 hours. About 5 minutes before serving, stir in the green onions, shrimp, and filé powder if using, and cook until the shrimp are cooked through. Serve over white rice with hot sauce on the side.

SERVES 6 TO 8

Monday is the traditional day for Red Beans and Rice in New Orleans, because Monday was traditionally laundry day and no one had time to cook. Sound familiar? Now that laundry is less time-consuming, though, there's more time for beans and rice, and we can have it any day and all day in the twenty-first century.

RED
BEANS AND RICE

2 tablespoons extra-virgin olive oil

1 onion, finely chopped

1 green bell pepper, finely chopped

2 stalks celery, finely chopped

2 cloves garlic, thinly sliced

1 pound dry red kidney beans

1 large smoked ham hock

1 tablespoon chili powder

1 tablespoon chopped fresh thyme

2 bay leaves

Kosher salt and freshly ground black pepper

Cooked white rice for serving

Hot sauce for serving

In a large, deep pot or Dutch oven, heat the oil over medium-high heat. Add the onion and sauté until soft, about 5 minutes. Add the bell pepper, celery, and garlic and sauté 3 minutes longer. Add the beans, hock, chili powder, thyme, and bay leaves and cover with water, about 8 cups. Bring to a boil, partially cover, and cook for 30 minutes. Reduce the heat to medium-low, cover, and simmer for 2 hours. The beans should be tender. Remove and discard the bay leaves. Remove the hock and mash the beans a bit with the back of a ladle.

Pull the meat off the hock, shred it, and return the meat to the pot. Discard the bone. Season with salt and freshly ground black pepper. Continue to simmer for at least 30 minutes longer.

Serve the beans over white rice with hot sauce on the side.

SERVES 6 TO 8

Any Floridian will tell you that a sweet, green Key Lime Pie is for tourists. A real one is a pale yellow and encourages a serious pucker. A lot of pies will be garnished with beautiful green slices of lime. But unless you did it wrong, there isn't any of that kind of lime in the pie. So don't do that.

KEY LIME PIE

Preheat the oven to 350°F.

In a bowl, mix together the graham cracker crumbs and melted butter. Press the mixture into a 9-inch pie pan, working it up the sides. Bake for 10 minutes, until the crust is set. Set aside to cool.

In a large bowl, whisk together the lime juice, condensed milk, and egg yolks. Pour into the crust and bake for 10 minutes.

Meanwhile, make the meringue. In a stand mixer with the whisk attachment, beat the egg whites and cream of tartar until peaks begin to form. Add the sugar and beat until the peaks are slightly stiff.

Add the meringue to the top of the pie and bake an additional 15 minutes, until the waves of meringue take on tones of sienna. Cool on the counter for at least 2 hours, then refrigerate for at least 8 hours before serving.

SERVES 8 TO 10

1½ cups graham cracker crumbs, from about 7 ounces of graham crackers

½ cup (1 stick) unsalted butter, melted

¾ cup fresh or bottled key lime juice

2 (14-ounce) cans sweetened condensed milk

3 large eggs, separated

½ teaspoon cream of tartar

1 tablespoon sugar

A French emissary in New Orleans in the 1700s allegedly asked his staff to whip up a confection that he could use to help woo the ladies. That's one story. There's a lot of sugar and pecans around New Orleans. That probably had more to do with the origin of this treat.

PRALINES

3 cups packed light brown
  sugar

1 cup cream

2 tablespoons corn syrup

2 tablespoons unsalted butter

1 teaspoon vanilla extract

2 cups pecans

In a medium saucepan over medium-high heat, cook the sugar, cream, corn syrup, and butter until the mixture reaches 240°F on a candy thermometer. Remove from the heat and let cool to 150°F.

Add the vanilla and stir in the pecans, continuing to stir until the candy becomes opaque, about a minute. Line a baking sheet with a silicone mat or wax paper and drop the mixture by the tablespoonful. The candy will firm up as it cools.

MAKES ABOUT 24 PRALINES

I might add some freshly ground black pepper on top of 6 of these while still warm, just for contrast. I think black pepper goes well with the rich caramel.

When someone's name is attached to a dish, it is so much easier to confirm the origin, right? Well, sort of. We know this dessert was created at Brennan's restaurant in New Orleans in the 1950s, and named for a friend of the owner. Some controversy has emerged about whose idea it was, but it's the dessert most associated with the city.

BANANAS
FOSTER

In a large skillet over medium-high heat, melt the butter and sugar, stirring until it becomes a sauce. Reduce the heat to low and add the bananas and cinnamon. Cook for about a minute, spooning the sauce over the bananas. Remove the pan from the heat and add the rum. Return to the heat and swirl the pan, and if you're feeling showy, carefully ignite the sauce to burn off the alcohol. Scoop ice cream into bowls and serve the bananas and sauce over it.

SERVES 4 TO 6

4 tablespoons unsalted butter

¼ cup firmly packed dark brown sugar

3 bananas, ripe but firm, peeled and cut in half lengthwise

½ teaspoon ground cinnamon

2 tablespoons dark rum

Vanilla ice cream for serving

When you buy or make a lot of bread, it isn't unusual to miscalculate now and then and have some that goes stale. Resuscitating it by soaking it in custard and baking it likely started in Europe centuries earlier, but it became an art form in New Orleans, where it is a full-on culture of its own.

BREAD PUDDING

FOR THE PUDDING

3 cups milk

½ cup (1 stick) unsalted butter, melted

4 large eggs, beaten

¾ cup granulated sugar

1 teaspoon vanilla extract

1 teaspoon ground cinnamon

1 teaspoon kosher salt

1 large loaf French bread, a day old, cut into 2-inch cubes (about 10 cups)

FOR THE BOURBON CARAMEL

½ cup (1 stick) unsalted butter

¾ cup packed light brown sugar

¼ cup bourbon

FOR THE PUDDING: Spray a 9-by-13-inch baking pan with cooking spray.

In a large bowl, whisk together the milk, melted butter, eggs, granulated sugar, vanilla, cinnamon, and salt. Add the bread and toss to coat. Pour the mixture into the baking pan. Refrigerate for at least 2 hours, or overnight, to let the bread soak up all the custard.

Preheat the oven to 350°F. Bake the pudding for 1 hour, until crusty bits begin to form on the surface.

FOR THE BOURBON CARAMEL: In a large skillet over medium-high heat, melt the butter and add the brown sugar. Stir until the butter and sugar have melted and incorporated. Remove from the heat and stir in the bourbon.

Spoon servings of the bread pudding into bowls and pour the bourbon caramel over.

SERVES 12

GREAT *Lakes*

WE ARE A NATION that has always been moved by our water. It's also a symbol of relaxation, of leisure, of freedom. If we are on the water, we are most likely not working and, oddly enough, we are connected to every other place on the planet that is also on the water.

For me, it's this concept and not mere size that makes the five bodies of water at the top of our national map spectacular and unique. Let's put aside for the moment that twenty-one percent of the world's freshwater supply is in our *Great* Lakes.

People from around the world came here to live and work, and they looked for people like themselves. Whether they came from Poland or Scandinavia, Greece or Germany, if they made it to the Great Lakes, it was only a short boat ride to find people who spoke like they did, who dressed like they did, who were working in an industry that required skills similar to theirs.

And mostly, they found people eating the food they liked. And it's still good today. While much of the industry the region was built on has faded (although in the case of the auto industry, it has made an excellent comeback), the food is still there. That's why we find pierogies in restaurants in Cleveland. And a parking lot full of football fans in Wisconsin will be fueling up on bratwurst. Or a church social in St. Paul that is not complete without a smorgasbord of pickled herring.

Today, we'll find fewer of the smokestacks and the mines that defined industry here for years. Now we find dairies making cheese, orchards providing cherries, and silos full of corn. We find hot chicken wings in so many places that it's easy to forget that they were born in the city they're named after. We find most of the Big Ten, and it seems every college town also sports a dish named after the local team. We find a region that is so genuinely wholesome that at the end of the biggest car race of the year in Indianapolis, the winner stands on the track guzzling a jug of milk.

Roadside treasures in the Great Lakes region are infinite, and from Buckeyes too! I can't drive through Cleveland without a tour of the justly mythical West Side Market for a **KIELBASA** on a hard roll, or the **HOT JERKY** from J and J Meats with my *Chew* buddy Michael Symon. We'll drop by his place, Lola, for a cocktail, or visit his neighbor, Jonathon Sawyer. And any trip to Milwaukee means a visit to Usinger's or a **FISH FRY** with Paul Bartolotta.

Chicago is one of my favorite cities in the country to be hungry in. But I'm never hungry for long, not with its namesake hot dogs and pizza, and the likes of Paul Kahan, Stephanie Izard, Rick Bayless, and Jimmy Bannos (both Senior and Junior) feeding my soul, and Grant Achatz giving me delicious things to eat and think about.

The water is still moving us. Personally, it moves me to get out of New York City for a couple of months every summer and spend some time with my toes in Lake Michigan. I see America cooking here, and I taste it. It is unique, yet recognizable. It is whitefish, cherry pie, and micro brew, it is pierogies and hanky pankies, it is cheese curds and Leinenkugel, it is hotdish and lefse, it is *wheeeeeeee!*

For decades, Sunday morning breakfast in Rockford, Illinois, has meant Swedish Pancakes at the Stockholm Inn. They resemble crepes but are a little eggier. Any tart berry jam is a perfect accompaniment, such as Traverse City Tart Cherry Preserves (page 253), but traditional would be lingonberry jam, which you can get at any monstrous blue-and-yellow furniture store.

SWEDISH
PANCAKES

In a blender, mix the eggs, milk, flour, granulated sugar, salt, and 2 tablespoons of the butter and blend until perfectly smooth. Pour the batter into a bowl or small pitcher, cover, and refrigerate for at least 2 hours. Even better: Do this the night before you plan to make the pancakes so the batter can rest overnight.

Preheat the oven to 200°F.

Add 1 teaspoon of the remaining butter to a 10-inch nonstick skillet, heat over medium heat, and swirl to coat the pan. Add about ¼ cup batter to the hot skillet and tilt the skillet in every direction necessary to get the batter to evenly distribute and form a beautifully round, thin pancake. Return to the heat and let it cook undisturbed for 2 minutes. With a long, thin spatula, work under an edge until you dislodge the pancake and flip it over, then cook 2 more minutes. The pancake will be set, but still quite blond. Move it to a heat-safe plate and keep warm in the oven while you repeat with the rest of the batter. Add more butter to the pan sparingly; after a few pancakes, it will become seasoned.

Fold the pancakes in quarters and serve dusted with confectioners' sugar and jam or syrup.

MAKES ABOUT 20 PANCAKES

3 large eggs

3 cups milk

1 cup all-purpose flour

2 tablespoons granulated sugar

1 teaspoon kosher salt

3 tablespoons unsalted butter, melted

Confectioners' sugar for dusting

Tart berry jam or syrup for serving

In July and August, the Leelanau Peninsula in Northern Michigan is packed with cherries and tourists, full force. Sweet cherries make up the bulk of the crop, and they're great, but my favorites—the ones most worthy of putting up to enjoy all year—are the tart ones. (Pickled Tart Cherries are pictured on page 254; Tart Cherry Preserves are pictured on page 250.)

PICKLED
TART CHERRIES

1 cup white balsamic vinegar

½ cup water

½ cup sugar

1 tablespoon kosher salt

1 tablespoon coriander seeds

1 teaspoon mustard seeds

2 cinnamon sticks

1 quart (about 1½ pounds) tart cherries, rinsed and pitted

1½-inch-long lobe fresh ginger, peeled and cut into wide strips with a vegetable peeler

Combine the vinegar, water, sugar, salt, coriander, and mustard seeds in a medium saucepan. Heat over medium heat, stirring, until the sugar and salt dissolve.

Put one cinnamon stick in each of 2 sterilized pint jars. Divide the cherries among the jars, layering in slices of ginger among the cherries. Pour the warm brine over the cherries and put lids on the jars. Let cure at least 48 hours before serving. Store in the refrigerator for up to 3 months or can according to the directions on page 9 for longer storage.

MAKES 2 PINTS

TRAVERSE CITY
TART CHERRY
PRESERVES

Place 2 small plates in the freezer.

In a large saucepan over medium heat, cook the cherries and sugar until the cherries break down and the mixture bubbles, about 10 minutes. Continue cooking for 20 to 30 minutes, until the mixture begins to look like a chunky syrup. Add the lemon juice and pectin and cook for 5 more minutes.

Do the frozen-plate test as described on page 9. When the jam is ready, skim any foam off the top, stir in the almond extract, and ladle the jam into sterilized half-pint or 4-ounce canning jars. Can according to the directions on page 9.

MAKES 6 HALF-PINTS

2 quarts (about 3 pounds) tart, or sour, cherries, stemmed, pitted, and chopped

2 cups sugar

Juice of 1 lemon

1 (3-ounce) pouch liquid pectin

2 teaspoons almond extract

If you don't live in Wisconsin, you might have trouble finding the signature brandy for this cocktail. Not because it's made locally; it's actually made by a big California winery. Some years, Korbel sends more of its brandy to the Badger State than it does to the rest of the country *combined*. And likely most of it goes into this cocktail.

WISCONSIN
OLD-FASHIONED

Put the sugar cube in a rocks glass and hit it with the bitters. Add the orange and 1 cherry to the glass, and muddle until the sugar dissolves. Add the brandy and stir until it is combined. Add crushed ice, garnish with the other cherry, and serve.

MAKES 1 COCKTAIL

1 sugar cube
2 dashes Angostura bitters
1 orange slice or twist
2 Pickled Tart Cherries (page 252) (may sub maraschino cherries)
2 ounces Korbel or other brandy
Crushed ice

How did people even watch football before 1964? That's when the Anchor Bar in Buffalo is credited with coming up with this dish. Various accounts give different inspirations, but my favorite is that the restaurant had to come up with a way to use a bunch of wings that were delivered by accident. Mistakes can be delicious!

BUFFALO
CHICKEN WINGS

FOR THE BLUE CHEESE DRESSING

½ cup mayo

½ cup sour cream

4 ounces blue cheese, such as Gorgonzola or Maytag blue, crumbled

1 tablespoon apple cider vinegar

½ teaspoon kosher salt

½ teaspoon white pepper

FOR THE WINGS

Canola or corn oil for frying

20 chicken wings, tips removed and saved for stock, flats and drumettes separated

Kosher salt

½ cup (1 stick) unsalted butter

¼ cup hot sauce, such as Tabasco or Frank's RedHot, or more to taste

Celery and carrot sticks

FOR THE BLUE CHEESE DRESSING: In a small bowl, combine all ingredients. Chill for at least 2 hours before serving.

FOR THE WINGS: Fill a large, heavy pot or Dutch oven about one-third full of oil and heat to 365°F. Working in batches to avoid crowding the pot, fry the wing flats for about 10 minutes, the drumettes 2 minutes longer, until the skin is brown and crispy. Remove to a paper towel–lined platter, drain well, and sprinkle with salt. Cover with foil while you fry the remaining batches.

In a small saucepan, melt the butter and whisk in the hot sauce.

Put the wings in a large bowl and pour the hot sauce butter over them. Toss to coat. Serve with the celery and carrot sticks and blue cheese dressing.

SERVES 2, HONESTLY

Holubki. Halupki. Galumpki. Golabki. Depending on where you grew up, these cabbage rolls might've had a different name. In some places, they're called Pigs in a Blanket, which must be confusing for the kids who think they're about to get a hot dog wrapped in croissant dough.

STUFFED CABBAGES

Kosher salt

1 large head green cabbage

1 pound ground beef

1 pound ground pork

2 cups cooked rice

2 medium onions, grated on a box grater

2 teaspoons fennel seeds

2 teaspoons ground coriander

2 teaspoons freshly ground black pepper

3 cups Basic Tomato Sauce (page 480)

½ cup water

Bring a large pot half-full of water to a boil over medium-high heat and add 2 tablespoons salt. Turn the cabbage upside down with the stem sticking up. With a long, thin knife, cut around the core, angling the knife slightly toward the center of the head. Remove the core and discard. Trim away any large veins remaining in the cabbage, then carefully drop in the boiling water, being careful to avoid splashing. Keep the head submerged for about 2 minutes. Carefully remove the cabbage and pull off the outer leaves, holding them on a towel-lined tray. The idea is to remove the leaves without tearing them. Return the cabbage to the pot, and after a couple of minutes pull off some more leaves and repeat until you've harvested as many large leaves as you can get. Cut thick veins away from the cooked leaves. Let the leaves cool and dry.

In a bowl, combine the beef, pork, rice, onions, fennel seeds, coriander, pepper, and 2 teaspoons salt and mix well.

Preheat the oven to 350°F.

Cover the bottom of a 9-by-13-inch baking pan with 1 cup of the tomato sauce. To stuff the cabbages, take a full leaf (or two smaller leaves) and lay it flat on a work surface. Put about ½ cup of the meat mixture on the leaf. Fold the sides of the leaf over the ends of meat, then roll the leaf to close. Put the cabbage rolls in the baking pan seam side down, and repeat to fill the rest of the leaves, making 3 rows of 4 rolls. In a bowl, mix the remaining 2 cups tomato sauce and the water and pour over the cabbage rolls. Pack any remaining cabbage leaves around the rolls. Cover the pan with foil. Bake for 1 hour and 10 minutes. Serve hot from the oven.

MAKES 12 CABBAGE ROLLS

I might make this with chorizo in place of the pork and spicy salsa instead of tomato sauce.

The good people of Cleveland and Pittsburgh may have little love for each other as a result of their football allegiances, but if they measured themselves by the contributions of their respective Eastern European communities, they'd find they had plenty in common. Take the noble pierogi: cheesy mashed potatoes stuffed in pasta dough. *Na zdorovie!*

PIEROGIES

In a medium skillet over medium-high heat, melt the 2 tablespoons butter and sauté the onion until softened but not browned, about 4 minutes.

Bring a large pot half-full of water to a boil. Add the potatoes and cook until soft, about 20 minutes. Drain the potatoes and pass them through a ricer into a large bowl. Add the sautéed onions, cheese, the 2 tablespoons sour cream, 1 teaspoon salt, and 1 teaspoon pepper and mix until the cheese is melted and well incorporated.

In the bowl of a stand mixer, combine the remaining ¼ cup sour cream, the flour, eggs, and warm water and mix until it becomes a pliable dough. Let the dough rest for 15 minutes.

Working with about one-fourth of the dough at a time, roll a piece out on a large, floured surface to about ⅛ inch thick. With a 3-inch round cookie cutter, cut out circles. On each round, place about a tablespoon of the potato mixture, just off center. Fold the dough over to enclose the potato and pinch all along the edge to seal. Repeat to use all the dough and potatoes.

Bring a large pot half-full of well-salted water to a boil over medium-high heat. Working in batches so as to not crowd the pot, drop several pierogies in the water and boil, stirring lightly so they don't stick together, for 3 minutes. They'll float as they finish cooking. Remove and continue cooking until all the pierogies are cooked.

At this point, the pierogies can be frozen, served as is, or pan-fried in the remaining 4 tablespoons butter and served with sour cream.

MAKES 36 TO 40 PIEROGIES, SERVING 6 TO 8

2 tablespoons unsalted butter plus optional 4 tablespoons for pan-frying

1 medium onion, finely diced

1 pound russet potatoes, peeled and cut into ½-inch dice

4 ounces sharp Cheddar cheese, shredded

2 tablespoons plus ¼ cup sour cream plus more for serving

Kosher salt and freshly ground black pepper

4 cups all-purpose flour

3 large eggs

¾ cup warm water

Wild rice comes from a grass that grows in lakes, creeks, and marshes of some of the coldest parts of the country and is best harvested by canoe. After a day of that, it's no wonder a warm bowl of Wild Rice Soup is so popular in Northern Minnesota. I cook this in a slow cooker, also known as a Crock-Pot.

WILD RICE
SOUP

1 cup uncooked wild rice

1 pound skinless chicken thighs

Kosher salt and freshly ground black pepper

1 tablespoon extra-virgin olive oil

1 small onion, finely chopped

2 stalks celery, finely chopped

¾ cup finely chopped carrot

6 cups Brown Chicken Stock (page 480)

4 tablespoons unsalted butter

½ cup all-purpose flour

1½ cups whole milk

2 tablespoons sherry wine

2 teaspoons fresh thyme leaves

Rinse the wild rice.

Season the chicken with salt and pepper. In a large skillet over medium-high heat, heat the oil and sauté the chicken until it's browned on each side, about 6 minutes total. Add to the slow cooker with the rice, onion, celery, carrot, 1 teaspoon salt, and the stock.

Cover and cook on the slow cooker's low setting for at least 7 hours. Remove the chicken, shred with two forks, and return the meat to the pot, discarding the bones.

In a small saucepan over medium heat, melt the butter and whisk in the flour. Cook for about 3 minutes, then slowly add the milk, continuing to whisk until the mixture thickens, about 6 minutes.

Stir the milk mixture into the rice and chicken in the slow cooker, add the sherry and thyme leaves, and stir to combine. Season to taste with salt and pepper and serve.

MAKES 2 QUARTS, SERVING 6 TO 8

The name isn't a trick: They're actually Swedish, making them a favorite of the Scandinavian population of the upper Midwest. But really, they've been a favorite everywhere since the days of go-go dances and psychedelic rock. Props to any food that can reasonably be served on a toothpick!

SWEDISH MEATBALLS

1 pound ground round

1 pound ground pork

1 pound ground veal

1 medium onion, grated

1 large egg

1 cup toasted bread crumbs

¼ cup cream

½ teaspoon allspice

Kosher salt and freshly ground black pepper

1 tablespoon unsalted butter

1 tablespoon extra-virgin olive oil

1 tablespoon all-purpose flour

2 cups half-and-half

1 shot aquavit (may sub brandy), optional

Combine the meats, onion, egg, bread crumbs, cream, allspice, and 1 teaspoon each salt and pepper. Form small meatballs, about the size of Ping-Pong balls. Refrigerate for at least a half hour.

In a large skillet over medium-high heat, heat the butter and oil. Working in batches, brown the meatballs, turning them to brown all sides, about 7 minutes per batch. Remove the meatballs to a platter and repeat to cook the rest.

Add the flour to the fat in the skillet and whisk it in for 1 minute. Add the half-and-half and scrape the bottom to deglaze, then add the aquavit, if using, and season to taste with salt and pepper. Return the meatballs to the skillet and toss to coat. Simmer for 5 minutes to heat through, and serve.

MAKES ABOUT 70 BALLS, SERVING 10 TO 12

While cheese curds may be hard to find in much of the country, in some places you can't go anywhere where they *aren't* available. These firm, crunchy, squeak-inducing nuggets of lactose love are worth seeking out. Look online, or ask your well-stocked cheese shop to get them for you—or you can find them at virtually every Midwestern state and county fair.

FRIED
CHEESE CURDS

In a large pot or Dutch oven, heat 2 inches of oil to 375°F.

In a medium bowl, combine the beer, egg, flour, baking powder, salt, and cayenne. Whisk to form a batter. Drop the curds in the batter and stir to coat.

Lift the curds out with a fork and, working a few at a time, carefully place in the oil. They'll quickly puff and are ready when they are golden brown, 2 to 3 minutes. Remove with a slotted spoon to a paper towel–lined plate. Season with salt.

Serve warm with tomato sauce for dipping, if you like.

SERVES 6 TO 8

Canola or corn oil for frying

12 ounces cold beer

1 large egg, beaten

1¼ cups all-purpose flour

1 teaspoon baking powder

1 teaspoon kosher salt plus more for seasoning

½ teaspoon cayenne

1 to 2 pounds fresh cheese curds

Basic Tomato Sauce (page 480) for serving, optional

Roast Beef Sandwiches

Honestly, the stories about how John Montagu—the Earl of Sandwich—may or may not have instigated putting meat between two slices of bread aren't very interesting. In eighteenth-century England, the best-case scenario is that that's probably all it was: meat and bread. What *is* very interesting is everything that's happened to that basic premise since then.

We can consider bread and beef—roasted or otherwise—a starting point. Add a small detail or a flourish, and a roadmap of America begins to emerge.

BUFFALO BEEF ON WECK (PAGE 270): In Buffalo, the wing is king, but locals will tell you their version of the roast beef sammie is just as much an icon. The game here is the bread—kummelweck—which is like a soft kaiser coated with salt and caraway. For added attitude, the sandwich is dressed with as much horseradish as it takes to get your undivided attention.

PHILLY CHEESESTEAK (PAGE 94): While Buffalo's beef sandwich has largely stayed a local landmark, cheesesteaks are so ingrained in the lexicon that "Philly" is attached more as a general descriptor than a geo-locator. Stories of abusive countermen are largely played up for travel show drama. Know what kind of cheese you want, and whether you want onions, and all will be fine.

PIT BEEF SANDWICH (PAGE 104): To obtain a classic Pit Beef Sandwich, you're pretty much going to have to be willing to get off the highway somewhere within about a two-and-a-half-hour radius of Baltimore. For the best one, it'll feel more like you walked into a friend's cookout than a business. The meat will be seasoned mostly with fire, then topped with a horseradish mayo and raw onion.

PO' BOY (PAGE 231): Few cities sport as much character as the Big Easy, so we would expect no less of its entrant on this tour. The Po' Boy has many iterations, but chief among them is this juicy one defined by the addition of all the remnants—solid and liquid—in the pan after the beast is roasted. Every cook who has picked at the pan knows these are the best parts.

ITALIAN BEEF SANDWICH (PAGE 272): For a city so defined by its relationship with beef, it's sort of funny that the unmitigated star of Chicago's favorite beef on bread is the vegetable salad that gets piled on top. The pack of pickled cherry peppers, olives, and cauliflower makes this sandwich. And napkins. Lots and lots of napkins.

SANTA MARIA TRI-TIP (PAGE 450): California checks in with another entry that's simply seasoned and kissed by fire. Tri-tip is a cut of the sirloin more likely to be readily available west of the Rockies than east of them. At a cookout in Santa Maria, your sandwich would be on a tortilla and adorned with bacon-y beans and pico de gallo.

ITALIAN BEEF SANDWICH

PIT BEEF SANDWICH

BUFFALO BEEF ON WECK

PHILLY CHEESESTEAK

PO' BOY

Beef on Weck is all about the bread. The kummelweck roll is a unique vehicle, crowned with a delicious layer of coarse salt and caraway seeds. Never fear if you can't find them. It's easy enough to doctor some kaiser rolls. This beef is the same as in Chicago's Italian Beef Sandwich (page 272), which is pretty similar to what's used in New Orleans's Po' Boy (page 231). There is quite a bit of the broth left over if you want to make a French dip, too.

BUFFALO
BEEF ON WECK

FOR THE ROAST BEEF

1 boneless top round or chuck roast, 3 to 4 pounds

6 cloves garlic, halved

Kosher salt and freshly ground black pepper

3 tablespoons extra-virgin olive oil

1 onion, thinly sliced

½ bunch thyme

1½ cups red wine

FOR THE KUMMELWECK CLONES

¼ cup coarse sea salt

¼ cup caraway seeds

1 large egg white

1 tablespoon water

12 kaiser rolls, or other firm sandwich bun

Prepared horseradish for serving

FOR THE ROAST BEEF: Preheat the oven to 350°F. With a sharp knife, cut 12 slits in the roast and insert a piece of garlic in each. Liberally season the beef with salt and pepper on all sides.

In a roasting pan, heat the olive oil over medium-high heat. Sear each side of the beef, about 5 minutes per side. Drop the onion in the pot around the beef and add the thyme. Add the wine and about 4 cups water to come about an inch up the side of the beef. Cover the pan with foil and put the roast in the oven. Roast, checking each hour to maintain the water level and adding more as necessary, for about 3 hours.

Carefully transfer the roast to a plate and let it rest for about 30 minutes. Strain the cooking liquid, discarding the solids, and keep warm in a saucepan over low heat.

FOR THE KUMMELWECK CLONES: Preheat the oven to 350°F.

Mix the salt and caraway in a small, shallow bowl. In another small, shallow bowl, beat the egg white with the water until slightly foamy. Brush the egg white mixture on the top of each roll and set them on a baking sheet. Liberally sprinkle the rolls with the salt-caraway mixture so that it sticks to the egg. Bake for 5 minutes, just to set the seasoning mix. (You can bake these as soon as you take the roast out of the oven.)

TO ASSEMBLE: Move the rested roast beef to a cutting board and slice the meat against the grain as thinly as possible. Cut a roll in half and stack several slices of beef on the bottom piece, then top with horseradish. Briefly dip the cut side of the roll's top in the warm broth, top the sandwich, and serve with a bowl of the broth for dipping.

MAKES 12 SANDWICHES

¾ cup apple cider vinegar

¾ cup extra-virgin olive oil

2 tablespoons kosher salt

1 tablespoon celery seed

*1 tablespoon chopped
    fresh oregano*

*1 teaspoon crushed red
    pepper flakes*

*6 ounces hot cherry peppers,
    sliced*

*4 ounces small cauliflower
    florets, no large stems*

*½ cup green olives, pitted
    and coarsely chopped*

*½ green bell pepper, finely
    minced*

*½ red bell pepper, finely
    minced*

*1 medium carrot, peeled
    and shredded*

2 stalks celery, finely minced

FOR THE ROAST BEEF

*1 boneless top round or chuck
    roast, 3 to 4 pounds*

6 cloves garlic, halved

*Kosher salt and freshly
    ground black pepper*

*3 tablespoons extra-virgin
    olive oil*

1 onion, thinly sliced

½ bunch thyme

1½ cups red wine

6 soft sub rolls

Few sandwiches are as ritualistic as the Chicago Italian Beef. Elbows on counter. Step back. Go. If you are not up for making the giardiniera, you can sub sliced pickled hot cherry peppers and sweet peppers, mixed to your own preference of heat. But remember, if you make your own giardiniera, you should make it at least 3 days ahead of time.

ITALIAN BEEF
SANDWICHES

FOR THE GIARDINIERA: In a bowl, whisk together the vinegar, oil, salt, celery seed, oregano, and pepper flakes. Set the dressing aside.

In a large bowl, toss together the remaining giardiniera ingredients. Put the vegetable mixture in a large jar and pour the dressing over it. Refrigerate for at least 3 days. Longer is better. The salad will last about a month in the refrigerator. Bring to room temperature before serving.

FOR THE ROAST BEEF: Preheat the oven to 350°F. With a sharp knife, cut 12 slits in the roast and insert a piece of garlic in each. Liberally season the beef with salt and pepper on all sides.

In a roasting pan, heat the olive oil over medium-high heat. Sear each side of the beef, about 5 minutes per side. Drop the onion in the pot around the beef and add the thyme. Add the wine and about 4 cups of water to come about an inch up the side of the beef. Cover the pan with foil and put the roast in the oven. Roast, checking each hour to maintain the water level and adding more as necessary, for about 3 hours.

Carefully transfer the roast to a plate, cover with foil, and refrigerate for several hours. Strain the cooking liquid, discarding the solids, and refrigerate it for several hours.

Skim the fat off the top of the liquid and reheat in a large saucepan over medium heat. Thinly slice the beef against the grain and warm it in the broth. Pile the beef on the rolls and spoon on the giardiniera.

MAKES 6 SANDWICHES (WITH LEFTOVER GIARDINIERA)

I had Michael Symon explain Hanky Pankies to me. They happen at parties in Cleveland all the time. Clearly Cleveland rocks!

HANKY PANKIES

8 ounces ground beef

8 ounces hot Italian sausage, removed from casings

1 cup ricotta, at room temperature

4 ounces Gouda cheese, shredded

¼ cup chopped fresh oregano

4 slices good rye bread

Preheat the oven's broiler.

In a large skillet over medium-high heat, brown the beef and sausage together and use a potato masher to break up the chunks to make a crumbly, browned mixture. Transfer to a bowl and stir in the cheeses and oregano. Divide the mixture evenly among the slices of bread, place on a baking sheet, and broil for 3 to 4 minutes, until the cheese starts to bubble and turn golden brown.

Cut each piece of bread in half on the diagonal and serve immediately.

MAKES 4 SLICES, SERVING 8

Walleye is a favorite target of anglers around the Great Lakes, and the secret I've heard is that the biggest fish are caught at night. Although not traditional, this potato-bud crust is loved by every single Great Lakes inhabitant or aficionado I have ever cooked it for!

POTATO-CRUSTED
WALLEYE

Set up a breading station with three wide, shallow bowls: Mix the flour with 1 teaspoon each salt and pepper in one, beat the eggs in another, and combine the potato flakes and chopped dill in the third.

Rinse the fish fillets and dry them with a paper towel. Heat the olive oil in a large skillet over medium-high heat.

One at a time, dredge each fish fillet in the flour, patting off excess, then dip in the beaten egg, then gently press the fish in the potato-dill. Two at a time, carefully add to the pan and fry for 3 to 4 minutes per side, until the crust is golden and crispy. Drain on paper towels, season with salt and pepper, and serve with lemon wedges.

SERVES 4

½ cup all-purpose flour

Kosher salt and freshly ground black pepper

3 large eggs

1 cup instant mashed potato flakes

2 tablespoons chopped fresh dill

4 walleye fillets, or other firm, white-fleshed fish, about 8 ounces each

½ cup extra-virgin olive oil

Lemon wedges for serving

There was a day before mass production when chicken was prohibitively expensive and veal and pork saved the day for many families on tight budgets. So a popular dinner in the Rust Belt was this way of "faking" fried chicken. Today, it's an extravagance!

CITY CHICKEN

Season the meat cubes aggressively with salt and pepper. Using 6-inch bamboo or metal skewers, thread 3 or 4 pieces of meat onto each skewer.

Set up a breading station with three wide, shallow bowls: Season the flour with 1 teaspoon each salt and pepper in one, beat the egg in another, and season the panko with paprika in the third.

In a large skillet, heat ½ inch of oil to 375°F. Alternately, preheat the oven to 400°F.

Dip the skewers of meat into the flour, roll to cover, then shake off excess. Dip in the egg and let the excess drip off. Then roll the skewers in the panko, pressing so the crumbs adhere.

If frying, carefully place the skewers in the hot oil in batches and fry for 4 to 5 minutes on each side, until golden brown. Remove from oil with tongs to a plate lined with paper towels and season with salt.

If baking, place the skewers on a baking sheet and spray with cooking spray. Bake for 10 minutes, until the crumbs start to brown. Turn the skewers over and bake an additional 10 minutes, until golden.

Serve hot.

MAKES 12 TO 15 SKEWERS, SERVING 4

1½ pounds veal roast or pork loin, or a combination, cut into 1-inch cubes

Kosher salt and freshly ground black pepper

½ cup all-purpose flour

1 large egg

1 cup panko bread crumbs

1 teaspoon paprika

Canola or corn oil for frying, optional

Akron claims to be the home of Sauerkraut Balls, and the one-bite party fave has migrated around the Buckeye State, but not too far outside of it.

SAUERKRAUT BALLS

In a large skillet over medium-high heat, cook the sausage, onion, and garlic until the sausage is lightly browned. Drain excess fat and transfer the cooked sausage to a bowl. Add the cream cheese and mix well. Stir in the sauerkraut, ¼ cup of the bread crumbs, the dry mustard, and about ½ teaspoon each salt and pepper. Refrigerate until the mixture cools.

Roll the meat mixture into about 24 orbs about the size of a golf ball.

In a large, deep-sided skillet, heat about 1 inch of oil to 340°F.

In a shallow dish, mix the flour with ½ teaspoon each salt and pepper. In another, lightly beat the eggs. In a third, spread out the remaining ¾ cup bread crumbs. Working in batches, roll the balls in the flour, then the egg, then the bread crumbs. In batches to avoid crowding the pan, fry the balls, flipping them halfway through, until golden brown, about 4 minutes. Drain on a paper towel–lined platter and season to taste with salt. Serve hot with mustard for dipping.

MAKES ABOUT 24 BALLS

8 ounces Italian sausage, removed from casings

¼ cup finely chopped onion

1 clove garlic, minced

3 ounces cream cheese

1 pound Fermented Sauerkraut (page 72), rinsed, drained, and chopped

1 cup bread crumbs

1 teaspoon Colman's dry mustard

Kosher salt and freshly ground black pepper

Canola or corn oil for frying

½ cup all-purpose flour

2 large eggs

Spicy mustard, such as Bertman Ball Park Mustard

An Old World favorite that lives on in the strong Hungarian community of Toledo, this is one of those dishes easily found at church socials and festivals throughout the city. Spaetzle is the traditional starch with this stew, and it's easy to make. But these days it's just as legit to serve egg noodles or white rice alongside.

CHICKEN
PAPRIKASH

FOR THE CHICKEN: Season the chicken pieces liberally with salt and pepper.

In a large skillet over medium-high heat, heat the oil and, working in batches if necessary, brown the chicken, about 7 minutes. Remove to a platter. Add the onion, garlic, and green pepper to the skillet and sauté until the onion is soft, about 5 minutes. Add 1 cup of the stock and the paprika. Stir, then return the chicken to the pan and bring to a boil. Cover, reduce the heat to medium-low, and cook for 20 minutes. Remove the lid and raise the heat to medium and cook for 10 minutes. The chicken should be cooked through.

In a bowl, whisk together the remaining 1 cup stock, the sour cream, and flour.

Raise the heat under the chicken to bring to a slight boil, pour in the sour cream mixture, and cook, stirring constantly, until thickened, about 2 minutes.

FOR THE SPAETZLE: In a large bowl, whisk together the eggs, milk, caraway, and salt. Add the flour, a little at a time, stirring as you go. When the dough comes together, set aside and let rest for 30 minutes.

Bring a large pot half-filled with water to a boil. Pour the spaetzle dough onto a cutting board. Working over the boiling water, use a bench scraper to push small, irregular bits of dough into the water. Work fast. They should not look consistent. Stop about a third of the way through the dough, and remove the cooked spaetzle (they are cooked when they float) with a slotted spoon, draining well, then repeat until all the dough is cooked.

Serve the chicken over the spaetzle, garnished with chopped parsley.

SERVES 4 TO 6

FOR THE CHICKEN

1 chicken, 3½ to 4 pounds, cut into 10 pieces

Kosher salt and freshly ground black pepper

2 tablespoons extra-virgin olive oil

1 medium onion, diced

2 cloves garlic, thinly sliced

1 green bell pepper, diced

2 cups Brown Chicken Stock (page 480)

2 tablespoons Hungarian paprika

½ cup sour cream

2 tablespoons all-purpose flour

FOR THE SPAETZLE

3 large eggs, beaten

½ cup milk

1 tablespoon caraway seeds

1 teaspoon kosher salt

2½ cups all-purpose flour

Chopped parsley for garnish

In Cincinnati, it's perfectly acceptable to go into a chili joint and ask for a three-way (spaghetti, chili, and cheese). It's every bit as sexy as it sounds. They won't even flinch if you ask for a four-way (add onion or beans) or a five-way (add onion *and* beans).

CINCINNATI CHILI

2 tablespoons extra-virgin olive oil

2 pounds ground beef

3 medium onions, finely chopped

4 cloves garlic, thinly sliced

2 cups water

2 cups Basic Tomato Sauce (page 480)

1 teaspoon hot sauce, or more to taste

2 tablespoons chili powder

2 teaspoons ground cinnamon

1 teaspoon ground cumin

1 tablespoon fresh oregano leaves, chopped

1 (1-pound) package spaghetti

1 (16-ounce) can kidney beans, drained and heated, optional

12 ounces Cheddar cheese, finely shredded

Oyster crackers for serving

In a large pot or Dutch oven over medium-high heat, heat the oil and brown the ground beef. When the beef is well broken up, add two-thirds of the onions and the garlic and sauté until the onion softens, about 5 minutes. Add the water, bring to a boil, and reduce to a simmer. Cook, stirring regularly to break up the beef, for about 20 minutes. Add the tomato sauce, hot sauce, chili powder, cinnamon, and cumin. Cover and simmer for at least 2 hours. Stir in the oregano.

Cook the spaghetti according to the package directions.

To serve, put a serving of spaghetti on a plate and top it with a generous ladleful or two of chili. Customize each dish with beans and/or some of the remaining chopped raw onion. Cover each plate with a handful of cheese and serve with oyster crackers.

SERVES 6 TO 8

Why do we have to make a contest about whether Chicago or New York has the best pizza? They're different, delicious things! Just remember that Chicago pizza is deep-dish with a much thicker, more substantial, and longer-cooking crust. It takes some time, so plan accordingly.

CHICAGO DEEP-DISH PIZZA

FOR THE CRUST

1 envelope (2¼ teaspoons) active dry yeast

½ cup warm water

1 cup water

¼ cup shortening, melted

3 cups all-purpose flour, or more as needed

¾ cup cornmeal

2 teaspoons kosher salt

FOR THE TOPPING

1 tablespoon extra-virgin olive oil

1 small onion, finely chopped

1 green bell pepper, finely chopped

Kosher salt and freshly ground black pepper

1½ cups Basic Tomato Sauce (page 480)

1 pound Italian sausage, casings removed

8 ounces cremini mushrooms, sliced

1 pound fresh mozzarella cheese, cut into ½-inch slices

1 cup grated Parmigiano-Reggiano

FOR THE CRUST: Spray an 11-inch round pan that's 2 inches deep with cooking spray.

In the bowl of a stand mixer with the dough hook, combine the yeast with the ½ cup warm water and set aside for 10 minutes. Add the 1 cup water, shortening, flour, cornmeal, and salt. Beat slowly until the flour is damp, then increase the speed to form a dough. On a floured surface, knead the dough for 5 minutes, until it feels smooth. Add more flour if necessary, ¼ cup at a time. Put the dough in an oiled bowl, cover with a towel, and let rise in a warm place in the kitchen for 90 minutes.

Preheat the oven to 425°F.

Punch the dough down. Put it in the prepared pan and, with your fingertips, work it out from the center to the edges and up the sides of the pan. Bake for 5 minutes, then remove and allow to cool.

FOR THE TOPPING: In a large skillet over medium-high heat, heat the olive oil, then sauté the onion and green pepper until the onion is soft, about 5 minutes. Season with salt and pepper and add the tomato sauce. Stir and cook for about 10 minutes.

Tear bits of sausage with your fingers and spread it around the pizza crust. Spread the mushrooms on top of the sausage and cover with slices of mozzarella, overlapping them if necessary to use it all. Press the meat and mozzarella down into the dough to make room for the sauce, then pour the tomato mixture over the top. Bake for 35 minutes. Add the Parmigiano-Reggiano over the pizza and bake 10 more minutes, until the cheese melts and the sauce is bubbling. Let the pizza rest 10 minutes before cutting it.

SERVES 6, OR 2 HUNGRY BEARS

The defining characteristic of Indiana's favorite sandwich is simple: The pork tenderloin must hang outside the perimeter of the bun on every side. It manages to be exceedingly simple and gloriously unique at the same time, for the same reasons. Although not traditional, you can make these your own by adding your favorite grated cheese to the bread-crumb mixture—say, pecorino Romano—or maybe even ground Ritz crackers? The possibilities are endless.

BREADED
PORK TENDERLOIN
SANDWICHES

1½ pounds pork tenderloin (may sub pork loin)

Kosher salt and freshly ground black pepper

¾ cup all-purpose flour

1 teaspoon cayenne

2 large eggs

2 cups panko bread crumbs

Canola or corn oil for frying

4 hamburger buns

Lettuce, tomato, onion, pickles, mustard, and/or mayonnaise for serving

Cut the pork crosswise into 4 equal portions. Place 1 portion between 2 pieces of plastic wrap and pound until it is very thin and considerably larger than the bun it will be served on. Repeat with the rest of the pork. Season both sides of each piece with salt and pepper.

Set up a breading station with three wide, shallow bowls: Combine the flour, cayenne, and 1 teaspoon each salt and pepper in one, beat the eggs in another, and put the panko in the third.

In a large, straight-sided skillet, heat about ½ inch of oil to 350°F. Preheat the oven to 200°F.

Working with one piece of pork at a time, dip it in the flour mixture on both sides, and pat off the excess. Dip it in the egg and let the excess run off. Place it in the panko and cover both sides, pressing the panko into the meat.

Working in batches, carefully place the breaded pork in the hot oil and fry for 3 minutes on each side, until golden. Transfer to a paper towel–lined tray and season with salt, then keep warm in the oven while you repeat with the remaining pork.

Serve on regular hamburger buns, with the meat hanging over, with a choice of toppings.

MAKES 4 SANDWICHES

I might add some sautéed hot chiles or spicy pepper relish to this, and I would definitely add deli mustard as well.

The Amish community in central Pennsylvania gets a lot of pop culture attention, but there are also plenty of adherents in a pocket of Ohio and northern Indiana, where this dish is popular. The broth is almost miraculously rich and delightful.

AMISH
BEEF AND NOODLES

Season the roast with a liberal amount of salt and pepper on all sides. Preheat the oven to 325°F.

In a large, deep ovenproof pot or Dutch oven, heat the oil over medium-high heat. Sear the meat, deeply browning it on each side for 5 to 6 minutes, about 25 minutes total. Add the onion, garlic, half the carrots, half the celery, the parsley stems, and the bay leaves to the pot, then the water. Bring to a boil and cover. Transfer to the oven and bake for 3 hours.

Carefully lift the roast from the pan and put on a platter. With a slotted spoon, remove the parsley stems, onion, bay leaves, and any of the other vegetables that may come up with them. Add the remaining carrots and celery to the pot and bring to a boil over medium-high heat. Add the noodles and cook until tender, 7 to 10 minutes, adding more water if necessary. The noodles should soak up most of the liquid and be left coated in the remaining broth. Chop or shred the meat, discarding any bones. Season the meat with salt and black pepper, then return it to the pot. Stir and serve, garnished with chopped parsley leaves.

SERVES 4 TO 6

1 beef chuck roast, about 3 pounds, preferably bone-in

Kosher salt and freshly ground black pepper

3 tablespoons extra-virgin olive oil

1 large onion, quartered

5 cloves garlic, thinly sliced

2 large carrots, chopped into ½-inch half-moons

4 stalks celery, chopped

1 bunch fresh parsley, leaves and stems separated

2 bay leaves

8 cups water

1 (1-pound) package egg noodles, preferably hand-cut Amish noodles

Hand Pies

There is nothing more egalitarian than the hand pie. It's the lunch of the workingman, a self-contained meal of meat, potatoes, and/or vegetables wrapped in an edible package that fits in a pocket until it is time for a short respite from the backbreaking rigors of the day.

But there is also nothing more exclusive than the hand pie. It's yours. It's designed to be a single serving. Single. One. You aren't going to share it. It would be awkward even if you wanted to share it. And you don't.

And that just covers the savory options. Virtually any baked pie can be turned into a hand pie. Fast-food chains figured that out years ago, but there's absolutely no reason to wait for a trip through the drive-through to get in on that.

U.P. PASTIES (PAGE 295): Their expertise as miners and their recipe for pasties—beef and root vegetable pies—weren't the only things Cornish miners brought to Michigan's Upper Peninsula. They also brought the superstition that it was best to not eat the last bite of a pasty, but instead drop it and leave it for the spirits that might otherwise wreak havoc in the mines.

RUNZAS (PAGE 353): It's a similar story in the Midwest, where the immigrants were Eastern European and the vocation was working the fields. The runza is unique among hand pies in that it's wrapped in a yeasted dough, as opposed to pie dough. Throughout the heartland, you'll find similar beef-and-cabbage pies going by other names, including bierocks, kraut strudel, and cabbage burger.

NATCHITOCHES MEAT PIES (PAGE 232): In Louisiana, the origin story gets flipped around. Spanish explorers wandered into the Cane River area and found Native Americans making a meat-filled pie. It looked a lot like the empanadas they loved at home, so they adopted them, with the local flavor eventually becoming the defining trait.

DEVIL CRAB (PAGE 211): The hand pie that's still famous in Tampa is delicious. But even if it wasn't, it would make me smile because of the way it uses commercial white bread, returning it to the dough from which it came.

FRIED PEACH PIES (PAGE 174): Dessert hand pies had regional popularity for a long time before McDonald's introduced its apple pie in the 1960s and made them a global favorite. By the 1990s, the clown started baking them, but the oil stayed hot at smaller and regional chains, including the Varsity in Atlanta, where the Fried Peach Pie is a menu favorite.

NATCHITOCHES MEAT PIES

DEVIL CRAB

RUNZAS

FRIED PEACH PIES

U.P. PASTY

When copper mines were being developed in Michigan's Upper Peninsula in the mid-1800s, Cornish immigrants lent the expertise they brought with them to teach the locals the ins and outs of the job. Apparently, that extended to lunch, and the Cornish Pasty, a pocket-size meat-and-vegetable hand pie, became the U.P. Pasty. Pasties are often served with canned gravy, but I like them with ketchup.

U.P. PASTIES

Preheat the oven to 375°F. Line two baking sheets with silicone mats or parchment paper.

In a large bowl, combine the beef, pork, rutabaga, onion, carrots, sour cream, rosemary, salt, and pepper and mix well.

Divide the dough into 8 equal pieces and roll each into a 7-inch round. Mound one-eighth of the filling onto each crust, fold the crust into a half-moon, and crimp the edge closed. With the tip of a small, sharp knife, poke each pie 2 or 3 times to vent. Arrange the pies on the baking sheets.

Brush the pasties with the egg wash and sprinkle with salt. Bake for 30 to 35 minutes, until golden brown. Serve immediately, pack for lunch, or freeze.

MAKES 8 PASTIES

1 pound ground beef

8 ounces ground pork

1½ cups grated rutabaga (may sub potato)

1 medium onion, finely chopped

2 medium carrots, finely chopped

2 tablespoons sour cream

1½ teaspoons minced fresh rosemary

¾ teaspoon coarse sea salt plus more for seasoning

½ teaspoon freshly ground black pepper

2 recipes Basic Pie Crust (page 481)

1 large egg, beaten with 1 tablespoon water

If I had access to some fresh venison or elk, I might sub that for the beef or the pork, but I would definitely use two different meats.

Hotdish is really just the word Minnesotans use in a generic sense for casserole, but ever since the advent of Tater Tots, the meaning has gotten a little more specific. The standard ingredients are a baking pan, starch (usually tots), meat (usually ground beef), sauce (usually cream of mushroom soup), and sometimes a vegetable (usually from a can). Michael Symon and I have a long-running dispute over the nature of the casserole. I contend that the presence of cream of mushroom soup qualifies any dish as a casserole, and this recipe is merely part of my discovery.

TATER TOT
HOTDISH

Preheat the oven to 400°F. Spray a 9-by-13-inch baking pan with cooking spray.

In a large skillet over medium heat, heat the oil and brown the ground beef. Season with salt and pepper. Add the onion and celery and sauté until the onion softens, about 5 minutes. Add the vegetables and the soup and stir to incorporate.

Cover the bottom of the pan with the meat mixture, then top with the cheese. Add the Tater Tots in an even layer. Bake for 30 to 40 minutes, until bubbly and irresistible.

SERVES 6 TO 8

1 tablespoon extra-virgin olive oil

1 pound ground beef

Kosher salt and freshly ground black pepper

1 onion, finely chopped

2 stalks celery, chopped

1 cup fresh vegetable (anything in season: corn, peas, beans cut into ½-inch lengths)

3 cups Cream of Mushroom Soup (page 419); may sub 1 (10½-ounce) can condensed cream of mushroom soup reconstituted with 1 can milk

2 cups shredded Cheddar cheese

1 (32-ounce) package Tater Tots

Wisconsin cheesemakers produce more than 600 kinds of cheese, so it's always a little bit of a sport to get as many kinds into a pan of mac and cheese as possible. I stopped at three, but feel free to substitute—or add!—any of your favorites. My fave macaroni shape for mac and cheese is cavatappi, but elbows are classic.

MACARONI AND CHEESE

2 tablespoons kosher salt

1 pound dry elbow macaroni

½ small onion, finely chopped

4 tablespoons unsalted butter, melted

3 tablespoons all-purpose flour

1½ cups milk

¾ cup (3 ounces) shredded sharp Cheddar cheese

¾ cup (3 ounces) shredded smoked Gouda cheese

¼ cup panko bread crumbs

¼ cup grated Parmigiano-Reggiano

Bring 6 quarts of water to a boil in a pasta pot and add the salt. Set up an ice bath next to the stove. Cook the macaroni 2 minutes short of the package instructions, then drain, drop into the ice bath, and allow to cool for 2 minutes. Drain the macaroni and set aside.

Preheat the oven's broiler. Spray a 9-by-13-inch casserole with cooking spray.

In a large saucepan over medium heat, sauté the onion in 3 tablespoons of the butter until the onion softens, about 5 minutes. Whisk in the flour and cook, stirring, for an additional 3 minutes. Add ½ cup of the milk and whisk to incorporate with the roux. Add the remaining 1 cup milk, whisk, and cook until the mixture thickens, about 3 minutes. While continuing to whisk, add the Cheddar and Gouda and stir until all the cheese has melted. Add the cooked macaroni and stir until well coated. Pour into the prepared casserole.

In a small bowl, toss together the panko, Parmigiano, and remaining 1 tablespoon butter. Scatter the mixture over the top of the macaroni. Put the casserole under the broiler and broil until the topping browns and the cheese bubbles, about 3 minutes. Serve hot.

SERVES 4 AS A MAIN, 6 TO 8 AS A SIDE

The Finger Lakes region of New York has a growing reputation for wine grapes, but it has been known for its Concord grapes for decades. Growing up on the West Coast, we never really cared for Concord grape jelly, but tasting the fruit fresh after I arrived in NYC, I realized I had missed the boat for years. Irene Bouchard is widely credited with popularizing the pie made of these remarkable and geo-specific gems. If the process of skinning the grapes seems tedious, it will all be worth it in the end.

CONCORD GRAPE
PIE

5 cups Concord grapes, about 2 pounds

½ cup sugar

6 tablespoons cornstarch

Zest and juice of 1 lemon

Basic Pie Crust (page 481), one crust in a 9-inch pan, second crust rolled out

Remove the skins from each grape by pinching the end opposite the stem. Pop the pulp into a medium saucepan; reserve the skins in a bowl.

Preheat the oven to 375°F.

Bring the pulp to a boil over medium heat and reduce the heat to low; cook for 8 minutes. Strain the pulp into the bowl with the skins, pushing the pulp through and discarding the seeds. Add the sugar, cornstarch, and lemon zest and juice.

Pour the filling into the pie shell and cover with the top crust, crimping closed. With a sharp knife, cut slits in the top crust to vent. Bake for 30 to 40 minutes, until the crust is golden and the filling bubbles up through the vents and anywhere you didn't crimp well enough.

Let the pie cool before serving.

SERVES 6 TO 8

I might whip 2 cups of cream and add ¼ cup crushed roasted and salted peanuts to it, adding a dollop on each slice to create a fancy PB&J.

The Shakers are a small sect that branched off from the Quakers in the nineteenth century and were known for their gardening, furniture making, and celibacy. Their movement never really caught on, for some reason, but their Lemon Pie did.

SHAKER
LEMON PIE

3 lemons

2 cups granulated sugar

5 large eggs

½ teaspoon kosher salt

Basic Pie Crust (page 481), one crust in a 9-inch pan, second crust rolled out

Demerara sugar for sprinkling

Wash the lemons and cut a little off each end. Cut very thin slices, with either a knife or a mandoline. Catch and reserve any juice, but remove seeds as you see them. Combine the slices and their juice in a bowl with the granulated sugar and let stand at room temperature for several hours or overnight.

When ready to assemble, preheat the oven to 450°F.

Beat the eggs with the salt in a small bowl and toss with the lemons. Pour the mixture into the pie shell, then top with the second crust, crimping closed. Use the tip of a sharp knife to cut three slits in the top crust. Dust with a little Demerara sugar.

Bake for 15 minutes, then reduce the oven temperature to 375°F and bake for 30 minutes, until the crust is golden. Let cool to room temperature before serving.

SERVES 6 TO 8

This is the first of two desserts in the Great Lakes that share a name with a local college sports team. This one's a peanut-butter-and-chocolate candy meant to be a doppelganger for the nut of Ohio's state tree. I first tasted these in the second season of *The Chew* and simply do not know how I missed them for fifty years, but I suspect that my Pac-10 roots may have blinded me to the greatness of this particular kind of Buckeye.

BUCKEYES

In the bowl of a stand mixer, combine the butter, sugar, peanut butter, and vanilla and stir until incorporated. Roll the mixture into 1-inch balls and place on a baking sheet lined with waxed paper. Freeze for at least an hour.

Melt the chocolate in a double boiler, stirring until smooth. Using a fork or skewer, transfer each peanut butter ball into the chocolate, dipping to cover most of the peanut butter, but leave a small area exposed so the candy resembles a buckeye nut. Return the balls to the waxed paper, with the peanut butter opening on top, and chill until firm. Store in an airtight container in the fridge for up to 4 weeks.

MAKES 40, PLUS A FEW EXTRA FOR "TASTING"

½ cup (1 stick) unsalted butter, melted

3 cups confectioners' sugar

2 cups creamy peanut butter

1 teaspoon vanilla extract

2 cups semisweet chocolate chips

Even in times of scarcity, people want their dessert. The Hoosier Sugar Cream Pie served that purpose on farms across Indiana, the goal being a little bit of a treat made only with things that were always on hand at a farm. Strikingly similar to Kentucky's Chess Pie (page 194), the Hoosier pie uses cornstarch as a thickener instead of eggs. Also, while Chess Pie is often the jumping-off point for a lot of flavor embellishments, Sugar Cream Pie is all about the dairy.

HOOSIER
SUGAR CREAM PIE

Preheat the oven to 400°F.

Prebake the pie shell for 10 minutes. Set aside to cool.

In a bowl, whisk ½ cup of the half-and-half with the cornstarch until smooth.

In a large saucepan over medium heat, mix together the remaining 2 cups half-and-half, the sugar, and butter. Cook, continuing to whisk, until the butter melts and the sugar dissolves, about 5 minutes. Remove from the heat. Stir the cornstarch mixture and whisk it into the saucepan. Return the pan to the heat and continue whisking until the mixture is smooth and begins to thicken, about 8 minutes. Remove from the heat and stir in the vanilla and salt.

Pour the filling into the prebaked pie crust, sprinkle with nutmeg, and bake for 20 minutes, until the filling is almost set, but a bit jiggly. Cool to room temperature, then refrigerate overnight before serving.

SERVES 6 TO 8

½ recipe Basic Pie Crust in 9-inch pan (page 481)

2½ cups half-and-half

¼ cup cornstarch

¾ cup sugar

½ cup (1 stick) unsalted butter

1 teaspoon vanilla extract

Pinch kosher salt

Freshly grated nutmeg

A staple in the Amish kitchen, this pie has a list of ingredients similar to the Hoosier Sugar Cream Pie (page 307), with egg replacing most of the cornstarch. It would be typical to top with either a meringue or a dollop of whipped cream.

BUTTERSCOTCH PIE

½ recipe Basic Pie Crust in 9-inch pan (page 481)

2 cups milk

2 tablespoons all-purpose flour

1 tablespoon cornstarch

2 large egg yolks

4 tablespoons unsalted butter

1 cup firmly packed dark brown sugar

Preheat the oven to 400°F. Prebake the pie shell for 12 minutes, until the crust on the rim has browned.

In a bowl, combine the milk, flour, and cornstarch. Whisk in the egg yolks until incorporated.

In a medium saucepan over medium-high heat, melt the butter then add the sugar and heat until the sugar softens and melts into the butter. Off the heat, slowly whisk in the milk mixture. Put back over medium heat and cook, whisking, until it is smooth. Cook for 5 minutes longer, until the mixture begins to thicken.

Pour the mixture into the prebaked pie crust and refrigerate for at least 3 hours before serving.

SERVES 6 TO 8

I might serve this with a wee glass of "Southern" whiskey made at the secret distillery in Lawrenceburg, Indiana. Sssssshhh!

When settlers moving west in the 1700s found their way into southern Indiana, they found persimmon trees. They also found Native Americans who taught them to wait for the fruit to fall from the tree, and then how to make a pudding from it.

PERSIMMON
PUDDING

5 or 6 small, ripe persimmons

1 cup milk

3 large eggs, beaten

2 tablespoons unsalted butter, melted

½ teaspoon vanilla

1 cup all-purpose flour

¾ cup sugar

1 teaspoon baking soda

½ teaspoon ground cinnamon

½ teaspoon kosher salt

Whipped cream for serving

Preheat the oven to 350°F. Spray an 8-by-8-inch pan with cooking spray.

Cut the persimmons in half and scoop the pulp out into a bowl. You should get about 2½ cups of pulp. Discard the skins.

Add the remaining ingredients to the bowl and mix until well incorporated. Pour the batter into the pan and bake until dark brown and set, about 1 hour. Allow to cool and serve with whipped cream.

SERVES 6 TO 8

Persimmons have such a unique and delightful flavor that I would serve this with a dollop of really cold sour cream, then top that with a teaspoon of good balsamic and some freshly cracked black pepper.

Tart cherries have such a short season that it's good that someone had the forward thinking to dry them. Use them anywhere you might use a raisin, or in this case, someplace you might never have used a raisin.

CHERRY-CHOCOLATE
CHUNK COOKIES

2 cups quick-cooking oats

1 cup packed light brown sugar

1 cup (2 sticks) unsalted butter, softened

1 teaspoon vanilla extract

3 large eggs

1½ cups all-purpose flour

1 teaspoon baking soda

1 teaspoon kosher salt

1 cup dark or semisweet chocolate chunks

1 cup dried tart cherries

In a food processor, pulse 1½ cups of the oats until they're the consistency of bread crumbs. Mix in the unprocessed oats and set aside.

In a stand mixer with a paddle attachment or a large bowl with an electric mixer, cream the brown sugar and butter together, then add the vanilla, then the eggs, one at a time, and beat until thoroughly mixed. In a separate bowl, combine the oats, flour, baking soda, and salt, then gradually add that mixture to the creamed butter and sugar. Stir in the chocolate chunks and cherries. Cover the dough and refrigerate for at least 2 hours; longer is fine.

Preheat the oven to 350°F. Line two baking sheets with silicone baking mats or parchment paper.

Drop heaping tablespoonfuls of the dough onto the baking sheets, about 2 inches apart. Bake, rotating the pans after 5 minutes, for 10 to 12 minutes. Cool on a wire rack and wait patiently nearby with a glass of milk.

MAKES 24 COOKIES

I like to sprinkle each cookie with coarse sea salt before baking.

the HEARTLAND

WITH MOST AMERICANS living near the outside edges of the country, short shrift is sometimes given to those who inhabit the middle of it. "Flyover country," it's called, as the coasters jet between meetings in New York and Los Angeles. The term probably isn't meant to be as dismissive as it can sound, but the fact is that while the machers are flying over, they're also overlooking something important.

That's the land that's growing much of the food they're going to be eating out on those coastal edges. The people of the Heartland are the ones raising our beef. They are growing our wheat and potatoes. And in fields that stretch seemingly forever in every direction, they are growing the corn and soybeans that find their way into almost everything we eat, for better or worse. These are the fruited plains we sing about. This is where you find the amber waves of grain.

And all of that happens in the shadow of our purple mountains' majesty. As the Great Plains fuel our bodies, the Rocky Mountains have served to fuel our sense of adventure. Along the way, you can forage plenty of accompaniments for the trout in the clear streams.

There are plenty of opportunities for big-city refinery in population centers such as St. Louis and Denver, but plenty of enviable escapades are available outside the crowds as well. A hike through the trails on the side of a mountain in Aspen, or past the gurgling earth at Yellowstone. The South Dakota dance hall that celebrates the impact of corn on the region by being constructed of the grain.

Roadside treasures through this part of the country include the intensely **LOCAL FAST-FOOD STOPS** at places like Runza in Nebraska and Maid-Rite in Iowa. I want **RIBS** in Kansas City, and once we get to Colorado and Wyoming, the play is to grab some trail mix and get off the road to see the glorious mountains up close!

As we plan to meander through these states, we find that chefs are doing great things in every corner of the country, and we'll take the opportunity to seek out meals from such talents as Clayton Chapman in Omaha, Sean Wilson in Des Moines, Gerard Craft in St. Louis, Alex Seidel in Denver, and Kelly Liken in Vail.

Find a festival or fair and you'll find yourself at the intersection of history and innovation. Sure they celebrate the old ways of agriculture. But the St. Louis World's Fair of 1904 gets credit for being the place that the ice cream cone was invented. The ice cream cone! In Iowa each August at the State Fair, they figure out a new way to spear food on a stick and drop it in hot oil. And they've turned butter into an artistic medium.

On the surface, it may seem like a disparate, far-flung collection of states. It ranges from the swamps of Arkansas to the glacier-carved valleys of Idaho, from the Mississippi River to the Western Slope of the Rockies.

But put together, the Heartland is where America still exists in its ideal notion. And as a gastro-tourist, I always find big portions, big hearts, big laughs, and a few funny cracks about my shoes.

Alternately known as a Western Omelet, this dish probably originated as a sandwich for workers on the Transcontinental Railroad. And Denver was probably not the origin of its namesake omelet. It was probably a destination, the place the crews were working toward. Either way, it's a diner staple around the country now.

DENVER OMELET

In a bowl, beat together the eggs, milk, hot sauce, salt, and pepper until the eggs are well beaten.

Heat the oil in a 12- to 14-inch nonstick skillet over medium-high heat. Add the onion and bell pepper and sauté until the onion begins to soften, about 5 minutes. Add the ham and cook just until it warms through. Remove from the pan and set aside.

Lower the heat to medium and add the egg mixture to the pan. Let the egg cook for about 1 minute, then use a spatula to push the cooked curds to the middle of the pan. Let the egg cook another minute, then scatter the sautéed vegetables and ham over the egg. Add ½ cup of the cheese. Use the spatula to fold the omelet in half and sprinkle the rest of the cheese over the top. Cover and cook until the cheese melts, about 2 minutes. Transfer the omelet to a plate and garnish with green onion slices.

SERVES 2, OR 1 HUNGRY COWBOY

4 large eggs

2 tablespoons milk

1 teaspoon hot sauce

½ teaspoon kosher salt

½ teaspoon freshly ground
    black pepper

1 tablespoon extra-virgin
    olive oil

½ small onion, finely chopped

½ small red bell pepper,
    finely chopped

6 ounces ham steak, diced

¾ cup shredded Cheddar
    cheese

2 green onions, green parts
    only, thinly sliced, for
    garnish

Someone took a White Russian and added a little bit of Coke to the mix. I'm not one hundred percent sure the Dude would abide, but I'm in.

COLORADO BULLDOG

Ice
1½ ounces vodka
1½ ounces Kahlúa
1 ounce cream
1 ounce Coca-Cola

Fill a highball glass and a cocktail shaker each with ice. Add the vodka and Kahlúa to the shaker, cover, and shake. Strain over the ice in the glass. Add the cream to the glass, then top with the cola.

MAKES 1 COCKTAIL

Hiking through the mountains on a late spring day can result in a hiker coming across a field full of wild asparagus. Wherever you encounter your asparagus (even if it's in a grocery store), you'll want to have a plan to preserve as much of it as you can carry home with you.

PICKLED
ASPARAGUS

2½ cups white wine vinegar

2½ cups water

3 tablespoons kosher salt

2 teaspoons black peppercorns

2 teaspoons dill weed

6 dried chile peppers, or 2 teaspoons crushed red pepper flakes

6 cloves garlic, peeled

2 teaspoons juniper berries

3 pounds asparagus, thin to medium spears, trimmed to fit in your jars

In a medium saucepan over medium-high heat, bring the vinegar, water, salt, black pepper, dill weed, chile peppers, garlic, and juniper berries to a simmer. Reduce the heat to medium-low and simmer for 10 minutes, stirring to dissolve the salt. Cool until lukewarm.

Put 1 or 2 cloves garlic and 1 or 2 chile peppers from the brine into each jar, then tightly pack in the asparagus. The spears should not come any higher than ½ inch from the rim of the jar. Pour the brine over, evenly distributing the spices, and seal the jars. The pickles will be ready to eat after about 3 days, and will last in the refrigerator for about a week. For long-term storage, can according to the directions on page 9.

MAKES 3 TALL 24-OUNCE JARS, OR 6 TALL 12-OUNCE JARS

A mature buffalo can weigh 2,000 pounds. When early Americans took one down on the Great Plains, they needed to have a plan to make the most of the sacrifice. In the days before refrigeration, that meant drying the meat. Homemade jerky is infinitely lower in salt than commercial brands, and I like to make it a little bit softer than the jerky I buy at the 7-Eleven. Spice-wise, you can add 1 tablespoon of just about anything you like...ginger, hot sauce, celery seeds. Experiment and dream on. (Pictured on page 321.)

BEEF JERKY

2 pounds flank steak; can be beef, buffalo, venison

½ cup soy sauce

1 teaspoon crushed red pepper flakes

Preheat the oven as low as it will go, 150°F to 175°F, or set a dehydrator to 150°F.

Freeze the steak for 10 to 15 minutes to make it easier to slice. Cutting with the grain—exactly the opposite way that you've always heard to cut flank steak—make long slices of meat about ⅛ inch thick. Toss with the soy sauce and pepper. Lay the strips out on a rack over a baking sheet, or on the dehydrator tray, and dry out in the low oven or the dehydrator for 10 to 12 hours, until the strips are very dark and wrinkly, but still a bit chewy.

MAKES ABOUT 20 STRIPS

If you worry about slimy okra, use a sharp knife. The sharper your blade, the less slimy your okra will become, as it will slice more precisely. These nuggets make an indulgent garnish to the Chicken and Shrimp Gumbo (page 236) and are also an excellent substitute for popcorn shrimp as an appetizer. (Pictured on page 325.)

CRISPY
CORNMEAL OKRA

In a large, deep pot or Dutch oven, heat 2 inches of oil to 360°F.

Put the buttermilk in a wide, shallow bowl. In another wide, shallow bowl, mix the cornmeal, flour, salt, and cayenne. Place the okra in the buttermilk and toss to coat. Drain the okra and move it to the cornmeal mixture and toss to coat.

Working in batches as necessary to avoid crowding, fry the okra until crispy, 3 to 5 minutes. Drain on a paper towel–lined plate and season with salt. Serve warm with hot sauce.

SERVES 6 TO 8

Canola or corn oil for frying

1 cup buttermilk

1½ cups cornmeal

½ cup all-purpose flour

1 teaspoon kosher salt plus more for seasoning

1 teaspoon cayenne

2 pounds fresh okra, sliced into 1-inch pieces

Hot sauce for serving

Some states name an official food. In Oklahoma, the legislature cut right to the chase and, in 1988, declared an official meal. The centerpiece is Chicken Fried Steak, but it also includes Crispy Cornmeal Okra (page 323) and Pecan Pie (page 373), as well as BBQ pork, sausage, gravy, and black-eyed peas. To me, this was a much more significant piece of legislation than much of what happens around the country. Oklahoma, I'll be right over!

CHICKEN FRIED STEAK

FOR THE STEAKS

1 cup all-purpose flour

1 teaspoon Colman's dry mustard

½ teaspoon paprika

½ teaspoon onion powder

½ teaspoon kosher salt

½ teaspoon freshly ground black pepper

2 large eggs, lightly beaten

½ cup milk

Canola or corn oil for frying

4 beef cube steaks, about 8 ounces each; or 1 (2-pound) round steak, cut into 4 portions and beaten flat with a spiked meat mallet

FOR THE GRAVY

¼ cup all-purpose flour

2 cups milk

1 teaspoon kosher salt

2 teaspoons freshly ground black pepper

¼ cup chopped fresh parsley

FOR THE STEAKS: Combine the flour, mustard, paprika, onion powder, salt, and pepper in a shallow dish. In a separate shallow dish, beat the eggs with the milk.

In a large skillet, heat ½ inch of oil to 360°F. While the oil heats, dip each steak into the flour, shake off, then dip in the egg mixture, then back into the flour and again shake off the excess. When the oil is ready, gently place 1 or 2 steaks in the skillet and cook for 4 to 5 minutes. Carefully flip them and cook for another 4 to 5 minutes, until crispy and golden. Drain on paper towels. Repeat to cook the remaining steaks, keeping the cooked ones warm.

FOR THE GRAVY: Working in the same skillet you fried the steaks in, remove all but 2 tablespoons of the frying oil. Watch out for burned bits in the pan after sautéing the meat—remove them before making the gravy. Stir in the flour and cook over medium heat for about 3 minutes. Remove from the heat and slowly whisk in the milk, salt, and pepper. Return to the heat and continue whisking until the gravy is thick, about 1 minute. Serve the gravy over the steaks, garnished with parsley.

MAKES 4 OKLAHOMA-SIZED SERVINGS

Whether they're called Rocky Mountain Oysters, Prairie Oysters, or Lamb or Calf Fries, testicles seem to be best served covered in euphemism. But if eating something so definitively masculine gives you pause, think for a minute about how many eggs you eat.

ROCKY MOUNTAIN
OYSTERS

2 pounds calf testicles

2 cups buttermilk

Canola or corn oil for frying

2 cups all-purpose flour

1 cup cornmeal

½ teaspoon kosher salt

½ teaspoon freshly ground
    black pepper

4 large eggs, beaten

Hot sauce for serving

You're going to need a sharp knife and no conscience. There's a skin-like membrane surrounding the testicles. That has to go. Cut through it and peel it off. Do not think about what you are actually doing. You can leave them whole if they're small, or slice them in half or in about ½-inch-thick slices, all the while considering the implications of yesterday's big ball game. GAME! I meant just yesterday's *game*!

Depending on your constitution, the worst is over.

Put the slices in a bowl and cover them with the buttermilk. Refrigerate for at least 2 hours.

In a large, heavy pot or Dutch oven, heat 2 inches of oil to 370°F.

In a wide, shallow bowl, mix together the flour, cornmeal, salt, and pepper. In another wide, shallow bowl, beat the eggs. (What did I tell you about eggs?)

Dredge the "oysters" in the flour, then in the egg, then back in the flour.

Drop in the oil 3 or 4 at a time and fry for about 3 minutes, until golden. Drain on a paper towel–lined plate.

Serve bravely with hot sauce.

SERVES 6 TO 8

I might add some ancho chili powder or cayenne to the dredging flour.

Potatoes are grown in all fifty states, but Idaho is the only one they're synonymous with. If you have a ham bone in the house, now is the time to use it.

POTATO SOUP

2 tablespoons extra-virgin
    olive oil

1 medium onion, diced

4 stalks celery, diced

1 ham bone or smoked pork
    shank

8 cups water

3 pounds russet potatoes,
    peeled and cut into
    ½-inch dice

Kosher salt and freshly ground
    black pepper

1 cup sour cream

Snipped fresh chives for
    garnish, optional

Shredded Cheddar cheese for
    serving, optional

Heat the olive oil in a large pot or Dutch oven over medium-high heat. Add the onion and celery and sauté for about 5 minutes, then add the ham bone or shank and water. Cover the pot, reduce the heat to medium-low, and simmer for 3 hours.

Remove the bone, pick it clean of any meat, chop the meat, and return it to the pot. Raise the heat to medium, add the potatoes and 1 teaspoon each salt and pepper, and cook for about 30 minutes, until the potatoes are tender. Use a stick blender to puree the soup to the consistency you prefer, anywhere from quite chunky to velvety smooth. You may choose to skip this step if you like it chunky.

Take the soup off the heat and stir in the sour cream. Taste and reseason as necessary. Serve, topping individual bowls with a sprinkling of chives and a large pinch of shredded cheese, if you like.

MAKES 2 QUARTS, SERVING 6 TO 8

From a small area starting just north of Moscow, Idaho, stretching west into Washington, comes most of the U.S. lentil crop. Most of it gets exported, but the ones that stick around might end up in a soup like this one.

LEMONY
LENTIL SOUP

Heat the oil in a large, heavy pot or Dutch oven over medium-high heat. Add the onion, carrots, celery, garlic, rosemary, and salt and pepper to taste and sauté for 5 minutes. Stir in the lentils and add the broth. Bring to a boil, then reduce the heat to medium-low and simmer for 20 minutes, until the lentils are tender. Stir in the chard leaves and cook until they wilt. Add the lemon zest and juice and season well with salt and black pepper. Serve hot.

MAKES 2 QUARTS, SERVING 6 TO 8

2 tablespoons extra-virgin olive oil

1 small onion, finely diced

2 carrots, finely diced

2 stalks celery, finely diced

3 cloves garlic, thinly sliced

1 tablespoon fresh rosemary, chopped

Kosher salt and freshly ground black pepper

1 cup brown lentils, rinsed

6 cups vegetable broth

12 ounces Swiss chard (about 2 bunches), stems removed and discarded, leaves thinly shredded

Zest and juice of 2 lemons

I might make some crostini out of old bread, toast them under the broiler, and then rub them with raw garlic and float them in the soup right before I serve it.

At state fairs across the Midwest, the food courts feature various incarnations of corn and fried food. So it's only natural that you'll find some fried corn. These make excellent passed hors d'oeuvres and can make a pretty killer sammie with shredded lettuce, sliced tomatoes, and tartar sauce on a soft sub roll.

CORN FRITTERS

Canola or corn oil for frying

1 cup all-purpose flour

1 cup cornmeal

1 teaspoon baking powder

1 teaspoon kosher salt plus more for seasoning

1 teaspoon freshly ground black pepper

½ cup sour cream

2 large eggs, beaten

2 tablespoons unsalted butter, melted

2 ears fresh sweet corn, kernels cut off, and the "milk" scraped from the cobs with the back of a knife

1 jalapeño, finely chopped

Honey for serving

In a large, deep pot or Dutch oven, heat 2 inches of oil to 325°F.

In a large bowl, whisk together the flour, cornmeal, baking powder, salt, and pepper. Add the sour cream, eggs, butter, corn kernels and corn milk, and jalapeño, and mix thoroughly.

In batches, using two spoons, make round balls and drop by heaping spoonfuls into the oil. Fry until crisp and golden brown, 4 to 6 minutes. Drain the fritters on paper towels and season immediately with salt. Serve with a drizzle of honey.

MAKES 12 TO 15 FRITTERS

I might add ¼ cup chopped green onions to the batter just before frying.

The Hill is St. Louis's Little Italy, and one of the great neighborhood-specific dishes you'll find in the country is the Toasted Ravioli they make there. The legend is that it was invented accidentally, when someone tripped near a fryer. Sounds suspect, but who doesn't love a good legend? Start with homemade ravioli if you like—the Cheese Buttons (page 355) are a perfect option—but a store-bought brand, mine from Gia Russa, for example, makes this dish a breeze.

TOASTED RAVIOLI
FROM THE HILL

2 large eggs

1½ cups panko bread crumbs

Kosher salt and freshly ground black pepper

Canola or corn oil for frying

Cheese Buttons (page 355), cooked through to the boiling step, or 1 (9-ounce) package prepared fresh ravioli, any filling, thawed if frozen

¼ cup grated Parmigiano-Reggiano

2 cups Basic Tomato Sauce (page 480), warmed

2 teaspoons crushed red pepper flakes

Get two wide, shallow bowls. In one, beat the eggs. In the other, spread out the panko crumbs. Season the eggs and the panko with salt and pepper.

In a large, straight-sided skillet, heat about ½ inch of oil over medium-high heat.

Dip the ravioli in the egg, then dredge in the panko. Working in batches, fry them in the oil for about 2 minutes, then flip them and fry for an additional 2 minutes, until crisp. Remove to a paper towel–lined plate, and repeat to fry all the ravioli. Serve on a platter, dusting them with Parmigiano.

Mix the tomato sauce with the red pepper flakes and serve in a ramekin on the side.

SERVES 4 TO 6

The rivers and streams that wend their way through Arkansas and Missouri and back, without regard to the state line, are paradise for anglers set on rainbow and brown trout. But if the fish aren't biting—or the smokehouse is out of trout—this recipe works with whatever smoked fish is on hand.

SMOKED TROUT CAKES

¼ cup sour cream

1 large egg

2 tablespoons whole-grain mustard

Zest and juice of 1 lemon

¼ cup chopped fresh chives

½ red bell pepper, finely diced

2 tablespoons capers, drained

½ teaspoon cayenne

1 pound smoked trout, skin and bones removed, meat flaked

1 to 1¼ cups instant mashed potato flakes

Canola or corn oil for frying

Lemon wedges for serving

In a large bowl, combine the sour cream, egg, mustard, lemon zest and juice, chives, bell pepper, capers, and cayenne. Add the fish and ½ cup of the mashed potato flakes. Lightly toss to combine, cover with plastic wrap, and refrigerate for 30 minutes. If there is liquid in the bowl at that point, add ¼ cup of the remaining potato flakes and rest another 30 minutes.

In a large skillet over medium-high heat, heat about ¼ inch of oil. Spread ½ cup potato flakes in a wide, shallow bowl.

Form the mixture into 10 to 12 equal patties. Dredge each side of each patty in the potato. In two batches to avoid crowding the pan, carefully place patties in the oil and fry for 2 to 3 minutes, then flip and fry for 2 to 3 minutes more, until each side is golden brown and crispy.

Serve hot with lemon wedges.

MAKES 10 TO 12 CAKES

I might serve these with a sauce inspired by Southeast Asia: Mix ½ cup nuoc cham with ½ cup Sriracha, add 2 tablespoons chopped cilantro, and dip on, you crazy diamond.

Bernell Austin, affectionately known as Fatman around Atkins, Arkansas, is credited with inventing Fried Dill Pickles in 1963. He said he did it because there was a pickle factory across from his drive-in, the Duchess. Fry local!

FRIED
DILL PICKLES

In a large, deep, straight-sided skillet, heat about ¾ inch of oil to 360°F.

In a wide, shallow bowl, combine the pickle brine, buttermilk, flour, and paprika. Put the cornmeal in another wide shallow bowl.

Dip each pickle slice in the batter, then in the cornmeal. Working in batches to avoid crowding the pan, fry the pickles for about 2 minutes, then flip and fry for another 2 minutes. Remove to a plate lined with paper towel, season with salt, and serve hot.

MAKES 16 TO 20 SLICES

Canola or corn oil for frying

4 large dill pickles, cut crosswise into thick slices, ½ cup brine reserved

2 tablespoons buttermilk

½ cup all-purpose flour

½ teaspoon paprika

1 cup cornmeal

Kosher salt

I don't know if there was ever a chuckwagon jockey—let's call him Cookie—who prepped bison steaks with a coffee rub and seared them to a perfect medium-rare over an open campfire for the crew at the end of a long day. But it totally makes sense, as the coffee brings a smoky rich bitterness to the crust and transforms the meat into something almost brooding in its complexity.

BISON
RIB EYES

In a small bowl, combine the coffee, olive oil, brown sugar, salt, red pepper flakes, and black pepper to make a paste. Rub the paste evenly over the two steaks, put them in a zip-top bag, and refrigerate for at least 8 hours.

Preheat a grill or the oven's broiler.

Take the steaks from the bag and brush off some of the paste. Cook over the hottest part of the grill for about 15 minutes, turning every 4 to 5 minutes, until the internal temperature reaches 120°F for medium-rare.

Let the steaks rest for 10 minutes before serving.

SERVES 4 TO 6

¼ cup ground coffee

¼ cup extra-virgin olive oil

2 tablespoons brown sugar

1 tablespoon kosher salt

1 tablespoon crushed red pepper flakes

1 tablespoon coarsely ground black pepper

2 buffalo rib eye steaks, 20 ounces each

It's important to be prepared when going out on a fishing trip. Always remember to bring the rod and the reel, your flies, a pair of waders. And if you're thinking optimistically, you'll bring a cast-iron skillet, a few lemons, and some dill.

MOUNTAIN TROUT

2 whole trout, about 1 pound each, cleaned and deboned with heads on

Extra-virgin olive oil

Kosher salt and freshly ground black pepper

3 lemons, 1 sliced, 2 halved

1 bunch fresh dill

Preheat the grill or the oven's broiler.

Rub the trout with olive oil, inside and out, and season the flesh with salt and pepper. Line the inside of each fish with lemon slices and half the dill, then fold the fish to close it around the lemon and dill. Use kitchen twine to secure the fish.

Place the lemon halves (cut side toward the heat) and the fish on the grill or under the broiler and cook for about 6 minutes. Using a large spatula, lift each fish and carefully turn over to cook for another 6 minutes, until the flesh is firm. Take the lemons off the heat when they begin to char.

Serve the fish with the grilled lemon.

MAKES 2 TROUT, SERVING 4

If you're an average American, you'll eat almost 120 pounds of potatoes over the course of a year. Is average good enough? Strive for excellence!

SCALLOPED POTATOES

3 pounds russet potatoes, peeled and sliced ¼ inch thick

3 tablespoons unsalted butter

1½ cups half-and-half

1 teaspoon freshly grated nutmeg

Kosher salt and freshly ground white pepper

Preheat the oven to 375°F. Spray a 9-by-13-inch casserole with cooking spray.

Line the bottom of the casserole with one-third of the potatoes. Dot the potatoes with 1 tablespoon butter, drizzle with ½ cup half-and-half, and dust with nutmeg, salt, and pepper. Repeat to use the remaining potatoes, butter, and half-and-half, seasoning each layer.

Bake for 1 hour, until the top layer of potatoes is golden brown and the interior is tender. Cool for 10 minutes before serving.

SERVES 8 TO 10

I might sprinkle this with ½ cup freshly grated Parmigiano-Reggiano before placing it in the oven.

The Maid-Rite restaurants figured something out, creating these sandwiches that aren't quite a hamburger, and aren't quite a sloppy joe, and aren't quite anything else you've ever seen. It's the fast food of choice in Iowa, but don't forget to grab a fork. And repeat the name every hour on the day you make them. It's funny!

IOWA
LOOSE MEAT

In a large skillet over medium-high heat, heat the oil and sauté the beef and onion until the beef has browned. Vigorously stir while cooking, breaking up the meat as much as possible. Add the stock, vinegar, soy sauce, Worcestershire, sugar, salt, and pepper and stir to combine. Bring to a boil, then reduce the heat to medium-low and cook until the liquid has evaporated.

With a slotted spoon, place an overwhelming amount of meat in each bun, with a couple of pickle slices on top of the meat. Serve with ketchup and mustard on the side.

MAKES 6 SANDWICHES

2 tablespoons extra-virgin olive oil

2 pounds ground beef

1 medium onion, finely diced

1 cup Brown Chicken Stock (page 480)

2 tablespoons apple cider vinegar

1 tablespoon low-sodium soy sauce

1 tablespoon Worcestershire sauce

1 tablespoon light brown sugar

1 teaspoon kosher salt

1 teaspoon freshly ground black pepper

6 hamburger buns

Dill pickle slices

Ketchup and mustard for serving

I might add 1 chopped chipotle in adobo at the same time as the Worcestershire. Or I might add two.

In Kansas City, ribs get sauce, and people get passionate about whose ribs they want. For most, the competition comes down to Gates vs. Arthur Bryant's. But ribs are a religion there, and you can find really good ones in a lot of places.

KANSAS CITY
BBQ RIBS

FOR THE RIBS AND RUB

¼ cup smoked paprika

¼ cup packed brown sugar

¼ cup kosher salt

1 tablespoon freshly ground black pepper

1 tablespoon chili powder

1 teaspoon cayenne

1 teaspoon Colman's dry mustard

2 racks St. Louis cut pork spareribs, about 7 pounds total (may sub 5 pounds baby backs)

FOR THE BBQ SAUCE

2 tablespoons extra-virgin olive oil

1 small onion, grated

½ cup ketchup

¼ cup packed dark brown sugar

¼ cup molasses

Zest and juice of 1 lemon

1 teaspoon celery seed

1 teaspoon smoked paprika

1 teaspoon kosher salt

FOR THE RIBS AND RUB: Mix all the dry ingredients in a small bowl. Aggressively coat the ribs with the rub. Don't be afraid to massage it in. Let the ribs rest at room temperature for about an hour.

FOR THE BBQ SAUCE: In a medium saucepan over medium-high heat, heat the oil and sauté the onion until softened, about 5 minutes. Add the rest of the ingredients, bring to a boil, then lower the heat to medium-low and simmer for 15 to 20 minutes, until the sauce starts to thicken.

AT THE GRILL: Prepare your gas or charcoal grill for indirect cooking. If using charcoal, add a cup of soaked wood chips to the embers; if using gas, wrap some soaked wood chips in foil, poke holes in the foil, and before you light the grill, set the packet on one of the burners, under the grate.

Set the ribs over the unlit portion of the grill, close the grill, and cook for 2½ hours for spare ribs or 1½ hours for baby backs, replenishing the charcoal and/or wood chips as necessary throughout the process. The ribs are ready when they start to separate from the bone when tugged at. Brush the ribs on both sides with sauce, close the grill, and cook for 30 additional minutes.

Serve with more sauce on the side.

MAKES 2 RACKS OF RIBS, SERVING 4 TO 6

At amusement parks and festivals around the Ozarks, you can find vendors sautéing this colorful one-skillet meal in pans wide enough to take a nap in. Luckily, it's easy to approximate in your largest skillet.

CALICO POTATOES

2 tablespoons extra-virgin olive oil

1 medium onion, finely chopped

½ green bell pepper, finely chopped

½ red bell pepper, finely chopped

1 pound red-skin potatoes, thinly sliced

1 pound sweet potatoes, peeled and thinly sliced

1 pound smoked sausage, such as kielbasa or andouille, cut into ½-inch slices

1 teaspoon kosher salt

1 teaspoon freshly ground black pepper

1 teaspoon cayenne

¼ cup water

Heat the olive oil in a 12- to 14-inch skillet over medium-high heat. Add the onion and bell peppers and cook until they soften, about 5 minutes. Add the potatoes and sausage and toss everything until you've achieved a calico tapestry—it'll make sense when you see it. Season with salt, black pepper, and cayenne, then toss again, add the water, and cover. Reduce the heat to medium and cook, tossing the potatoes every 5 minutes, for 15 minutes, until the potatoes are cooked through. Take the skillet to the table and serve hot.

SERVES 6 TO 8

When Eastern Europeans started making their way to the Midwest in the mid-1800s, they brought with them these meat-and-cabbage hand pies that were a typical lunch for field workers. What they didn't bring is one name for them. They're called runzas in Nebraska, where a drive-through chain specializes in them, but in Kansas, they're called bierocks. And if you're in that general area and ask for a kraut strudel or a cabbage burger, you'll probably get one of these.

RUNZAS

Depending on the size runzas you want to make, divide the pizza dough into 8 (large), 12 (medium), or 16 (small) pieces. Roll into balls, cover with a towel, and let rise for 1 hour.

In a large skillet over medium-high heat, brown the ground beef, then add the onion and sauté for 5 minutes. Add the cabbage, sugar, salt, and pepper and cook, stirring frequently, until the cabbage has wilted down, 10 to 15 minutes. Drain as much liquid as possible from the filling and let cool.

Preheat the oven to 350°F. Line two baking sheets with silicone mats or parchment paper.

Take each piece of dough and flatten it out to a 5- to 7-inch round about ¼ inch thick (the diameter will depend on how many runzas you're making). Divide the filling, and cheese if using, evenly among the dough. Fold one side of the round over the filling, then fold the two ends in, and bring up the other side to enclose the filling. Pinch together the seams. They'll look something like an egg roll. Place the runzas on the prepared baking sheets seam side down as they're ready.

Brush each runza with the egg wash and sprinkle with salt. Bake until the dough is golden brown, about 35 minutes. Serve with mustard.

MAKES 8 TO 16 PIES

Basic Pizza Dough (page 481)

1 pound lean ground beef

1 medium onion, finely chopped

½ medium head cabbage, finely shredded; or substitute 1 cup Fermented Sauerkraut (page 72), well drained

1 tablespoon sugar

2 teaspoons kosher salt plus more for seasoning

1 teaspoon freshly ground black pepper

1 cup shredded cheese, such as sharp Cheddar or Emmenthaler, optional

1 large egg, beaten with 2 teaspoons water

Mustard for serving

Kase means cheese in German, and *knoephla* are dumplings, meaning that we aren't too far removed from a good-looking ravioli. Cheese Buttons can be served in soup or as a side dish with sour cream or gravy.

CHEESE BUTTONS
OR KASE KNOEPHLA

In a bowl, combine the cheese, 2 of the eggs, the salt, and pepper. Set aside.

In a bowl or stand mixer fitted with a paddle attachment, mix together the flour and remaining 2 eggs. Mix in ½ cup of the milk, then, if the dough seems dry, the remaining ¼ cup milk. Cut the dough into two pieces.

Bring a large, heavy pot half-full of water to a boil over medium-high heat. Add about a tablespoon of salt.

On a large, flour-dusted work surface, roll one piece of dough to a thickness of ⅛ inch. Cut the dough into 4-inch squares and place a heaping spoonful of the cheese mixture in the middle. Fold the dough over and pinch the edges lightly to close. Repeat to use the rest of the dough and cheese to make about 12 cheese buttons.

Add the cheese buttons to the boiling water in batches to avoid crowding the pot and cook for about 6 minutes. They're ready when they float. Remove with a slotted spoon to a plate.

In a large skillet over medium-high heat, melt the butter and sauté the onion until it softens, about 5 minutes. Toss the cheese buttons in the pan and sauté until browned on one side. Serve hot.

SERVES 4 TO 6

1½ cups cottage or farmer's cheese

4 large eggs

½ teaspoon kosher salt plus more for the pasta water

½ teaspoon freshly ground black pepper

3 cups all-purpose flour

¾ cup milk

6 tablespoons unsalted butter

½ small onion, finely chopped

There are a lot of theories about how this dish of simply fried meat on a stick came to be so popular in a very specific corner of southeastern South Dakota. My favorite: It was developed as an alternative for diners who didn't want Prairie Oysters. (See page 326 for more on those.)

CHISLIC

½ cup extra-virgin olive oil plus more for frying

3 cloves garlic, thinly sliced

1 pound boneless lamb, shoulder or leg, cut into 1½-inch cubes

Kosher salt and freshly ground black pepper

Hot sauce for serving

Crackers for serving

In a gallon zip-top bag, mix the ½ cup olive oil, garlic, and lamb. Massage the bag a little bit and refrigerate for at least 2 hours or up to 12.

In a large, straight-sided skillet, heat 1 inch of oil to 370°F.

Remove the lamb from the bag and thread the chunks on 6-inch bamboo skewers, 3 or 4 pieces per skewer. Using tongs and working in batches if necessary to avoid crowding the pan, carefully drop the skewers into the oil. Fry for 2 or 3 minutes, turning once, until cooked through. Drain on a paper towel–lined platter, season with salt and pepper, and serve with hot sauce and crackers.

MAKES 6 SKEWERS

Each August at the Peach Festival in Palisade, Colorado, there's an ice cream social. The featured sweet is vanilla ice cream with some of the starring fruit cut over the top. That sounds fantastic, but here, let's just put the peaches right in the ice cream.

PEACH
ICE CREAM

Sprinkle the peaches with the sugar and let stand at room temperature a few hours. In a small bowl, mix together the cream cheese and cornstarch. Set aside.

Heat the milk and cream over medium heat. Whisk in the honey. Raise the heat to medium-high and whisk in the cream cheese mixture until the milk thickens slightly. Remove from the heat and stir in the peaches. Refrigerate overnight. Freeze in an ice cream machine according to the manufacturer's instructions.

MAKES ABOUT 1 QUART

2 cups peeled and chopped peaches, about 3 large peaches

½ cup packed dark brown sugar

½ cup cream cheese, softened

2 tablespoons cornstarch

1 cup milk

1 cup heavy cream

¼ cup honey

I might top this with some sliced raw peaches tossed with a touch of balsamic vinegar and some freshly cracked black pepper.

Just outside Montana's Glacier National Park is Flathead Lake, which is ringed by orchards of sweet cherry trees. A travel website once ascribed a dessert of this profile to the state, which left residents scratching their heads, because most had never heard of it. I'm going to suggest they get some of their fine local cherries, make this, and start telling tales about its storied history.

SWEET AND SOUR CREAM

CHERRY TART

FOR THE CRUST

6 tablespoons very cold unsalted butter, cut into small cubes, plus more for the tart pan

½ cup blanched almonds, lightly toasted

1 cup all-purpose flour plus more as needed

½ cup confectioners' sugar

1 teaspoon kosher salt

1 large egg, lightly beaten with 1 tablespoon cold water

FOR THE FILLING

1 cup sour cream

2 large eggs, lightly beaten

½ cup cream

1 teaspoon vanilla extract

¼ cup sugar

2 cups sweet cherries, stemmed and pitted

Confectioners' sugar for dusting

FOR THE CRUST: Butter a 10-inch tart pan.

In the bowl of a food processor, pulse the almonds, breaking them into coarse crumbs. Add the flour, confectioners' sugar, and salt and pulse a few times to mix. Add the 6 tablespoons butter and pulse 10 to 12 times to create coarse crumbs. Add the egg and pulse 8 to 10 times, just until the pastry begins to come together.

Turn the mixture out onto a lightly floured work surface and form it into a ball. Flatten the ball with a floured rolling pin, and press the dough into the bottom and sides of the prepared tart pan. Cover with plastic wrap and place in the freezer for 30 minutes.

Preheat the oven to 400°F.

Take the crust out of the freezer and remove the plastic wrap. Prick the surface of the pastry all over with a fork. Prebake the crust for 12 to 14 minutes, until it is firm and pale golden brown. Let cool.

Reduce the oven temperature to 375°F.

FOR THE FILLING: In a bowl, whisk together the sour cream, eggs, cream, vanilla, and sugar. Scatter the cherries over the prebaked crust, then pour the cream mixture over the cherries.

Bake the tart for 35 minutes, or until the custard is set. Let cool for 10 minutes. Carefully remove the tart pan and let the tart cool for at least 20 minutes more before dusting with sifted confectioners' sugar and serving.

SERVES 6 TO 8

There is a town called Sunflower in Kansas. The sunflower is the state flower, and it's pictured on the state flag. It only makes sense that the state also would be famous for a cookie starring sunflower seeds.

SUNFLOWER SEED
COOKIES

Preheat the oven to 350°F. Line two baking sheets with silicone mats or parchment paper.

In a stand mixer or a bowl with an electric mixer, cream together the butter and sugar, beating for 5 minutes. Beat in the eggs, one at a time, then the salt and vanilla.

Mix together the oats, flour, baking powder, and cinnamon. Gradually add to the butter mixture until well incorporated. Add the coconut and sunflower seeds and mix just to combine.

Form cookies with a heaping tablespoonful, dropping them on the baking sheets about 2 inches apart. Press lightly with the palm of your hand to flatten them out and sprinkle a little coarse sea salt over them. Bake for 9 to 11 minutes, until the cookies turn golden. Cool on wire racks.

MAKES ABOUT 30 COOKIES

½ cup (1 stick) unsalted butter, softened

¾ cup packed light brown sugar

2 large eggs

½ teaspoon kosher salt

2 teaspoons vanilla extract

2 cups old-fashioned rolled oats

1½ cups all-purpose flour

1 teaspoon baking powder

1 teaspoon ground cinnamon

1 cup unsweetened shredded coconut

1 cup unsalted roasted sunflower seed kernels

Coarse sea salt for sprinkling

I might use these cookies to make ice cream sandwiches with the Peach Ice Cream (page 359).

The dessert alternately known as either Huguenot Torte or Ozark Pudding got a shot in the arm when it became known that President Harry S. Truman was a fan. Truman was from the Ozarks. When Bess Truman's recipe was published, using the region's name, that name stuck.

OZARK PUDDING

Preheat the oven to 350°F. Spray an 8-by-8-inch casserole with cooking spray.

In a stand mixer using the whisk attachment, beat the eggs, brown sugar, and vanilla together. Sift the flour, baking powder, and salt together into the bowl with the eggs and beat until well mixed. With a spatula, fold in the nuts and diced apple. Pour into the prepared casserole and bake for 30 minutes, until the surface has browned. Serve warm or at room temperature.

SERVES 6 TO 8

2 large eggs

¾ cup packed brown sugar

1 teaspoon vanilla extract

¼ cup all-purpose flour

1 teaspoon baking powder

½ teaspoon kosher salt

¾ cup walnuts or pecans, chopped

1 large apple, peeled, cored, and cut into fine dice

I might serve this with a rum-spiked whipped cream.

The original Gooey Butter Cake was reportedly an accident that the St. Louis baker recognized had potential, so he immediately set to work to replicate the gooey goof. He was right—it was a hit. It's more a coffee cake than a dessert, and it's also more goo than anything else.

GOOEY
BUTTER CAKE

FOR THE BUTTER CAKE BATTER

½ cup (1 stick) unsalted butter, softened

1 cup granulated sugar

1 large egg, beaten

2 cups all-purpose flour

2 teaspoons baking powder

¼ teaspoon kosher salt

FOR THE GOO

8 ounces cream cheese, softened

½ cup (1 stick) unsalted butter, softened

2 cups confectioners' sugar

2 large eggs, beaten

1 teaspoon vanilla extract

Preheat the oven to 350°F. Spray a 9-by-13-inch baking pan with cooking spray.

FOR THE BUTTER CAKE BATTER: In the bowl of a stand mixer with the paddle attachment, combine the butter and granulated sugar until creamy. Add the egg and beat until incorporated, then add the flour, baking powder, and salt and mix until it forms a batter. Pat this into the prepared pan.

FOR THE GOO: In the bowl of a stand mixer, beat the cream cheese with the butter until smooth. Beat in 1½ cups of the confectioners' sugar, then the eggs and vanilla. Spread the goo over the cake. Bake for 40 to 45 minutes, until lightly browned but still soft. Allow the cake to cool completely, then sift the remaining ½ cup confectioners' sugar over the surface. Cut into squares to serve.

SERVES 10 TO 12

When the leaves start falling in Missouri, so do the black walnuts. No area of the world harvests more black walnuts than Missouri, and almost half of the nuts that are commercially processed end up in ice cream.

BLACK WALNUT
ICE CREAM

In a bowl, whisk together the cream, egg yolks, sugar, and salt. In a large saucepan over medium heat, warm the milk to 180°F. Whisk the cream mixture in and bring to 170°F, whisking constantly. Remove from the heat and strain through a fine-mesh sieve into a container. Cover and refrigerate for several hours, until completely chilled.

Whisk in the liqueur, then freeze the ice cream in an ice cream maker according to the manufacturer's instructions.

Just before the ice cream is done turning, add the toasted walnuts and let the machine stir them into the ice cream. Freeze for at least 2 hours before serving.

MAKES ABOUT 1 QUART

1½ cups heavy cream

6 large egg yolks

½ cup sugar

¼ teaspoon kosher salt

1½ cups whole milk

2 teaspoons walnut liqueur, such as nocino; or black walnut extract

¼ cup chopped black walnuts, toasted in a 350°F oven for 6 minutes

Lefse came to America with Norwegian immigrants and acts as a vehicle for virtually any application, sweet or savory. A Lefse wrapped around fish salad is every bit as legitimate as one stuffed with fruit and whipped cream. One extremely easy and extremely traditional way to eat them is smeared with soft butter, sprinkled with cinnamon sugar, and rolled up like a sweet little burrito. You can use your standard rolling pin to form them, but know that decorative Lefse pins are family heirlooms and prized Internet finds.

LEFSE

OR POTATO CREPES

Bring a large pot of water to a boil. Add the potatoes and cook until tender, 15 to 20 minutes. Drain and pass through a ricer. Place in a large bowl and add the rye flour.

In a large pan over medium heat, warm the half-and-half, butter, salt, and sugar. Pour over the potatoes and flour and mix to incorporate. Divide the dough in half, form into two discs, wrap in plastic wrap, and let rest in the refrigerator for at least 30 minutes.

Working with one disc at a time, cut each into 8 equal pieces and roll each piece into a ball. Using a rolling pin, roll each ball out to a 6-inch round that is about ¼ inch thick.

On a griddle over medium-high heat, cook one lefse for a couple of minutes. With a long, thin spatula, turn the lefse. Cook until a few small brown spots appear. Continue cooking the lefse, stacking them on a plate and covering with a towel as they finish cooking. Repeat with the other disc.

Serve warm with any sweet or savory filling, but to totally understand them, try them simply with butter and sugar.

MAKES 16 CREPES

2 pounds russet potatoes, peeled and roughly diced

2 cups rye flour

½ cup half-and-half

4 tablespoons unsalted butter, melted

1 teaspoon kosher salt

1 teaspoon sugar

From Georgia to Texas, you'll find people who claim their Pecan Pie is the best. But Pauls Valley, Oklahoma, a small town between Dallas and Oklahoma City, lays claim to being the pie's original homeland.

PECAN PIE

Preheat the oven to 350°F.

In a stand mixer, cream together the butter, sugars, and salt. Add the eggs, one at a time, and beat until smooth. Stir in the vanilla and chopped pecans. Pour the filling into the pie shell and scatter the pecan halves over the top. Or arrange them neatly, if that's more your style. Bake for 55 to 60 minutes, until the filling is set. Cool to room temperature before serving.

SERVES 6 TO 8

½ cup (1 stick) unsalted butter, softened

½ cup granulated sugar

1 cup firmly packed light brown sugar

1 teaspoon kosher salt

5 large eggs, lightly beaten

1 teaspoon vanilla extract

1 cup chopped pecans

½ recipe Basic Pie Crust in 9-inch pan (page 481)

1 cup pecan halves

SOUTHWEST

Nevada

Utah

Arizona

New
Mexico

Texas

THE DISCUSSION OF AMERICAN FOOD would be incomplete without considering the food of actual Americans.

In the desert Southwest, we find the people and the food most closely aligned with what was here before settlers arrived to start forming the melting pot we've created. For many here, the area is an ancestral homeland. For others, it is where they were driven after being displaced in shameful ways, and it might be slightly more comforting if only there was evidence to suggest we've evolved to a point that nothing that terrible could ever happen again. Regardless, the perseverance of these people and their culture is inspiring.

No flavor will put my head in the Southwest faster than chile sauce. Equally useful as a braising liquid or a condiment, and as likely to be found at a fancy restaurant or burger shop as in some sweet abuela's casita, these simple sauces are easy to master and will transport me to Sante Fe no matter where I am.

The question I'll get when I order virtually any dish here is "red or green?" I don't feel put on the spot. My favorite answer is "Make it Christmas!!!"

The red sauce is made from the roasted pulp of the indigenous peppers and has a bold earthiness. You'll find the peppers being roasted in huge perforated drums in the parking lots of supermarkets, restaurants, and gas stations. The aroma becomes an integral part of the atmosphere.

The green sauce is made from the same plant, but fresh from the vine with a bright fruitiness. The beautiful thing—both literally and figuratively—is that you don't have to choose. Ask for yours to be "Christmas" and the dish will be draped with some sauce of each hue.

> Roadside treasures of the Southwest are **CHILES RELLENOS, TACOS, ENCHILADAS,** and every sort of food with a Hatch chile in or on it; here there is almost no chance to go wrong unless you can't stand the heat!

Next door in Texas, the independent spirit of the formerly autonomous republic lives on with its own cuisine. When I get off the plane in Texas, I grab a cowboy hat—which goes perfect with shorts and Crocs, thankyouverymuch—and start thinking about grabbing a seat at the table of one of my friends who are masters of the craft: Dean Fearing, Tim Love, Robert Del Grande, Chris Shepherd, Tyson Cole, Paul Qui, Bryce Gilmore.

But first I go find some brisket from Aaron Franklin or Louie Mueller or one of the spots in Lockhart, a little town that was built on BBQ smoke in houses with names including Smitty's, Black's, and Kreuz. Don't be turned off by the modesty of a roadside shack with questionable structural integrity. If there's a plume of sweet oak smoke billowing out of a vent, I'll stop in to give it a look. In Texas, it is cattle country and beef is what's for dinner, so find a truck stop or a diner or a place with an unlikely German or Czech name on the sign and cowboy types sitting in it, and saddle up for some 'cue and a bowl of red. In the rest of the Southwest, it's more about the chiles and the Latino flavors interpreted by a plethora of different immigrant cultures with their own take on the flavor of the local soil.

It took a hearty breakfast to fuel the work on the ranch, and this dish was standard fare for the hands. Now it's a mainstay of yuppie and traditional brunch menus around the region and beyond. Serve with a side of beans and a slice or two of avocado.

HUEVOS RANCHEROS
WITH CHILE SAUCE

Canola or corn oil for frying

4 (6-inch) corn tortillas

8 large eggs

Kosher salt and freshly ground black pepper

2 cups Green Chile Sauce or Red Chile Sauce (page 378), or 1 cup of each, warmed

4 green onions, green parts only, thinly sliced

¼ cup fresh cilantro leaves

½ cup sour cream

Heat ¼ inch of oil in a small skillet over medium-high heat. With tongs, lower a tortilla in the oil and fry for 30 seconds. Turn over and fry the other side for 30 seconds; it'll puff up. Remove to a paper towel–lined plate and repeat until all the tortillas are fried, placing paper towels between the layers as you go.

In another, larger skillet, heat a little oil over medium-high heat. Fry the eggs as you like them, sprinkling with a little salt and pepper. Sunny-side up for me!

On each of 4 plates, place 1 tortilla and top with 2 eggs. Spoon about ½ cup chile sauce over the egg whites. Toss on some green onions, some cilantro sprigs, and a dollop of sour cream.

SERVES 4

There are a lot of great things about the Green and Red Chile Sauces you'll see used in recipes throughout this chapter. But possibly the greatest thing: They're completely interchangeable. In any recipe that calls for one, feel free to substitute the other. The Green Chile Sauce (pictured on page 377) is good on any number of dishes, most notably on top of a cheeseburger, but I will also open the fridge first thing in the morning and take a shot of it, just for pure flavor. The Red Chile Sauce (pictured on page 415) is a standard accompaniment in New Mexico to everything from eggs to enchiladas.

GREEN CHILE SAUCE

MAKES ABOUT 3 CUPS

4 pounds fresh Hatch chiles; use New Mexico or
    Anaheim if those are easier to find
2 tablespoons extra-virgin olive oil
1 medium onion, finely diced
2 cloves garlic, thinly sliced
¼ cup chopped cilantro leaves
1 teaspoon ground cumin
1 teaspoon ground coriander seed
Kosher salt and freshly ground black pepper

Char the peppers, by putting them either over the open flame of a gas grill or under a broiler for a few minutes, turning them to make sure they don't burn. Put the charred peppers in a zip-top bag or a bowl covered with plastic wrap and let steam for 20 minutes. The skins should easily slip off. (If you can buy the chiles already roasted and peeled, by all means, do that.) Pull the stem off to remove the seedpod. Slit open the side of the chiles and scrape out the remaining seeds and veins. Discard the skins, pods, seeds, and veins. Chop the chile flesh into small dice. You should have about 3 cups.

In a large skillet over medium heat, heat the oil and sauté the onion and garlic until soft, about 5 minutes. Add the roasted peppers, cilantro, cumin, and coriander. Bring to a low boil and cook for about 15 minutes, until everything is soft. Transfer the sauce to a food processor or blender and, venting the lid, blend it until smooth. Season with salt and pepper to taste.

The sauce will keep in the refrigerator for about a week, or you can freeze it for up to six months.

RED CHILE SAUCE

MAKES ABOUT 3 CUPS

1 pound dried red chiles, preferably New Mexico
    (may sub ancho, pasilla, or use a combination)
2 tablespoons extra-virgin olive oil
1 medium onion, chopped coarsely
4 cloves garlic, thinly sliced
2 tablespoons fresh oregano, chopped
2 teaspoons kosher salt
2 tablespoons honey

Remove the stems and seeds from the chiles and tear into 3 or 4 pieces each.

In a deep, heavy pot or Dutch oven over medium-high heat, heat the olive oil and sauté the onion and garlic until the onion softens, about 5 minutes. Add the chiles and cover with water. Bring to a boil, then add the oregano and salt. Cover, reduce the heat to medium-low, and simmer for 45 to 60 minutes, until the chiles are soft. Using a slotted spoon, remove the chiles, onion, and garlic to a blender. Discard the cooking liquid. Add the honey to the blender and puree, adding 1 to 2 cups of fresh water to the mixture as needed.

The sauce will keep in the refrigerator for about a week, or you can freeze it for up to six months.

Replace common dill chips on your favorite sandwich with one of these and you'll instantly have an entirely new favorite sandwich. (Pictured on page 400.)

PICKLED
JALAPEÑOS

In a large saucepan, combine the vinegar, water, and salt. Bring to a boil, stirring to dissolve the salt.

If using whole peppers, puncture each pepper several times with the tip of a small knife. Pack the peppers into 4 or 5 sterilized pint jars and top each jar with 1 tablespoon each of coriander seed, peppercorns, and mustard seed. Carefully fill each jar with the hot brine, then seal the jars to store in the refrigerator for up to one month, or can according to the directions on page 9 for longer storage.

NOTE: Yield and amount of brine needed will vary depending on whether the peppers are whole or cut.

MAKES 4 OR 5 PINTS

3 cups white vinegar

3 cups water

¼ cup kosher salt

2 pounds jalapeños, whole if small, cut in half lengthwise or in ¼-inch rings if large

4 or 5 tablespoons coriander seed

4 or 5 tablespoons freshly ground black peppercorns

4 or 5 tablespoons mustard seed

There's no better way to start a day in the great Southwest than with a breakfast burrito, but they're less about a recipe than an opportunity.

BREAKFAST BURRITOS

You'll start with a large, 10- to 12-inch flour tortilla for each person. Actually, if you're thinking ahead, you'll start with 2 tortillas per person.

You'll want some potatoes. If you have some frozen hash browns in the freezer, they're fair game. Heat them up. No frozen spuds? Dice a small onion and 1 medium potato for every 6 burritos and sauté them together in some olive oil until the potato is tender.

Vegetarian? Skip this next step. Not? Find some meat. Like leftover roast beef or Carne Adovada (page 414). When I stay with my friends in New Mexico, there's usually some elk sausage in the freezer from the previous hunting season. Sauté that up for a great taste of place. Or chorizo. Or Italian sausage. Whatever you have.

Scramble up some eggs: 1 egg for every 2 burritos.

Grate some sharp Cheddar or Jack cheese. And you've already made Green Chile Sauce, right? Get that. Unless you prefer the Red Chile Sauce. (Both recipes are on page 378.)

Put those ingredients together on a tortilla in your favorite proportions and in quantities that will allow you to enclose it all, then go out to the patio and watch the hot-air balloons rise with the sun over the mesa!

The saying goes that everything's bigger in Texas. That's largely a state of mind...except when it comes to breakfast pastries. Some places brag of 4-pound cinnamon rolls! Here's one that's more in proportion with the rest of the country. The dough recipe is also the base of the Hot Orange Rolls (page 201).

CINNAMON
ROLLS

FOR THE DOUGH

1 envelope (2¼ teaspoons) active dry yeast

¼ cup plus 1 teaspoon sugar

¼ cup warm water, about 110°F

1 cup milk

4 tablespoons unsalted butter, melted, plus 4 tablespoons to brush over the formed rolls

1 large egg, beaten

½ teaspoon kosher salt

3½ cups all-purpose flour plus more for rolling

FOR THE FILLING

1½ cups packed brown sugar

½ cup (1 stick) unsalted butter, melted

1 tablespoon ground cinnamon

FOR THE ICING

1½ cups confectioners' sugar

2 tablespoons milk

1 teaspoon vanilla extract

FOR THE DOUGH: In the bowl of a stand mixer with a dough-hook attachment, combine the yeast, 1 teaspoon sugar, and warm water. When it begins to foam, add the ¼ cup sugar, milk, 4 tablespoons melted butter, egg, and salt. Mix to combine. Gradually add the flour and slowly mix until damp, then mix on medium-high speed for 6 to 7 minutes, until the dough comes together. Continue to knead the dough for a few minutes, then put in a large, greased bowl, cover with a towel, and let rise in a warm place for about an hour, or until doubled in size.

FOR THE FILLING: Combine the brown sugar, butter, and cinnamon in a bowl.

TO ASSEMBLE: Spray a 9-by-13-inch baking pan with cooking spray.

On a floured work surface, roll out the dough to about a 12-by-18-inch rectangle. Spread the cinnamon-butter mixture over the dough, leaving a 1-inch bare border along one long side. Starting on the long side opposite the bare border, roll up the dough like a jelly roll. Seal the seam by pinching along the uncovered side.

Cut the log into twelve 1½-inch slices and place in the prepared pan. Cover with a towel and let rise for 45 minutes.

Preheat the oven to 350°F.

Brush the remaining butter over the top of the rolls. Bake for 30 minutes, until golden.

FOR THE ICING: In a bowl, whisk the confectioners' sugar, milk, and vanilla together. Drizzle over the warm rolls when they come out of the oven. Serve warm.

MAKES 12 ROLLS

Not much grows in the desert, which means locals have to make the most of whatever thrives. And figs thrive. The lemon provides the acidity needed for preservation, and it also tastes great with figs.

FIG-LEMON JAM

In a large saucepan, cook the figs, sugar, and lemon over medium heat, stirring constantly, for about 10 minutes. Reduce the heat to medium-low and simmer for an hour, stirring occasionally, until the fruit all breaks down and the mixture becomes quite thick. Can in sterilized half-pint or 4-ounce jars according to the directions on page 9.

MAKES 3 HALF-PINTS

1½ pounds fresh figs, washed, stemmed, and coarsely chopped

1½ cups sugar

1 large lemon, thinly sliced, seeds removed, then coarsely chopped

I might spread a little soft cow's or ewe's milk cheese when I serve this, because I love the way this jam pairs with dairy.

In the 1950s, Helen Corbitt moved from New York to take a job in Dallas as a chef at Neiman Marcus. She was asked to put together an all-Texas menu and include a black-eyed pea dish. This dish, which became known as Texas Caviar years later, was her attempt to cover up the flavor of an ingredient she didn't care for. Now it's a statewide favorite.

TEXAS
CAVIAR

In a bowl, combine the oil, vinegar, garlic, hot sauce, salt, and black pepper. Pour the dressing over the peas. Add the green pepper, jalapeño, and onion and toss to coat. Refrigerate for at least a few hours, or even a few days, before serving.

MAKES ABOUT 3 CUPS AS A DIP, SERVES 4 TO 6 AS A SIDE

¼ cup extra-virgin olive oil

2 tablespoons red wine vinegar

2 cloves garlic, thinly sliced

3 dashes hot sauce

1 teaspoon kosher salt

½ teaspoon freshly ground black pepper

2 (15-ounce) cans black-eyed peas, rinsed and drained

1 small green bell pepper, finely diced

1 jalapeño, finely diced

1 medium red onion, finely diced

Posole was a favorite of the Aztecs long before Europeans found their way to this part of the world. The term refers to the stew, which can be made with any number of meats, but is also synonymous with the hominy that's the star ingredient. In a pinch or a hurry, you can substitute 3 drained 15-ounce cans of hominy and use 6 cups chicken stock, then skip the first step. I use pork neck bones for added unctuousness and to give everyone something to gnaw on.

POSOLE

1 pound dried posole (hominy)

1 cup Red Chile Sauce (page 378)

2 pounds pork or lamb neck bones

1 large onion, diced

2 cloves garlic, smashed

2 jalapeños, stems removed, chopped with seeds

1 teaspoon oregano

1 teaspoon kosher salt

12 fresh corn tortillas

2 ripe avocados, diced

2 limes, cut into wedges

Rinse the posole and cover it with cold water in a large pot. Bring to a boil over medium-high heat, then reduce the heat to low and simmer for 2 hours.

Add the chile sauce, bones, onion, garlic, jalapeños, oregano, and salt and more water to cover. Cook over medium-low heat for 2 hours, until the posole and the meat are tender.

Skim the fat from the top. Remove the neck bones. Take the meat off the bones, shred, and return to the soup; or leave the bones intact if you want to gnaw on them.

Serve with hot corn tortillas, avocados, and lime wedges.

MAKES ABOUT 2 QUARTS, SERVING 6 TO 8

Those cacti growing in the desert aren't just there for the scenery. The leaves of the nopales have a ton of nutritional value and a flavor that evokes green beans, bell pepper, and okra, all at the same time. My pal Enrique Olvera makes these into a ceviche at his renowned Pujol restaurant in Mexico City.

NOPALES SALAD

Clean the nopales by putting one on the cutting board and carefully running a small knife parallel to the board, slicing off each of the small needles. Repeat on the other side and with the other paddles, then trim around each nopale to remove the outer edge. Rinse the nopales and discard the trimmed bits. Slice the nopales into thin strips.

In a large skillet over medium heat, heat the 1 tablespoon olive oil and sauté the nopales and onion. The mixture will get a little slimy, but that's OK. Keep sautéing for a few minutes, and the liquid will help cook the cactus. Reduce the heat to low, cover, and cook for 10 minutes, or until the cactus is softened.

In a large bowl, combine the ¼ cup olive oil, the nopales, tomato, jalapeño, oregano, lime zest and juice, and salt, tossing to combine, then chill for 2 hours. Garnish with radish slices.

MAKES 1½ QUARTS AS A CONDIMENT, SERVES 4 TO 6 AS A SALAD

5 nopales paddles

1 tablespoon plus ¼ cup extra-virgin olive oil

1 small onion, finely chopped

1 medium tomato, chopped

1 jalapeño, finely chopped

2 teaspoons fresh oregano, chopped

Zest and juice of 2 limes (if you don't get at least 2 tablespoons lime juice, add white wine vinegar to make up the difference)

½ teaspoon kosher salt

3 radishes, thinly sliced, for garnish

I might use this as an omelet filling or as a condiment on just about any sandwich.

Depending on who's making it, the tortillas in Tortilla Soup can be used as a thickener, a noodle, or a garnish. All three applications make sense. This soup is all about the chiles and the broth. The meat is almost an afterthought.

TORTILLA SOUP

2 tablespoons extra-virgin olive oil plus more for frying the tortillas

1 medium onion, finely diced

3 cloves garlic, thinly sliced

¼ cup tomato paste

1 canned chipotle in adobo, chopped; or 1 dried chipotle pepper, soaked in hot water 20 minutes, then stemmed, seeded, and chopped

2 teaspoons chile powder, preferably ancho or chipotle

2 teaspoons ground cumin

6 cups Brown Chicken Stock (page 480)

6 corn tortillas, cut into thin strips

Kosher salt

2 cups shredded cooked chicken, warmed

1 avocado, sliced

¼ cup fresh cilantro leaves

Lime wedges for serving

In a large, heavy pot over medium-high heat, heat the 2 tablespoons oil and sauté the onion and garlic until the onion softens, about 5 minutes. Add the tomato paste, chipotle, chile powder, and cumin and stir, then add the stock. Simmer for 20 minutes.

While the soup simmers, prepare the tortillas: In a large skillet, heat ½ inch of oil to 360°F. Working in batches if necessary, quickly fry the tortilla strips until they are crisp, about 30 seconds, then remove to a paper towel–lined plate. Season with salt.

Add about three-fourths of the tortillas to the soup and let them simmer for about 5 minutes. Puree the soup with a stick blender until it becomes smooth and somewhat thick.

Serve in wide, shallow bowls garnished with some of the reserved tortilla frizzles, the chicken, a luxurious slice of avocado, some cilantro leaves, and a lime wedge.

MAKES 2 QUARTS, SERVING 6 TO 8

All credible evidence points to Mexico as the origin of the Margarita, but a couple of (unlikely) versions of the tale have Texas angles to them. Regardless, the drink's attachment to the state is undeniable. And it isn't disputed that the first time a batch went through a slushie machine, that happened in Dallas.

MARGARITA

PRICKLY-PEAR STYLE

FOR THE PRICKLY PEAR SYRUP

3 to 4 prickly pears, peeled and chopped (see note)

½ cup sugar

Juice of 1 lime

FOR THE MARGARITA

Kosher salt

Lime wedge

3 ounces silver tequila

1 ounce triple sec

1 ounce Prickly Pear Syrup

Ice

FOR THE PRICKLY PEAR SYRUP: Put the chopped prickly pears in a medium saucepan over medium-high heat and add just enough water to cover. Bring to a boil, then simmer for about 15 minutes. Strain the liquid to remove the seeds, pressing to squeeze any liquid from the pulp, then rinse the saucepan and return the juice to the pan on the cooktop. Add the sugar and lime juice and stir until the sugar dissolves. Let cool and store in the refrigerator for up to a week. Makes about 1 cup syrup.

FOR THE MARGARITA: Spread a layer of salt on a small plate. Circle the rim of a glass with the lime wedge to wet it. Invert the glass into the salt to coat the rim.

In a cocktail shaker, combine the tequila, triple sec, syrup, and ice. Shake it like you're excited about it, because you should be! Strain the drink into the glass, taking care not to disturb the salt, and drop the lime wedge in.

NOTE: Any tart, tangy juice can be substituted for the Prickly Pear Syrup. Try a citrus juice, such as blood orange, or pomegranate juice.

MAKES 1 COCKTAIL

The roads of Gillespie County, Texas, turn into a tourist attraction in early spring when the county's 1,400 peach trees are in bloom. Pair Peach Salsa with grilled pork, chicken, or fish. Setting out a bowl with tortilla chips is a totally legitimate strategy, too. (Pictured on page 395.)

PEACH SALSA

1 pound peaches (2 large),
   peeled and chopped

¼ cup chopped fresh cilantro

2 tablespoons finely diced red
   onion

1 jalapeño, finely diced

2 tablespoons freshly squeezed
   lime juice

1 tablespoon honey

1 teaspoon kosher salt

Toss together all the ingredients. Let stand at least 1 hour before serving.

MAKES ABOUT 2 CUPS

The barbecue joints of Central Texas are multigenerational family businesses, and many of those families are German. When you go in and order your brisket, there aren't a lot of side dish options. There's usually German Potato Salad, though. (Pictured on page 398.)

GERMAN
POTATO SALAD

Preheat the oven to 350°F.

In a small saucepan, cover the eggs with water and bring to a boil over medium-high heat. Once the water boils, cook for 1 minute, then turn the heat to low and cover the pan. Cook for 7 minutes. Drain and set aside to cool.

In a bowl, toss the potatoes with ¼ cup of the olive oil and salt and pepper to taste. Turn them out onto a baking sheet and roast for 30 to 40 minutes, until tender and slightly browned at the edges.

In a large skillet over medium-high heat, sauté the bacon until crisp. Use a slotted spoon to remove the bacon to a paper towel–lined dish, leaving the fat in the skillet. To the skillet, add the whites of the green onions and sauté for 2 minutes. Add the remaining ¼ cup oil, the vinegar, and mustard and stir to incorporate. Turn the heat to low to keep warm.

Peel the eggs and chop them.

When the potatoes are roasted, add them to the skillet and toss to dress them. Add three-fourths of the chopped eggs and the greens of the onions and toss again. Season with salt and pepper and put in a serving bowl. Garnish with the remaining egg and the crisped bacon.

SERVES 6 TO 8

4 large eggs

3 pounds small fingerling potatoes, cut in half lengthwise

½ cup extra-virgin olive oil

Kosher salt and freshly ground black pepper

6 ounces bacon, chopped

4 green onions, thinly sliced, whites and greens separated

½ cup apple cider vinegar

2 tablespoons whole grain mustard

More power to everyone who puts together a bunch of secret herbs and spices to make their BBQ rubs, but if you go to the tiny Texas brisket capital of Lockhart, you'll find that for the most part, the beef there is seasoned with three things: salt, pepper, and smoke.

LOCKHART

BBQ BRISKET

Mix the salt and pepper together and liberally coat the brisket on all sides. Press the seasoning in, and let the meat sit at room temperature for about 90 minutes.

Soak 6 cups of wood chips, preferably oak, in water for at least 30 minutes, then drain.

If you have an offset smoker—and 12 hours—this is the time to use it. But if you have an offset smoker, you know that.

If you don't have an offset smoker, set up your charcoal or gas grill for indirect heat. If using charcoal, scatter about 2 cups of the chips over the coals. If using gas, wrap about 2 cups of chips in aluminum foil, poke holes in the foil, and set them under the grate, on top of one of the burners that will be lit.

Put the brisket on the unlit portion of the grill, fat side up, close the grill, and let it cook until the temperature of the meat hits about 200°F, probably 4 hours or more. (Be careful. The temperature may begin to climb quickly after it reaches about 180°F.) Monitor the coals, and replenish the wood chips about every 2 hours.

Let the meat rest for 30 minutes or so. In fact, you'll want to rest for 30 minutes or so, too. Slice the meat against the grain and serve with the white bread, onions, and pickles. If you'd like some sauce, I'd suggest going to Kansas City.

SERVES 6 TO 8

¼ cup kosher salt

¼ cup coarsely ground black pepper

6- to 8-pound brisket, trimmed of excess fat, but leave a good ¼ inch of it

White bread, sliced white onion, and dill pickle slices for serving

Several people claim to have invented this famous iteration of meat on a stick, but there's no disputing the fact that the Texas State Fair is the most famous place for anything to get fried. Growing up in Washington, we knew these as Pronto Pups at the Central Washington State Fair just outside of Yakima.

TEXAS STATE FAIR
CORN DOGS

In a large, deep pot or Dutch oven, heat 3 inches of oil to 350°F.

In a large bowl, combine the cornmeal, flour, baking soda, salt, and dry mustard. In another bowl, whisk together the eggs, buttermilk, and honey. Pour the wet mixture into the bowl with the dry and mix to form a batter.

Insert thick, round skewers into 2 or 3 hot dogs and dip into the batter, then put them straight into the oil. Fry for about 5 minutes, or until golden. Drain on a paper towel–lined platter. Repeat to batter and fry them all. Let cool and serve with a squiggle of brash yellow mustard.

MAKES 10 CORN DOGS

Canola or corn oil for deep-frying

2 cups yellow cornmeal

1 cup all-purpose flour

1 teaspoon baking soda

1 teaspoon kosher salt

½ teaspoon Colman's dry mustard

2 large eggs, lightly beaten

1¾ cups buttermilk

2 tablespoons honey

10 hot dogs

Yellow mustard for serving

I might serve these with a bowl of chopped Pickled Jalapeños (page 379) and spoon them on top of each bite.

It's hard to improve on the original Chiles Rellenos (page 417), peppers stuffed with meat or cheese, then battered and fried. When people started turning those flavors into pies and casseroles, the special occasion favorite became something you could whip up on a Wednesday.

CHILES RELLENOS PIE

Preheat the oven to 350°F. Spray a 9-by-13-inch baking pan with cooking spray.

In a large skillet over medium-high heat, brown the ground beef, onion, and garlic. Add the chili powder, cumin, and salt to taste.

Arrange half the chiles in a single layer on the bottom of the prepared pan. Top with the ground beef mixture. Arrange the remaining chiles on top of the beef. Combine the two cheeses and sprinkle about three-fourths of it over the top. In a bowl, beat the milk, eggs, cilantro, and flour together. Pour the mixture over the top of the casserole. Top with the salsa and sprinkle with the remaining cheese. Bake for 40 to 45 minutes, until the edges are brown. Turn on the broiler and put the casserole under for 6 to 8 minutes, until bubbling and golden brown.

Let rest for 10 minutes. Cut into squares and serve with sour cream, raisins, and pecans.

SERVES 8 TO 10

1 pound ground beef

1 large onion, chopped

2 cloves garlic, thinly sliced

4 teaspoons chili powder

1 teaspoon ground cumin

1 teaspoon kosher salt, or more to taste

10 to 12 peppers, either Hatch or Anaheim, roasted, peeled, and seeded (instructions on page 378)

10 ounces Cheddar cheese, shredded

10 ounces Monterey Jack cheese, shredded

1 (13-ounce) can evaporated milk

4 large eggs, beaten

½ cup chopped fresh cilantro

1 tablespoon all-purpose flour

2 cups salsa as spicy as you like, jarred or homemade (or Red Chile Sauce, page 378)

Sour cream, raisins, and pecans for garnish

There are rules about chili in Texas. The first one is no beans. When you run into some-one who's hard-core, there are no tomatoes. And for the purists, there's no chili powder. This is meant to express the flavor of the fields of chiles on a hot, end-of-summer after-noon, fragrant with the heat punch of the hot breeze.

8 dried ancho peppers (may substitute a mix, includ-ing pasilla and/or guajillo peppers), stems and seeds removed, flesh reconstituted in boiling water for 30 min-utes, and drained

3 canned chipotles in adobo

1 cup water

2 tablespoons extra-virgin olive oil, or more if necessary

3½ pounds chuck roast, cut into ¼-inch dice, or coarsely ground

1 large onion, chopped

4 cloves garlic, thinly sliced

1 (12-ounce) can of beer, preferably Pearl, Lone Star, or Shiner

1 cup Brown Chicken Stock (page 480) plus more if needed

1 tablespoon honey

1 tablespoon ground cumin

2 teaspoons kosher salt, or more to taste

1 teaspoon ground cinnamon

¼ cup masa harina or cornmeal, optional

Sour cream, lime wedges, and tortillas for serving

TEXAS
"BOWL OF RED"

In a blender, puree the reconstituted chiles with the chipotles and water until smooth. Set aside.

In a large, heavy pot or Dutch oven, heat the olive oil over medium-high heat. Working in batches, brown the meat and transfer to a bowl. When all the meat is browned, sauté the onion and garlic until the onion has softened, 5 to 6 minutes. Return the meat to the pot along with the pureed chiles, beer, stock, honey, cumin, salt, and cinnamon. Stir to incorporate. Bring the chili to a boil, then reduce the heat and simmer, uncovered, for 3 hours. If the chili gets too thick, add more stock and cover the pot.

If you'd like the chili a little thicker, ladle about 1 cup of liquid from the pot into a bowl and whisk in the masa harina. Pour the mixture into the chili and stir it in. Raise the heat and stir until it thickens.

Serve with sour cream, lime wedges, and tortillas on the side.

SERVES 6 TO 8

Like the Chiles Rellenos Pie (page 403), this adaptation takes a traditional favorite and makes it something that doesn't take hours of prep work. This isn't the same thing as a real tamale (see page 410), and there is value in those hours of prep work. But this is a spectacular alternative when the time isn't there.

TAMALE PIE

4 cups water

2 teaspoons kosher salt

1½ cups cornmeal

3 tablespoons extra-virgin olive oil or bacon fat

2 pounds ground pork

1 pound fresh chorizo

1 onion, chopped

3 cloves garlic, thinly sliced

2 jalapeños, finely chopped

2 cups fresh corn kernels (may sub frozen)

1 (14½-ounce) can diced tomatoes

2 tablespoons chili powder

1 teaspoon freshly ground black pepper

2 cups shredded Cheddar cheese

In a 3-quart saucepan, bring the water to a boil and add 1 teaspoon salt. While whisking, slowly add the cornmeal and continue whisking until the mixture is smooth. Reduce the heat to low, cover, and cook until the mixture is thick, about 30 minutes.

Preheat the oven to 350°F. Grease a 9-by-13-inch baking dish.

Heat the oil in a 12- to 14-inch sauté pan and add the pork, chorizo, onion, and garlic. Cook until the meat is browned and onions are soft, about 8 minutes. Add the jalapeños, corn, tomatoes, chili powder, black pepper, and remaining 1 teaspoon salt. Mix well and set aside.

When the cornmeal mixture is ready, spread the meat evenly in the baking dish. Spread the cornmeal mixture evenly over the meat. Top with the shredded cheese. Bake for 45 minutes, until the crust is set and nicely brown. Remove from the oven and let rest for 15 minutes before cutting and serving.

It'll be even better the next day.

SERVES 8 TO 10

Frybread goes back less than two centuries in Navajo culture, but in that time it has become embraced as a symbol of perseverance. Borne of the ingredients Navajos were given to survive on after their forced move to the Southwest, it was adapted to various dishes, including as a replacement for tortillas in this simple taco.

NAVAJO
FRYBREAD TACOS

FOR THE FRYBREAD: In a bowl, mix together the flour, baking powder, and salt. Add the warm water and knead the dough until soft but not sticky. Divide into 6 to 8 pieces and roll out each to about a 6-inch round. Poke a hole in the center of each with your finger.

In a large skillet, heat ½ inch of oil to 350°F. Add a frybread and fry for about 2 minutes on each side, until it puffs up. Drain on paper towels. Repeat to fry them all.

FOR THE TACOS: In a saucepan, heat the chili until bubbling. Top a piece of frybread with ¼ cup chili and spoonfuls of onion, tomato, lettuce, cheese, sour cream, and hot sauce, as desired.

MAKES 6 TO 8 TACOS

FOR THE FRYBREAD

2 cups all-purpose flour

1½ teaspoons baking powder

½ teaspoon kosher salt

¾ cup warm water

Canola or corn oil for frying

FOR THE TACOS

1½ cups Texas "Bowl of Red" chili (page 404)

1 small red onion, chopped

1 large red tomato, chopped

½ head iceberg lettuce, shredded

1 cup shredded Cheddar cheese

½ cup sour cream

Hot sauce, optional

Tamales are a festive food, and it's more likely that someone making them around a holiday or for a party would make 300 rather than 30. Pork is a favorite filling, but anything goes.

PORK TAMALES

30 dried corn husks

½ recipe Carne Adovada (page 414)

4 cups masa harina

1 cup lard or shortening

1 teaspoon kosher salt

2½ cups Brown Chicken Stock (page 480), hot

Green Chile Sauce (page 378) for serving

Soak the husks in warm water for at least 30 minutes.

Separate the meat and sauce of the carne adovada. Shred the meat and add sauce, ¼ cup at a time, until the meat is coated but not saucy. Set aside.

In a food processor, combine the masa, lard, and salt and pulse until you get a crumbly texture. Place the masa mixture in a bowl and mix in half the stock. Continue stirring in stock a little at a time until a dough is formed.

Drain the husks and lay one flat on the work surface. Spoon about ¼ cup of the masa dough onto the husk and flatten it with your fingers, leaving about ¼ inch clear on each side, and about 1 inch at the bottom of the husk where it tapers. Add 2 tablespoons of the shredded pork in a line down the middle of the masa. Roll the husk, enveloping the meat in the masa. Fold the bottom of the husk up and set open side up in a steamer basket. Repeat until you've used all the ingredients to make 30 tamales.

Put 1 to 2 inches of water in a pot and set the steamer basket inside. Cover the pot, bring to a boil, and reduce to a simmer. Steam the tamales for 50 to 60 minutes, until the masa is firm.

Serve with the remaining warmed adovada sauce and Green Chile Sauce on the side.

MAKES 30 TAMALES

Sheep ranching was a huge industry in New Mexico from the 1600s up until the time of the U.S. Civil War. And lamb is still a favorite dish, especially when paired with other beloved regional flavors.

GREEN CHILE–BRAISED
LAMB SHANKS

Preheat the oven to 375°F.

Season the lamb shanks with salt and pepper. Dredge the shanks in the flour, shaking off the excess.

Heat the olive oil in a large braising pot over medium-high heat until just smoking. Add the shanks and brown on all sides, 12 to 15 minutes total. Transfer to a plate.

Add the onions and carrots to the pan and cook, stirring occasionally, until the onions soften, 5 minutes. Add the garlic and oregano and cook for 1 minute. Stir in the chile sauce and wine and bring to a boil. Return the shanks to the pan, cover, and transfer to the oven. Braise, turning the shanks every 45 minutes, until the meat is fork-tender and begins to fall off the bone, 2½ to 3 hours. Transfer the shanks to a platter.

Skim any fat off the chile sauce. Spoon the sauce over the shanks, top with cilantro leaves, and serve with warm corn tortillas.

MAKES 4 SHANKS, SERVING 4 TO 8

4 lamb shanks, about 1½ pounds each

Kosher salt and freshly ground black pepper

½ cup all-purpose flour

¼ cup extra-virgin olive oil

2 medium onions, cut into ½-inch dice

2 carrots, coarsely chopped

4 cloves garlic, thinly sliced

2 tablespoons chopped fresh oregano

3 cups Green Chile Sauce (page 378)

1 cup white wine

¼ cup chopped cilantro leaves

Warm corn tortillas for serving

What started out as a way to preserve meat with chiles and salt evolved over the years into a slow, unctuous braise that can be used any number of ways: in a burrito, taco, enchilada, tamale, omelet, or sopapilla, or on a platter over rice with beans.

CARNE ADOVADA

4 pounds boneless pork shoulder, cut into ¾-inch cubes

Kosher salt and freshly ground black pepper

2 tablespoons extra-virgin olive oil

1 large onion, chopped

2 cloves garlic, thinly sliced

2 tablespoons sherry vinegar

1 tablespoon honey

1 teaspoon ground cumin

2 cups Red Chile Sauce (page 378)

Cooked white rice for serving

¼ cup toasted pumpkin seeds

Season the pork generously with salt and pepper.

Heat the oil in a large 12- to 14-inch skillet over medium-high heat. Working in batches, sauté the pork until browned. Transfer the pork to a bowl. Sauté the onion and garlic in the pan until the onion softens, about 5 minutes. Add the vinegar, honey, and cumin and scrape the pan bottom with a wooden spoon to deglaze the pan. Pour over the pork.

Pour the Red Chile Sauce over the pork mixture and toss to coat. Cover and refrigerate overnight.

Preheat the oven to 350°F.

Pour the pork and sauce mixture into a casserole or Dutch oven, cover, and bake for 2 hours. Serve over cooked rice and garnish with pumpkin seeds.

SERVES 6 TO 8

The name means nothing more than "stuffed chile," and can be appropriately applied to any number of stuffed pepper variations. As is often the case, simple is best, and in this case probably closest to its origin.

CHILES RELLENOS

Roast and peel the peppers as instructed on page 378. Make a lengthwise slit in each pepper and remove the seeds and as much of the seedpod as possible while keeping the pepper mostly intact.

Once the peppers are roasted and peeled, heat about 1 inch of oil in a large, straight-sided skillet to 375°F.

Fill the peppers with the cheese strips. In a bowl, whip the egg whites until stiff peaks form. Mix in the yolks one at a time to form a batter. Put the flour in a wide, shallow bowl. Roll the peppers in the flour, then dip in the egg mixture. Working in batches, fry the peppers until golden, 2 or 3 minutes per side. Drain on a paper towel–lined plate and season with salt as soon as they come out of the oil.

Serve draped with chile sauce.

MAKES 10 PIECES

10 chile peppers, either Hatch or Anaheim

Canola or corn oil for deep-frying

12 ounces Monterey Jack or Oaxacan cheese, cut into long strips

8 large eggs, separated

¾ cup all-purpose flour

Kosher salt

1 cup Red or Green Chile Sauce (page 378), warmed

Depending on what part of the country you're from, this crowd-pleaser might be known as Heavenly Potatoes, or have attached to them the name of a favorite aunt who makes them for family gatherings. In Utah, they have a name that evokes mortality in an interesting way. They are good enough *to die for.* There is cream of mushroom, so as far as I'm concerned, it's a casserole. You don't have to make your soup, but you won't regret it.

FUNERAL
POTATOES

2 tablespoons kosher salt

4 pounds potatoes, peeled and cut into ½-inch dice

1½ cups sour cream

2 cups Cream of Mushroom Soup (page 419); may sub 1 (10½-ounce) can condensed cream of mushroom soup reconstituted with 1 can milk

1 small onion, finely minced

2 cups shredded sharp Cheddar cheese

1 cup (2 sticks) unsalted butter, melted

3 cups corn flakes, just crushed

Preheat the oven to 350°F. Spray a 9-by-13-inch casserole dish with cooking spray.

In a large pot over medium-high heat, boil water with 2 tablespoons salt. Add the potatoes and cook for about 10 minutes. Drain. In a large bowl, combine the potatoes, sour cream, mushroom soup, onion, cheese, and half the butter. Toss to mix without breaking the potatoes and pour into the casserole. In a bowl, toss the corn flakes with the remaining butter, then scatter over the potatoes. Bake for 1 hour, until the crust is brown, and serve.

SERVES 8 TO 10

CREAM OF MUSHROOM SOUP

MAKES 5 CUPS

6 tablespoons unsalted butter

1 medium onion, finely chopped

2 stalks celery, finely chopped

1 pound cremini mushrooms, chopped

⅓ cup all-purpose flour

1 tablespoon fresh thyme, chopped

1 cup Brown Chicken Stock (page 480)

1 cup milk

1 cup cream

Kosher salt and freshly ground black pepper

In a Dutch oven over medium-high heat, melt the butter. Add the onion and sauté for 2 minutes. Add the celery and mushrooms and continue to sauté for 10 minutes, until the mushrooms release their liquid and it evaporates. Stir in the flour to coat the vegetables. Add the thyme and chicken stock and cook until the stock is reduced by half. Stir in the milk and cream and bring to a boil. Reduce the heat to low and simmer for 10 minutes. The soup should be thick. Season with salt and pepper to taste.

The Bizcochito is an anise-flavored shortbread that is also known as the Mexican Wedding Cookie, and has been the state cookie of New Mexico since the 1980s. Sometimes they're cut into squares or diamonds with a knife, but often they are cut with cookie cutters and served at Christmas.

BIZCOCHITOS

Preheat the oven to 325°F. Line 2 baking sheets with silicone mats or parchment paper.

In a stand mixer, cream together the butter and ½ cup of the sugar. Add the eggs, liqueur, anise seed, baking powder, and salt. When incorporated, gradually add the flour, a cup at a time.

In a small bowl, stir together the remaining ¼ cup sugar and the cinnamon.

Using a 1½-inch ice cream scoop, scoop the cookie dough and roll the balls in the cinnamon-sugar. Place on the baking sheet and lightly press the cookies to flatten them slightly. (Alternately, the dough can be rolled out on a floured work surface and cut into shapes with cookie cutters, with the cinnamon-sugar sprinkled on top.)

Bake for 12 to 14 minutes, until the edges begin to tan. Cool on racks and store in an airtight container.

MAKES ABOUT 30 COOKIES

1 cup (2 sticks) unsalted butter, at room temperature

¾ cup sugar

2 large eggs

2 tablespoons anise-flavored liqueur, such as anisette, Pernod, or Herbsaint

1 tablespoon ground anise seed

1 teaspoon baking powder

1 teaspoon kosher salt

2½ cups all-purpose flour

1 teaspoon ground cinnamon

Sometimes used as a sandwich wrap or as bread with a stew such as Carne Adovada (page 414), this puffy fried dough is most prevalent as a dessert treat. When a basket of the confectioners' sugar–covered squares comes to the table, rip off a corner and drizzle some honey inside.

SOPAPILLA

3 cups all-purpose flour

2 tablespoons baking powder

1½ teaspoons kosher salt

2 tablespoons shortening or lard

1¼ cups water

Canola or corn oil for frying

Confectioners' sugar for dusting

Honey for serving

Into a bowl, sift together the flour, baking powder, and salt. Cut in the shortening with a fork, stirring until the mixture looks like a coarse meal. Add the water, ¼ cup at a time. When the dough comes together, knead on a flour-dusted work surface for about 5 minutes. Let rest for 30 minutes.

In a Dutch oven, heat 2 inches of oil to 375°F.

Roll the dough out ⅛ inch thick. Cut into approximate 3-inch squares. Fry the squares, 4 or 5 at a time, until they puff up and turn golden, 2 to 3 minutes. Drain on paper towels.

Lightly dust with confectioners' sugar and serve with honey.

MAKES 24

I might omit the confectioners' sugar and honey and use sopapilla as hamburger buns, or stuff with Carne Adovada (page 414).

The haul of raspberries in Bear Lake, Utah, each summer is so great that it's a tourist attraction, and the favorite delivery system is a milk shake. Virtually every place in town offers them, and locals all have their favorites. Here's one to try if you can't make it to Bear Lake this year.

BEAR LAKE
RASPBERRY SHAKES

Reserve the two most pristine raspberries and put everything else in a blender. Puree until smooth. Pour into two tall glasses and insert a straw in each. Top each with a raspberry.

MAKES 2 SHAKES

½ pint raspberries

1 pint vanilla ice cream, softened

¼ cup milk

I might add 1 teaspoon almond extract to the blender before zapping to give the shake a nutty perfume.

Pacific
COAST

Washington

Oregon

California

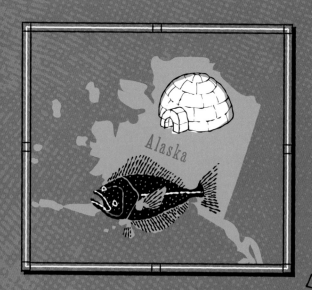

Alaska

Hawaii

VIVA TACOS

TORTAS

EVEN IN THE EARLIEST DAYS of America, when the budding nation of a few East Coast colonies was finding its way, the assumption was that we Americans would ultimately find our way as far west as there was to go. It was the manifest destiny.

It's hard to imagine the American food culture without the impact of the West Coast: the oysters that taste just a little bit different as I travel the Pacific Coast Highway from Willapa Bay in my home state of Washington down to Tomales Bay near San Francisco. The ingenuity of immigrants in Los Angeles and their forebears to meld their treasured dishes with those of their new neighbors. The towns that proclaim to be the home of whatever vegetable grows rampant there. The smell of garlic that is so pervasive as I drive through Gilroy, California, I'm certain that it's permanently embedded in my cargo shorts and probably my Crocs, too. And I'm OK with that. Then a few hours later, on the same road, I encounter a twenty-foot-tall artichoke that makes me want to find the world's largest lemon. Going farther north, I meander past a fruit that is fairly unique to the area, Oregon's marionberry, then one that is shipped all over the country (even Michigan...sssshhhhh!) for most of the summer, Washington's cherries.

Roadside treasures are found all along the Pacific Coast Highway. It's every American's birthright to drive up Highway 1 at least once, stopping at every farmers' market along the way to pick up just enough **FRESH FRUIT** and **LOCAL DELIGHTS** to get you to the next farmers' market. Find a **TACO VENDOR** at one, an **OYSTER FARMER** at the next, and a **CHEESE MAKER** somewhere else. You'll never eat better!

We extended our destiny beyond what was originally manifest to include Hawaii and Alaska, adding unique seafood and tradition to our national menu.

The chefs of the area were among the first in the country to embrace the idea that it's best to cook with ingredients that grow as close to their kitchens as possible. Visionaries such as Alice Waters, Wolfgang Puck, and Jeremiah Tower started the new language of Californian cuisine. Their groundwork inspired the next wave that gave us Nancy Silverton, Traci Des Jardins, my two hot tamales Mary Sue Milliken and Susan Feniger, Suzanne Goin, and the late, great Judy Rodgers. When I visit family in the Northwest, I see what my pals Tom Douglas, Matt Dillon, and Thierry Rautureau are up to in Seattle and drive down to Portland, where Jenn Louis and Naomi Pomeroy work their crafts. And you can bet my carry-on will be packed with salumi from my sister Gina's shop, Salumi.

What these chefs and others have done is to make the farmers' market the place to be seen. The proper vacation rental on the West Coast will include a kitchen, so that you can spend a morning at the farmers' market, and return with the makings of a fine meal to share with family and friends.

When one of the winners of the California Gold Rush showed up at a bar in Hangtown—now Placerville—and asked for the most expensive dish in the house, that meant oysters and eggs, and a legend was born.

HANGTOWN FRY

½ cup all-purpose flour

Kosher salt and freshly ground black pepper

9 large eggs

1 cup panko bread crumbs

12 oysters, shucked and drained

3 pieces bacon, chopped

In a shallow bowl, season the flour with 1 teaspoon each salt and pepper. In a second shallow bowl, beat one of the eggs. In a third, place the panko.

In a separate bowl, beat the remaining 8 eggs and season with salt and pepper. Set aside.

Dredge an oyster in the seasoned flour, patting off any excess. Dip in the single beaten egg and let excess drip off, then roll in the panko. Repeat to coat all the oysters.

In a 10- to 12-inch nonstick skillet over medium-high heat, cook the bacon until crisp. Remove the crisp pieces and mix them into the 8 beaten eggs, leaving the bacon fat in the skillet.

Fry the dredged oysters in the bacon fat for 2 minutes on each side, until crispy. Pour the eggs over the oysters, lower the heat to medium, and cook until the eggs have set like an omelet, about 7 minutes. Flip the eggs (I place a large plate on top of pan, flip it, and slide the eggs back into the pan) and cook on the other side for 2 minutes. Slide out onto a plate, slice, and serve.

SERVES 6

BELLINI

MAKES 4 COCKTAILS

Very few things are as refreshing as fruit and bubbles, and both are available in abundance in California's wine country.

2 ripe peaches
Chilled prosecco or California sparkling wine

Peel and pit the peaches, capturing any juice that runs off. Chop the peaches and puree them with their juices in a blender or food processor until very smooth. Divide among four champagne glasses and fill with prosecco.

There are many stories about the origin of this quintessential Bay Area breakfast. A prevalent one has a 1920s jazz musician coming into a restaurant after his set late one night and asking for a spinach omelet. He asked the cook if there was anything that could make it more filling. The cook saw some leftover hamburgers. Any origin story that involves making a musician happy is good by me.

JOE'S
SPECIAL

In a large skillet over medium-high heat, heat the oil and sauté the onion and garlic until the onion softens, about 5 minutes. Add the ground beef and season with salt and pepper. Sauté until the beef browns, about 8 minutes. Add the spinach and stir until wilted.

In a bowl, combine the eggs, milk, and hot sauce. Reduce the heat under the pan to medium and add the egg mixture. Cook, stirring constantly, until the eggs are set, 2 to 3 minutes. Scatter cheese over the top and serve with sourdough toast.

SERVES 4

1 tablespoon extra-virgin olive oil

1 small onion, finely chopped

2 cloves garlic, thinly sliced

8 ounces ground beef

Kosher salt and freshly ground black pepper

1 pound baby spinach, chopped

6 large eggs, lightly beaten

2 tablespoons milk

Hot sauce to taste, a few dashes; I would use Sriracha

¼ cup grated Parmigiano-Reggiano

Sourdough bread, toasted, for serving

With all due respect to the king crab and the blue crab, the Dungeness is true royalty and the revered favorite of the Pacific Northwest. I like to think that crab breakfast iterations were born because fishermen checked their crab pots early in the morning, then couldn't wait to start eating their catch when they got back to shore.

DUNGENESS CRAB
QUICHE

½ cup mayonnaise

½ cup milk

4 large eggs, well beaten

1 tablespoon sherry

2 tablespoons all-purpose flour

8 ounces fresh crabmeat

6 ounces Swiss cheese, shredded

½ cup chopped green onions (about 4)

Kosher salt and freshly ground black pepper

½ recipe Basic Pie Crust in 9-inch pan (page 481)

Preheat the oven to 350°F. Combine the mayonnaise, milk, eggs, sherry, and flour, mixing thoroughly. Stir in the crab, cheese, green onions, and salt and pepper.

Pour the mixture into the pie shell. Bake for 30 to 40 minutes, until the quiche is firm in the center.

SERVES 8 TO 10

I might go further into total celebration and add a few smoked oysters to the egg mixture.

We Can Pickle That

The brilliant *Portlandia* skit celebrating/mocking the region's pickle ubiquity was funny because it's basically true. Pickling is your best friend for enjoying the bounty of one season in a comparatively bare one. Try different herbs and spices in the brine if you like.

FOR BASIC BRINE: In a large saucepan, combine 3 cups water, 2 cups white wine vinegar, ¼ cup kosher salt, and ¼ cup sugar over medium-high heat and heat until the salt and sugar dissolve. This will be enough brine to pickle 4 to 5 pints of vegetables.

Now pick what you want to pickle.

FOR GREEN BEANS, FIDDLEHEAD FERNS, CARROTS, BABY ZUCCHINI, RAMPS, OR GARLIC SCAPES, get a few sterilized pint jars. Add a clove or two of garlic, 1 teaspoon black peppercorns, and ½ teaspoon fennel seed to each jar. Fill with one of the vegetables or a combination of them (you'll need about 1 cup vegetables per pint), then top with the Basic Brine and can according to the directions on page 9. Don't want to hassle with the sealing process? Put the jar in the fridge. The pickles will be ready in a few days and will still be good for about a month.

FOR CAULIFLOWER, break down a head of cauliflower into small florets. Once the core and large stems are removed, you can expect a 3-pound head to yield about 3 pints of cauliflower pickles. Put the florets in the jars, add a half-dozen cardamom pods and 2 teaspoons curry powder and top with Basic Brine. Then can according to the directions on page 9, or refrigerate.

FOR TURNIPS, peel about 1 pound of turnips and 1 medium red beet. Slice into matchsticks and fill two 1-pint jars with the vegetables, evenly dividing the beet between the jars. Top with Basic Brine and can according to the directions on page 9, or refrigerate.

MAKES 4 OR 5 PINTS

In search of a different way to preserve a bumper crop of apricots and apples, a couple of enterprising orchard owners in eastern Washington took a cue from Turkish Delight.

APLETS AND COTLETS

4 cups grated cored apples (about 4 large apples) or grated pitted apricots (about 24 apricots)

4 cups sugar

¾ cup apple cider or juice

¼ cup unflavored gelatin

2 cups confectioners' sugar

Line a 9-by-13-inch pan with plastic wrap.

In a large saucepan over medium heat, cook the grated apples or apricots, the sugar, and ½ cup cider until the fruit breaks down and begins reducing, about 40 minutes.

In the remaining ¼ cup cider, soften the gelatin for at least 2 minutes. Reduce the heat to low, add the gelatin mixture, and whisk together.

Pour the fruit mixture into the prepared pan and refrigerate several hours until set. Remove from the pan and invert onto a cutting board. Peel the plastic wrap off and cut into small cubes.

Before serving, put the confectioners' sugar in a wide bowl and roll the squares in the sugar to coat. The Aplets and Cotlets will keep in the refrigerator for up to a month.

MAKES ABOUT 8 DOZEN BITE-SIZE CANDIES

A restaurant owner is hungry at the end of the night. She scavenges the kitchen to put together something that passes for dinner. It works. It goes on the menu at the Brown Derby in Los Angeles, then down in history. For a properly dramatic presentation, compose this salad on a large platter, big enough for two or more people.

COBB SALAD

FOR THE DRESSING: Whisk together the lemon zest and juice, olive oil, and mustard in a small bowl and season to taste. The dressing can be refrigerated for up to 3 days.

FOR THE SALAD: Toss the lettuce with a bit of the dressing, then spread it over a platter. Add each ingredient in a neat row over the lettuce, arranging them to contrast the colors and textures as you go. When it is sufficiently beautiful, drizzle more dressing over the top and serve.

SERVES 2

FOR THE DRESSING

Zest of 2 lemons

¼ cup fresh lemon juice

½ cup extra-virgin olive oil

1 teaspoon Dijon mustard

Kosher salt and freshly ground black pepper

FOR THE SALAD

1 head romaine or butter lettuce, chopped or torn into bite-size bits

¼ cup crumbled Gorgonzola cheese

2 strips bacon, cooked and crumbled

2 large eggs, boiled and chopped

2 Roma tomatoes, chopped

4 ounces cooked chicken, cubed or shredded

1 small avocado, diced and spritzed with fresh lemon juice

The Star of Castroville

Just a short detour off Highway 1 in Castroville, California, you'll find the famous Giant Artichoke. Such is the connection between produce and place that a monument was built to it.

The best way to celebrate an artichoke is to let it shine. Here are two simple preparations, grilled or fried.

But first, we'll need to clean them.

To prep an artichoke for grilling or frying, start by getting two large bowls: one empty, one three-fourths full of water. Cut a lemon in half, squeeze both halves into the water, then drop the halves in.

Pick artichokes that are no bigger than a baseball and have tight leaves. With a serrated knife, cut off the top quarter of the artichoke, then pull off several layers of the outer leaves and deposit them in the empty bowl. The artichoke should have tight leaves and form a torpedo shape.

With a sharp paring knife, cut around the base of the artichoke to remove the remnants of the leaves you removed. Use the knife to peel the stem, then cut the very tip of it off.

Return to the serrated knife and cut the artichoke in half lengthwise. With a spoon or paring knife, scoop out the fuzzy choke from the middle and discard, then dunk the cleaned half in the lemon water and repeat with the other half. You want to work quickly, as exposure to the air will turn the artichoke brown.

You can also use baby artichokes. For those, just pick off any loose leaves, peel the stem, and trim the top and stem ends. Quarter longways and drop in the lemon water.

So go ahead, turn the page, and grill or fry your artichokes.

AIOLI

MAKES ABOUT 1 CUP
A citrusy aioli is totally appropriate with artichokes cooked in any manner!

2 large egg yolks

2 cloves garlic, minced

Zest and juice of 1 lemon (at least 2 tablespoons juice)

1 cup extra-virgin olive oil

Kosher salt

In a food processor, combine the yolks, garlic, and lemon zest and juice. As the processor continues to run, slowly drizzle in the oil to make an emulsified sauce. Taste and add salt as necessary.

GRILLED ARTICHOKES

4 medium artichokes, cleaned
and halved
Extra-virgin olive oil
Kosher salt and freshly ground
black pepper
Lemon slices for serving
Aioli (page 440) for serving

Bring a large pot of water to a boil over medium-high heat. Cook the artichokes for 15 to 20 minutes, until tender.

Set up a gas or charcoal grill for direct cooking.

Brush the cut side of the artichokes with oil, then season all over with salt and pepper. Place on the hottest part of the grill, cut sides down, and cook for 5 minutes, until burnished with grill marks. Flip them over, partly to heat them through from the other side, partly so you can admire the grill marks. Cook for a couple of minutes and serve warm with lemon slices and aioli.

SERVES 4

FRIED
ARTICHOKES

In a large, deep pot or Dutch oven, heat 3 inches of oil to 350°F. Line a plate with paper towels.

In a bowl, combine the flour and ½ teaspoon each salt and pepper. Toss the artichoke quarters and the lemon slices in the seasoned flour.

One by one, drop the lemon slices in the oil and fry for 1 to 2 minutes, until they begin to brown at the edges. Remove with tongs or a spider strainer and drain on the paper towels.

Working in batches to avoid crowding, drop the artichokes in the oil and fry until the leaves start to frizzle and the hearts become tender, about 3 minutes. Remove to the plate and season with salt and pepper. Repeat to fry all the artichokes and serve with the fried lemon slices and aioli.

SERVES 4

Extra-virgin olive oil for frying
1 cup all-purpose flour
*Kosher salt and freshly ground
    black pepper*
*4 medium or 8 baby
    artichokes, cleaned and
    quartered*
1 lemon, sliced
Aioli (page 440) for serving

The key with Garlic Fries is you want to be aggressive. If you can do that without being offensive, great, but it's more important to be aggressive. Err on the side of too much garlic.

GILROY

GARLIC FRIES

2 pounds russet potatoes (3 or 4 medium potatoes), cut into even fries, about ⅜ inch thick, soaked in ice water for at least an hour

Canola or corn oil for frying

3 tablespoons extra-virgin olive oil

1 head garlic, peeled and minced, about ¼ cup

1 teaspoon chopped fresh thyme

1 teaspoon kosher salt plus more for seasoning

1 teaspoon freshly ground black pepper

Remove the potatoes from the ice water and place on a clean kitchen towel, getting them as dry as possible.

Line a baking sheet with newspaper and top with a wire rack. In a deep, heavy pot or Dutch oven, heat 2 inches of frying oil to 300°F.

Heat the olive oil in a medium skillet over medium-high heat. Add the garlic and cook for about 45 seconds, then add the thyme, salt, and pepper and stir. Keep this mixture warm while you make the fries.

Working in batches, carefully add the potatoes to the frying oil and cook for 5 to 8 minutes, until the fries are starting to cook but aren't browned. Remove the fries from the oil and scatter on the wire rack. Repeat to cook all the fries.

Increase the oil temperature to 375°F, then return the fries to the oil and cook until they're golden brown, just a minute or two. Remove to a paper towel–lined plate to drain.

Put the fries in a large bowl and pour the warm garlic-oil mixture over them, tossing as you go. Season with salt and serve.

SERVES 4

HAWAIIAN LUAU FISH DISHES

There are a few dishes that no Hawaiian luau would be complete without, and these two raw fish preparations are among them. *Lomi lomi* means "to massage," which is how the salmon is broken up for preparation. That process was brought to the islands by Western sailors, but Ahi Poke (page 449) is a truly native dish, pre-dating the arrival of Captain Cook.

LOMI LOMI
SALMON

1 pound salmon fillet

1 cup Hawaiian red salt (Alaea) or kosher salt

4 Roma tomatoes, seeded and chopped into ¼-inch dice

½ cup finely diced sweet onion, such as Maui, Vidalia, or Walla Walla

1 green onion, thinly sliced

2 serranos or 1 jalapeño, seeded and finely diced

2 tablespoons extra-virgin olive oil

2 teaspoons sesame oil

Set a piece of plastic wrap on the counter and put the fish on it. Cover one side with half the salt, then flip it over and coat the other side with the remaining salt. Wrap the fish tightly in the plastic wrap and refrigerate for 2 to 4 days.

Remove the fish from the wrap and rinse it under cold running water. Pat dry with paper towels. Cut the fish into about ¼-inch dice, the same size as the tomato.

When ready to serve, lightly toss the fish, tomatoes, onions, and chiles together in a bowl. Drizzle the oils over and give one last light toss, then serve immediately.

SERVES 4 TO 6 AS AN APPETIZER

AHI POKE

In a large bowl, combine all ingredients and gently mix. Cover and refrigerate for at least 2 hours before serving.

SERVES 4 TO 6 AS AN APPETIZER

1 pound fresh sashimi-quality ahi tuna, cut into ½-inch dice

¼ cup finely diced sweet onion, such as Maui, Vidalia, or Walla Walla

3 tablespoons soy sauce

2 green onions, thinly sliced

1 tablespoon seaweed flakes

2 teaspoons sesame oil

2 teaspoons toasted sesame seeds

1 teaspoon grated fresh ginger

1 teaspoon Sriracha

Along the Central California coast, you'll find a barbecue style all its own. Cuts of tri-tip are cooked on a large grate that can be raised or lowered over a red oak fire, then served with salsa and beans. It's a meal borne of cowboys, yet just as romanticized today.

SANTA MARIA
TRI-TIP

FOR THE TRI-TIP

1 tablespoon kosher salt

1 tablespoon freshly ground black pepper

2 teaspoons garlic powder

1 tri-tip steak, 2 to 3 pounds

Warm tortillas for serving

Frijoles Pinquito (page 451) for serving

FOR THE PICO DE GALLO

3 tomatoes, chopped

1 small onion, finely diced

1 jalapeño, finely diced

¼ cup chopped fresh cilantro

1 teaspoon kosher salt

FOR THE TRI-TIP: In a small bowl, mix the salt, pepper, and garlic powder. Rub over the meat and let stand at room temperature for 60 to 90 minutes.

If you can make a wood fire of red oak, perfecto! If not, set up a gas or charcoal grill for indirect cooking, with optional smoking chips—again, preferably red oak, but any kind you like—that you've soaked for a half hour. Put the meat on the grill over the hot fire and let it char for about 5 minutes, then turn and char the other side. Move the meat to the side of the grill without the fire, cover the grill, and cook for about 40 minutes, until it reaches an internal temperature of about 130°F for medium-rare, turning the meat every 10 minutes or so.

Let the steak rest on a cutting board for about 15 minutes. After resting, slice against the grain into ¼-inch slices. Watch the grain carefully; due to the shape of the steak, it changes direction.

FOR THE PICO DE GALLO: Toss together all the ingredients in a bowl.

Serve the steak with warm tortillas, beans, and pico de gallo.

SERVES 6 TO 8

FRIJOLES PINQUITO

MAKES ABOUT 7 CUPS

*1 pound dried small, pink beans, such as pinquito,
    rinsed and picked over*

6 ounces bacon, cut into ¼-inch dice

1 small onion, finely diced

½ cup Basic Tomato Sauce (page 480)

1 tablespoon chile powder, such as ancho or chipotle

1 teaspoon kosher salt

In a large, heavy pot or Dutch oven, combine the beans and enough cold water to cover by about an inch. Bring to a boil over medium-high heat, cover, reduce the heat to low, and simmer for about 2 hours, until the beans are tender and most of the liquid is absorbed. Replenish the water as necessary.

Meanwhile, in a large skillet over medium-high heat, sauté the bacon until crisp. Remove the bacon and sauté the onion in the grease until soft, about 5 minutes. Add the tomato sauce, chile powder, and salt. Return the bacon to the mixture.

When the beans are tender, add the tomato sauce mixture and a little water to loosen (between ¼ and ½ cup) and simmer for 20 minutes.

Hazelnuts are the top crop in Oregon and pears aren't far behind. You know what else is big in Oregon? Pinot noir. If there is a better celebration of one state's agricultural prowess on one plate, I'm not aware of it.

PEAR AND HAZELNUT
SALAD

In a saucepan large enough to fit the pear halves in one layer, pour in the wine, add the bay and cinnamon, and bring to a boil. Add the pears, reduce heat to low, and simmer for 20 minutes. The pears will be soft and have taken on the hue of the wine.

Preheat the oven to 400°F.

Remove the pears and let cool. Remove the cinnamon and bay from the wine and raise the heat to bring the wine to a boil. Reduce the wine until it is syrupy, about 15 minutes. Whisk in the olive oil and honey and season with salt and pepper to taste. Set the dressing aside to cool.

Meanwhile, spread the hazelnuts in a single layer on a baking sheet. Toast in the oven for 8 to 10 minutes, watching them to make sure they don't burn. They're ready when you can smell them. Chop coarsely.

Toss the arugula in the dressing and divide among four salad plates. Slice each pear half into 6 slices and arrange over the arugula. Crumble the blue cheese and scatter it and the hazelnuts over the salads. Season to taste and serve.

SERVES 4

1 bottle pinot noir or other dry red wine

2 bay leaves

1 cinnamon stick

2 Anjou pears (or other firm pears), peeled, cored, and halved

¼ cup extra-virgin olive oil

2 tablespoons honey

Kosher salt and freshly ground black pepper

1 cup blanched hazelnuts

10 ounces arugula

4 ounces blue cheese

Oyster BBQ

The Pacific Northwest Oyster BBQ is not altogether unlike the Oyster Roast of South Carolina (see page 158), but maybe not quite as fussy. Here, you set up your grill—gas or charcoal—and set the unshucked oysters over a hot spot. The oysters will tell you when they're ready; just take them off the grill as they pop open. If they don't open, don't eat them. Have hot sauce or lemon butter at the ready, if you like. I definitely use my chipotle Tabasco with abandon here.

At Spago in Hollywood in the early 1980s, pizza chef Ed LaDou and Wolfgang Puck turned California pizza into a whole new genre of pie. The most famous one on that menu, and one that has since gone around the country, is the BBQ Chicken Pizza.

BBQ CHICKEN
PIZZA

1 tablespoon extra-virgin olive oil

6 boneless, skinless chicken thighs, cut into ½-inch dice

Kosher salt and freshly ground black pepper

Basic Pizza Dough (page 481)

Cornmeal for dusting

1½ cups BBQ Sauce (page 348) (may sub your favorite store brand)

2 cups shredded mozzarella cheese

1 small red onion, thinly sliced, soaked in ice-cold water until ready to use, then drained and dried on paper towels

½ cup chopped fresh cilantro leaves

Preheat the oven to 500°F. Place a pizza stone or a cast-iron griddle in the oven to heat.

Heat the oil in a large skillet over medium-high heat. Season the chicken with salt and pepper, then add to the skillet and sauté until it begins to brown and is cooked through, about 8 minutes. Set aside.

Form the pizza dough into 4 rounds, each about 10 inches wide. Dust a pizza peel or the back of a baking sheet with cornmeal and place one of the pizza rounds on it. Spread ¼ cup of the BBQ sauce over the dough, then add ½ cup of the cheese and one-fourth of the cooked chicken. Drizzle a little more sauce over the pizza.

Transfer the pizza to the pizza stone in the oven and bake for about 10 minutes, until the crust browns and the cheese bubbles. Scatter some onions and cilantro over the top, slice, and serve.

Repeat with the remaining ingredients to make 4 pies.

MAKES 4 INDIVIDUAL PIZZAS

Linguistics can be pretty funny. The story goes that fishermen at San Francisco's wharf would return from a day at sea and contribute some of their catch to a community stew that they'd all share. Everyone would "chip in." Another version is that wharf folks—many of them Italian immigrants living in the city's North Beach section—would walk around the returning fishing boats and ask for "a little," or "c'e un pò." You can decide.

FISHERMAN'S WHARF
CIOPPINO

¼ cup extra-virgin olive oil

2 large onions, chopped

3 stalks celery, finely diced

4 cloves garlic, thinly sliced

Kosher salt and freshly ground black pepper

3 cups Basic Tomato Sauce (page 480)

2 cups water

2 tablespoons fresh thyme, chopped

1 teaspoon cayenne

2 pounds small clams in shells, scrubbed

1 Dungeness crab, cracked, or 3 blue crabs, halved

2 pounds fish fillets, such as halibut or rockfish

1 cup white wine

2 tablespoons fresh basil chiffonade

12 medium shrimp, preferably head-on

¼ cup chopped fresh parsley leaves

In a large pot or Dutch oven, heat the olive oil and sauté the onions, celery, garlic, and 1 teaspoon each salt and pepper until the onion is soft, about 5 minutes. Add the tomato sauce, water, 1 tablespoon of the thyme, and the cayenne. Reduce the heat to low and simmer with the pot partially covered for 30 minutes.

Add the clams and crab and cook for 10 minutes. Add the fish fillets, wine, basil, and remaining 1 tablespoon thyme and cook for 5 more minutes. Add the shrimp and cook for 5 more minutes, until they are opaque.

Serve in wide, shallow bowls, making sure each bowl has some of each kind of seafood (if the fish fillets haven't broken up, portion them by cutting with a spoon). Garnish with parsley, and serve with rustically torn pieces of sourdough.

SERVES 4 TO 6

I would love to tell you to go dig a deep hole in your backyard, start a fire, and bury some pork, then dig it up later in the day for this Hawaiian luau classic. If you can do that, more power to you. If you have a smoker, that's the way to go. If you don't, we can get this done in the oven or the Crock-Pot.

KALUA PORK

FOR THE PORK: Preheat the oven to 250°F.

In a small saucepan, warm the tamarind paste and soy sauce and whisk to combine. If your tamarind paste is particularly thick, add a tablespoon or so of water to loosen it. With a fork or small knife, puncture the roast all over. Don't get all stabby, but make a lot of little holes around the roast. Rub the roast all over with the salt, then the tamarind-soy mixture. Wrap the pork in banana leaves to cover, and tie it tight with twine. Wrap the roast in foil and put it in a 9-by-13-inch baking pan.

Pour 1 or 2 cups of water in the pan and bake for 8 to 10 hours. Let it rest for 30 minutes, then unwrap and shred the pork.

Alternately, prepare the pork the same way, but cook in a slow cooker set on low. (You might need a smaller piece of pork to fit in your slow cooker.)

FOR THE SLAW: While the pork roasts, in a large bowl, whisk together the olive oil, sesame oil, vinegar, and sesame seeds. Toss the cabbage in the dressing to coat. Cover and refrigerate for several hours before serving.

Serve the pork with the slaw on soft hamburger rolls.

SERVES 8 TO 10

FOR THE PORK

2 tablespoons tamarind paste (get seedless)

2 tablespoons sweet soy sauce (kecap manis)

1 large pork butt or shoulder roast, 5 to 6 pounds

3 tablespoons Hawaiian red salt (Alaea) plus more as needed (may sub kosher salt)

Banana leaves

FOR THE SLAW

¼ cup extra-virgin olive oil

2 tablespoons sesame oil

2 tablespoons rice wine vinegar

2 tablespoons sesame seeds

½ head red cabbage, shredded

Hamburger rolls for serving

I might serve this with hot Chinese mustard and hoisin sauce on the side.

The halibut is a giant fish and a huge part of the Alaskan economy. It's an incredibly versatile fish, but it benefits from being treated simply to star on its own merits.

GRILLED HALIBUT

In a small bowl, combine the butter and dill. Refrigerate until ready to use.

Prepare a grill for direct grilling, or preheat a grill pan over medium-high heat. Rub the halibut with olive oil and add salt and pepper. Toss the green onions in a tablespoon of olive oil.

Grill the halibut over high heat for about 5 minutes on each side, until you've achieved beautiful grill marks and the fish is firm. After turning the fish, add the green onions to the grill to char them.

Place the green onions on a platter and arrange the halibut steaks on top of them. While the fish is hot, put about a tablespoon of the dill butter on each piece and let it melt over the fish.

SERVES 4

4 tablespoons unsalted butter, softened

¼ cup fresh dill fronds or 1 tablespoon dried dill

4 halibut steaks, 8 ounces each

Extra-virgin olive oil

Kosher salt and freshly ground black pepper

2 bunches green onion, roots trimmed

I might serve this with a little bowl of BBQ sauce (page 348) on the side.

At a traditional Native American salmon bake in the Pacific Northwest, the filleted fish are pinned onto a stake that stands in the ground next to an alderwood fire, flying in the hot air like a delicious flag. The stake is tilted and rotated to regulate the heat during the bake. The easiest way to approximate this at home is with a cedar plank on a grill. You can pick up untreated cedar shingles at a hardware store or online. You can also roast in a 450°F oven with similar results.

CEDAR-PLANKED
SALMON

Prepare your charcoal or gas grill for direct grilling. Place the soaked planks on the grates and close the grill.

Finely chop the lemon zest and mix it into the butter. Set aside.

After the planks have preheated for about 10 minutes, season the salmon with salt and pepper, then put it on the cedar, skin side down. Top each with 1 tablespoon of the lemon zest butter, close the grill, and cook for 12 minutes, until the fish is opaque and firm.

Place the lemon halves, cut sides down, over the hottest part of the fire and grill for 2 minutes. Serve the salmon on the plank with the grilled lemon.

SERVES 4

Untreated cedar planks large enough to accommodate your salmon, soaked in water for an hour

2 lemons, zested and cut in half

4 tablespoons unsalted butter, softened

1 side of salmon fillet, skin on, pinbones removed; or 4 fillets, 6 to 8 ounces each, with or without skin

Kosher salt and freshly ground black pepper

Tacos and Burritos

California's close kinship with Mexico has resulted in a lot of culinary adoption and adaptation. In Los Angeles, tacos served out of trucks were first the lunch of the workingman, then became a cross-cultural phenomenon driven by genius and social media. And in San Francisco, vendors in the Mission rebuilt the humble burrito into a self-contained meal that would later become the basis of a new age in fast food. Here's how to assemble some favorites. On the next few pages are recipes you'll need to pull off some of the fillings.

CARNE ASADA TACO

THE OUTSIDE: Doubled corn tortillas, about 6 inches, warmed over an open flame or on a hot, dry skillet
THE INSIDE: Carne Asada (page 470)
THE TOPPINGS: Pico de Gallo (page 450), shredded cabbage, a slice of avocado, shredded radish, a lime wedge for squeezing

CARNITAS TACO

THE OUTSIDE: Doubled corn tortillas, about 6 inches, warmed over an open flame or on a hot, dry skillet
THE INSIDE: Carnitas (page 470)
THE TOPPINGS: Pickled Red Onion (page 471), a slice of avocado, chopped cilantro, a lime wedge for squeezing

L.A. BULGOGI STREET TACO

THE OUTSIDE: Flour or doubled corn tortillas, about 6 inches, warmed
THE INSIDE: Bulgogi Beef (page 470)
THE TOPPINGS: Quick Kimchi (page 471), a squirt of sour cream mixed with a little lime juice, toasted sesame seeds, thinly sliced green onion greens

SAN DIEGO FISH TACO

THE OUTSIDE: Flour tortilla, about 6 inches, warmed
THE INSIDE: Fried Fish Strips (page 470)
THE TOPPINGS: Shredded cabbage, thinly sliced radish, sour cream or Greek yogurt mixed with a little cayenne, a wedge of lime for squeezing

TOFU TRUCK TACO

THE OUTSIDE: Doubled corn tortillas, about 6 inches, warmed over an open flame or on a hot, dry skillet
THE INSIDE: Taco Truck Tofu (page 471)
THE TOPPINGS: Quick Kimchi (page 471), a squirt of sour cream mixed with a little lime juice, toasted sesame seeds, thinly sliced green onion greens

S.F. MISSION BURRITO

(Not pictured)
THE OUTSIDE: Flour tortilla, 10 to 12 inches, warmed
THE INSIDE: Equal parts Rice for Burritos (page 471), Frijoles Pinquito (page 451), and any meat or tofu listed above
ADDITIONAL FILLINGS: A little sour cream, Pico de Gallo (page 450), and shredded Jack cheese
TO ASSEMBLE: Line everything up in the middle of the tortilla, fold each end in, then roll to enclose

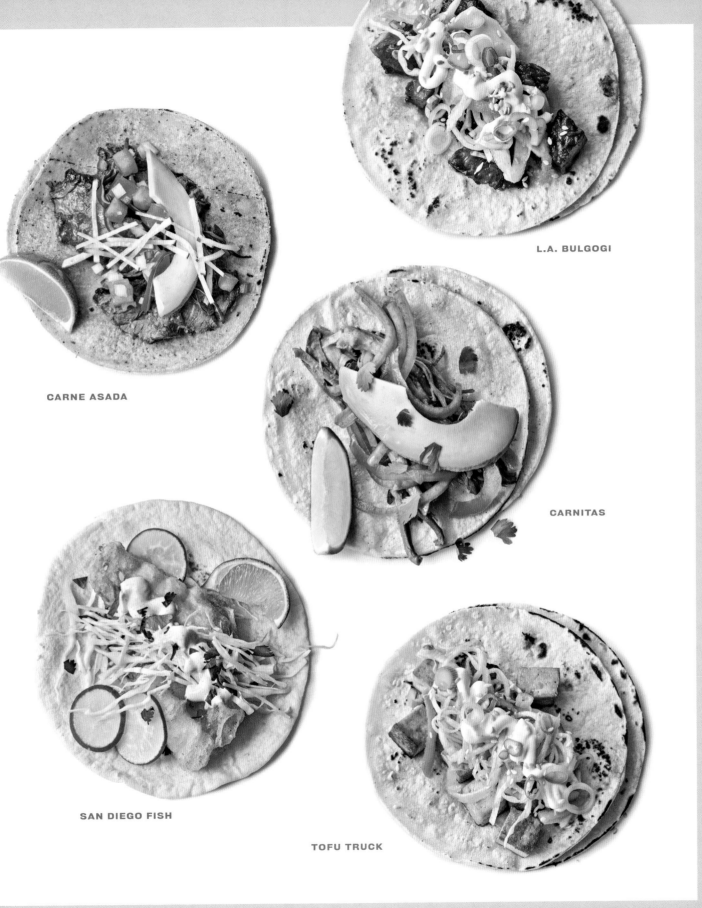

CARNE ASADA

L.A. BULGOGI

CARNITAS

SAN DIEGO FISH

TOFU TRUCK

FRIED FISH STRIPS

MAKES ENOUGH FOR ABOUT 6 TACOS

Canola or corn oil for frying

1 cup beer

½ cup all-purpose flour

½ teaspoon kosher salt

½ pound white, flaky fish, such as snapper, tilapia, or mahi mahi, cut into thin strips

In a deep skillet, heat about ½ inch of oil to 370°F. In a bowl, combine the beer, flour, and salt. Dip the fish strips in the batter, then place in the oil. Fry for 3 to 4 minutes, until crisp. Drain on paper towels.

CARNE ASADA

MAKES ENOUGH FOR ABOUT 12 TACOS

Juice of 2 limes

¼ cup extra-virgin olive oil

2 cloves garlic, thinly sliced

1 flank or skirt steak, about 1½ pounds

Kosher salt and freshly ground black pepper

Combine the lime juice, olive oil, and garlic. Season the steak with salt and pepper and put in a zip-top bag. Pour the marinade in and press the air out of the bag. Refrigerate for 2 to 4 hours.

Prepare a grill for direct heat, heat a stovetop grill pan, or preheat the broiler in your oven. Discard the marinade and grill the steak for 5 or 6 minutes per side, until you start seeing some char marks. Let rest for 5 minutes before cutting ¼-inch slices against the grain to serve on tacos.

CARNITAS

MAKES ENOUGH FOR ABOUT 12 TACOS

1 pork shoulder roast, about 2 pounds, cut into 2-inch cubes

Kosher salt and freshly ground black pepper

2 tablespoons extra-virgin olive oil or lard

1 cup water

Zest and juice of 2 oranges

1 bunch thyme

Generously season the pork with salt and pepper. Heat the oil in a large saucepan over medium-high heat and brown the pork chunks on several sides, 2 to 3 minutes per side, for a total of 10 to 12 minutes. Add the water, orange zest and juice, and thyme. Reduce the heat to medium and cook until the cooking liquid evaporates and the pork begins frying in its own fat, a little over an hour. The pork is ready when you can easily shred the chunks with a fork.

BULGOGI BEEF

MAKES ENOUGH FOR ABOUT 12 TACOS

½ cup soy sauce

¼ cup packed brown sugar

¼ cup rice wine vinegar

2 tablespoons toasted sesame oil

1½ pounds skirt steak or sirloin, thinly sliced

Mix the soy sauce, brown sugar, vinegar, and sesame oil. Put the beef slices in a zip-top bag and pour the marinade over them. Press out the air, seal the bag, and marinate in the refrigerator overnight.

Remove the beef from the bag (save the marinade). In a large skillet over medium-high heat, stir-fry the beef until cooked through, about 5 minutes total. Set aside.

In a small saucepan, bring the marinade to a boil and reduce it until it becomes a thick glaze, about 10 minutes.

Cut the meat into small cubes and toss in the glaze.

TACO TRUCK TOFU
MAKES ENOUGH FOR ABOUT 8 TACOS

½ cup soy sauce

¼ cup packed brown sugar

¼ cup rice wine vinegar

2 tablespoons toasted sesame oil

1 pound extra-firm tofu, cut into ½-inch cubes

2 tablespoons extra-virgin olive oil

Mix the soy sauce, brown sugar, vinegar, and sesame oil. Put the tofu cubes in a zip-top bag and pour the marinade over them. Press out the air, seal the bag, and marinate in the refrigerator for 1 or 2 hours.

In a large skillet over medium-high heat, heat the olive oil. Discard the marinade and sear the tofu on one side, leaving it undisturbed for 2 minutes or so until a crust forms. Stir and let sear on another side. The tofu is ready when it's heated through.

RICE FOR BURRITOS
MAKES ENOUGH FOR ABOUT 6 BURRITOS

1 tablespoon extra-virgin olive oil

½ small onion, finely diced

2 cloves garlic, thinly sliced

½ green bell pepper, finely diced

1 teaspoon kosher salt

1 cup white rice, such as basmati or jasmine

½ cup Basic Tomato Sauce (page 480)

1½ cups water

2 green onions, thinly sliced

Heat the oil in a large saucepan over medium-high heat and sauté the onion until it begins to soften, about 5 minutes. Add the garlic, bell pepper, and salt and continue to sauté for another minute or two. Add the rice and stir, then add the tomato sauce and water. Stir and bring to a boil. Cover, reduce the heat to medium-low, and simmer for 18 to 20 minutes, until the liquid is absorbed and the rice is tender. Toss in the green onions.

PICKLED RED ONION
MAKES ABOUT 1 CUP

1 teaspoon kosher salt

1 teaspoon sugar

½ cup hot water

½ cup red wine vinegar

1 red onion, thinly sliced and rinsed under cold water

Dissolve the salt and sugar in the hot water. Add the vinegar and pour over the onion slices in a sealable container. Make sure the onions are covered; press them down or add a little more water to make sure they're submerged. Let stand in the refrigerator for at least an hour before using. They'll keep for a week in the fridge.

QUICK KIMCHI
MAKES ABOUT 3 CUPS

½ head cabbage, either napa or red, thinly shredded

1 carrot, peeled and shredded

2 green onions, thinly sliced

¼ cup rice wine vinegar

2 tablespoons gochujang, or other hot chili sauce, such as Sriracha

1 tablespoon toasted sesame oil

1 teaspoon kosher salt

In a large bowl, toss together the cabbage, carrot, and green onion. In a small bowl, whisk together the vinegar, chili sauce, sesame oil, and salt. Pour the dressing over the vegetables and toss. The kimchi will be ready to eat in about a half hour, but will be better the next day.

What happens when a doughnut shop in Glendora takes a standard glazed doughnut, cuts it in half, and stuffs it with fresh strawberries? It becomes the perennial favorite in contests that celebrate L.A.'s culinary icons.

STRAWBERRY

DOUGHNUTS

FOR THE STRAWBERRIES: Toss the strawberries with the granulated sugar and set aside at room temperature for at least an hour.

FOR THE DOUGHNUTS: In a small bowl, sprinkle the yeast over the warm milk and set aside for 10 minutes as the yeast blooms.

In a large bowl or stand mixer, combine the butter, granulated sugar, eggs, vanilla, and salt. Beat until creamy, add the yeast mixture, then gradually add the flour. Knead the dough, either by hand or with the hook attachment of the stand mixer, for 5 to 6 minutes. Lightly oil a bowl, add the dough, and cover with a towel. Let the dough rise in a warm place until doubled in size, about 90 minutes.

Dust an open countertop with flour. Punch down the dough and roll it out to about ½ inch thick. Cut doughnuts with a 3-inch round cookie cutter and put them on a baking sheet, giving them some space to expand. Cover the baking sheet with a towel and let them rise again, for about 45 minutes.

In a large, heavy pot or Dutch oven, heat about 2 inches of oil to 340°F.

Cooking 2 or 3 at a time, carefully slide the doughnuts into the oil and fry for about 2 minutes per side, until golden. Remove them to a paper towel–lined platter and allow them to cool while you make the glaze. Allow to cool at least 30 minutes before glazing.

FOR THE GLAZE: In a bowl, whisk together the confectioners' sugar and milk.

TO ASSEMBLE: Put the glaze in a wide, shallow bowl and dip one side of the doughnut in the glaze. Put the doughnuts on a wire rack, glazed side up, for about 30 minutes, until the glaze sets. Cut each doughnut in half like a hamburger bun and stuff it with strawberries.

MAKES 12 DOUGHNUTS

FOR THE STRAWBERRIES

1 pound strawberries, hulled and sliced

½ cup granulated sugar

FOR THE DOUGHNUTS

1 envelope (2¼ teaspoons) active dry yeast

1 cup warm milk, 110°F

6 tablespoons unsalted butter, softened

¼ cup granulated sugar

1 large egg plus 1 yolk

1 teaspoon vanilla extract

1 teaspoon kosher salt

3 cups all-purpose flour plus more for dusting

Canola or corn oil for frying

FOR THE GLAZE

2 cups confectioners' sugar

¼ cup milk

For some people, a trip through the Coachella Valley isn't complete without a stop at one of the many date shake stands for their favorite treat. For others, the shake is the reason to make the journey.

COACHELLA
DATE SHAKES

1 cup dates, such as medjool

1 cup milk

2 cups vanilla ice cream

Pit the dates, then chop them. In a blender, puree the dates, then add the milk and puree. Add the ice cream and blend until smooth. Serve with a wide straw.

MAKES 2 SHAKES

Tucked at the bottom of the menu of Hobee's restaurant, suspiciously under the heading of "Light Bites," is the reason a lot of people are there in the first place: the blueberry coffee cake. It's the thing people who leave the southern San Francisco Bay Area say they miss and they try to replicate.

SOUR CREAM AND BLUEBERRY
COFFEE CAKE

FOR THE CAKE

1½ cups fresh blueberries, stems removed

2 cups all-purpose flour

2 teaspoons baking powder

½ teaspoon baking soda

½ teaspoon kosher salt

2 large eggs, beaten

1 cup sour cream

1 teaspoon vanilla extract

1 cup granulated sugar

FOR THE BROWN SUGAR TOPPING

½ cup packed brown sugar

2 tablespoons unsalted butter, softened

1 teaspoon ground cinnamon

FOR THE SOUR CREAM TOPPING

1 cup sour cream

3 tablespoons granulated sugar

Preheat the oven to 350°F. Spray a 9-by-9-inch baking pan with cooking spray.

FOR THE CAKE: Rinse the berries in cold water and then toss them in ½ cup of the flour. Pour the berries in a sieve and shake the excess flour off into a bowl. Set the berries aside.

Add the remaining 1½ cups flour to the bowl, along with the baking powder, baking soda, and salt.

In a separate bowl or stand mixer, beat together the eggs, sour cream, vanilla, and granulated sugar until well combined. Gradually add the flour mixture and beat until a smooth batter forms.

Pour half the batter in the pan and scatter most of the berries over. Pour in the rest of the batter and drop the rest of the berries on top.

FOR THE BROWN SUGAR TOPPING: In a small bowl, mix together the brown sugar, butter, and cinnamon. Spread over the top of the batter. Bake the cake for 30 to 35 minutes or until the top is uniformly brown. Let cool before serving.

FOR THE SOUR CREAM TOPPING: Whisk together the sour cream and granulated sugar. Serve each slice of cake with a dollop of the cream on top.

SERVES 6 TO 8

The marionberry is a specific and majestic kind of blackberry that grows in a concentrated area around Salem, Oregon. It looks like an elongated blackberry; if you can't get them where you are, blackberries are a perfect substitute.

MARIONBERRY COBBLER

Preheat the oven to 350°F. Spray a 9-by-9-inch baking pan with cooking spray.

In a large saucepan over medium-high heat, combine ¾ cup of the sugar and the cornstarch, then add the water and bring to a boil. Add the berries and return to a boil. When the mixture thickens, about 10 minutes, pour into the prepared pan.

In a stand mixer with the paddle attachment or a large bowl with an electric mixer, cream the butter with the remaining ¼ cup sugar. Mix together the flour, baking powder, and salt. Beat the flour mixture into the butter mixture and then gradually add the milk, beating until well combined.

Drop dollops of the batter over the surface of the berries. Lightly sprinkle pinches of sugar over the batter. Bake for 45 minutes, until the batter has browned. Serve warm.

SERVES 6 TO 8

1 cup sugar plus more for sprinkling

2 tablespoons cornstarch

1 cup water

1 quart (about 1 pound) marionberries, fresh or frozen, or substitute blackberries

4 tablespoons unsalted butter

1½ cups all-purpose flour

1 tablespoon baking powder

1 teaspoon kosher salt

⅔ cup milk

Basic Recipes

BASIC TOMATO SAUCE

MAKES ABOUT 4 CUPS

¼ cup extra-virgin olive oil

1 large onion, cut into ¼-inch dice

4 cloves garlic, thinly sliced

½ medium carrot, finely shredded

3 tablespoons chopped fresh thyme leaves,
or 1 tablespoon dried

2 (28-ounce) cans peeled whole tomatoes,
crushed by hand, juices reserved

Kosher salt

In a 3-quart saucepan, heat the olive oil over medium heat. Add the onion and garlic and sauté until soft and light golden brown, 8 to 10 minutes. Add the carrot and thyme and cook 5 minutes more, until the carrot is quite soft. Add the tomatoes and their juice and bring to a boil, stirring often. Lower the heat and simmer for 30 minutes, until the sauce is as thick as hot cereal. Season with salt.

This sauce holds for 1 week in the refrigerator or up to 6 months in the freezer.

BROWN CHICKEN STOCK

MAKES ABOUT 6 CUPS

2 tablespoons extra-virgin olive oil

3 pounds chicken backs, bones, wings, and scraps
(from about 3 chickens), excess fat removed

3 carrots, coarsely chopped

2 onions, coarsely chopped

4 celery ribs, coarsely chopped

3 quarts water

2 tablespoons tomato paste

1 tablespoon black peppercorns

Stems from 1 bunch flat-leaf parsley

In a large, heavy-bottomed pot, heat the olive oil until smoking. Add the chicken parts and cook over moderately high heat, stirring frequently, until well browned all over. Transfer the chicken parts to a plate.

Add the carrots, onions, and celery to the pot and cook until softened and lightly browned. Return the chicken to the pot. Add the water, tomato paste, peppercorns, and parsley stems and stir to release any browned bits stuck to the bottom of the pot. Bring to a boil, reduce the heat, and simmer gently over moderately low heat, skimming occasionally, until reduced by half, about 2 hours.

Strain the stock, pressing hard to extract the liquid from the solids. Let cool, then refrigerate. Skim the fat from the surface before using.

The stock can be refrigerated for 2 days or frozen for up to 1 month.

BASIC PIZZA DOUGH

MAKES ABOUT 2 POUNDS, ENOUGH DOUGH FOR FOUR 10-INCH PIZZA CRUSTS

3¼ cups all-purpose flour plus extra for dusting

2 teaspoons instant or rapid-rise yeast

1 tablespoon sugar

1 tablespoon kosher salt

1 cup warm water

¼ cup dry white wine, at room temperature

2 tablespoons plus 1 teaspoon extra-virgin olive oil

In a large bowl, combine the flour, yeast, sugar, and salt and mix well. Make a well in the center of the dry ingredients and add the warm water, wine, and all the olive oil. Using a wooden spoon, stir the wet ingredients into the dry until the mixture is too stiff to stir, then mix with your hands in the bowl until the dough comes together and pulls away from the sides of the bowl.

Lightly dust a work surface with flour and turn out the dough. Knead gently, dusting the work surface lightly with more flour as necessary, for 5 minutes, or until the dough is smooth, elastic, and only slightly sticky.

Oil a large clean bowl, add the dough, and turn to coat. Cover the bowl with plastic wrap or a kitchen towel, set in a warm part of the kitchen, and let the dough rise until doubled in size, about 1 hour.

Punch down the dough, and it is ready to use.

Stored in a plastic bag in the refrigerator, the dough will last a week.

BASIC PIE CRUST

MAKES TWO 9-INCH DEEP-DISH PIE CRUSTS, OR 1 DOUBLE CRUST

3½ cups all-purpose flour

1 teaspoon kosher salt

½ teaspoon baking powder

1½ cups (3 sticks) very cold unsalted butter, cut into small cubes

½ cup ice water, or more as needed

In a large bowl, combine the flour, salt, and baking powder. Add the butter and toss to coat in the flour, then mix with a pastry blender—or the back of a fork, though that will take longer—until the butter is cut into tiny bits and incorporated through the dough. Add 6 tablespoons of the ice water and mix in until the dough just comes together, adding more water a tablespoonful at a time, if necessary. (The ingredients can be mixed in a food processor but should be done in two batches.)

Dust a work surface with flour and turn the dough out of the bowl. Cut it in half and form 2 discs. Dust them with more flour, then wrap in plastic wrap and refrigerate for at least 2 hours or up to 2 days.

When ready to roll out the crust, dust your work surface and use a rolling pin to roll out the dough to at least 12 inches across. Carefully line a pie pan with the dough and cut away any excess hanging over the sides. Refrigerate the crust until ready to fill. The second disc can be used for another pie, or as a top crust in double-crusted pies.

Acknowledgments

WITHOUT MY TEAM I AM NOTHING.

SUSI, **BENNO**, and **LEO**, family truly is everything.

My communications and chicharrón team led by **PAMELA MURPHY**, with **DAVID GRUBER**, **KATY-JO PREVITE**, and **TESS KOENIG**, for making everything work smoothly with aplomb, poise, and style.

My coauthor, **JIM WEBSTER**, whose pork wrapped in pork started a lifelong and joyous collaboration.

Designer **DOUGLAS RICCARDI** and his team at **MEMO** for making the pages smart and beautiful.

Photo shoot art director, food artist, and Zen mistress of all edible beauty **KRISTA RUANE**.

Shopper **LIZ TARPEY**, and chefs **MARYANN POMERANZ**, **KOREN GRIEVSON**, and **PANCHO GATCHALIAN**.

Recipe test team **PATTI NUSSER** for excellence in temperature control.

Prop stylist **RICK GILBERT** and his team **GINE FREEDMAN** and **ALEX DORMAN** for truly being the coolest prop people on this planet.

My editor **KAREN MURGOLO** at **GRAND CENTRAL LIFE & STYLE** for making this a smooth and delightful process. And kudos to her team, **MATTHEW BALLAST** in publicity, **AMANDA PRITZKER** in marketing, and **MORGAN HEDDEN** and **KALLIE SHIMEK** in editorial.

Zen master photographer **QUENTIN BACON** and his assistant **KRISTEN WALTHER** for brilliance on the page and in the kitchen studio.

For lending their geographic expertise, **NASTAZIA BRICK**, **OPAL CURLESS** (via **AMY WIMMER SCHWARB**), **DAWN OWCZARZAK**, **HEATHER MEDINA**, and **MATTY EGGELSTON**.

My business partners **JOE BASTIANICH**, **LIDIA BASTIANICH**, **NANCY SILVERTON**, **JOHN FARBER**, **MARY GIULIANI**, and the **FARINETTI** and **SAPER** clans, plus the teams at **SUMMER GARDEN FOODS**, **MADEIRA HOUSEWARES**, and **BEL CAMPO**.

The hardworking teams at my restaurants and at **EATALY** for exceeding all expectations and understanding the importance of our collaboration; and more importantly, their families, for tolerating the amount of hard work we all put into our days, every day.

CATHY FRANKEL for keeping it all under one roof and consistent.

TONY GARDNER for persevering in the truly intense and silly grind that contracts have become in a way that always impresses me.

SUSAN MARZANO at my foundation for working hard to raise money to help share our joy.

REYNA MASTROSIMONE for constantly keeping the digital and entertainment world near.

The Chew crew—**DAFO**, **SYMON**, **CLINTON**, and **CARLA**—for making every day at work fun and funny at the same time.

To **JIM HARRISON** and **MICHAEL STIPE** and **BONO** and president **BILL CLINTON** for the voices in my head reminding me to love life and to give unconditionally, every day and every night…

Jim Webster would like to thank: **PAM WEBSTER**, the team at *The Washington Post,* including **JOE YONAN**, **BONNIE BENWICK**, **COURTNEY RUKAN**, and **TRACY GRANT**; **MELANIE STARKEY**; **CAROL BLYMIRE**; **JEREMY AND BECKY BOWERS**; **LAURA REILEY**; **RONNIE PERKINS**; and **MICHELLE AND GREG BAKER**.

Index

About the Authors

MARIO BATALI counts twenty-six restaurants, ten cookbooks, numerous television shows, and four Eataly marketplaces among his ever-expanding empire of deliciousness.

His cookbooks include the James Beard Award–winning *Molto Italiano: 327 Simple Italian Recipes to Cook at Home* and *America—Farm to Table: Simple, Delicious Recipes Celebrating Local Farmers*. Batali appears daily on ABC's *The Chew*, a daytime talk show that celebrates and explores life through food. He and his co-hosts won their first Emmy for Outstanding Informative Talk Show Hosts in 2015.

To learn more about Mario Batali, visit mariobatali.com. To learn more about the Mario Batali Foundation, visit mariobatalifoundation.org.

JIM WEBSTER works at *The Washington Post* as a copy editor and a contributing writer to the Food section. Webster is the co-author, with Batali, of *America—Farm to Table: Simple, Delicious Recipes Celebrating Local Farmers*. He lives in Washington, D.C.

ALABAMA

ALASKA

ARIZONA

ARKANSAS

CALIFORNIA

HAWAII

IDAHO

ILLINOIS

INDIANA

IOWA

MASSACHUSETTS

MICHIGAN

MINNESOTA

MISSISSIPPI

MISSOURI

NEW·MEXICO

NEW YORK

NORTH CAROLINA

NORTH DAKOTA

OHIO

SOUTH DAKOTA

TENNESSEE

TEXAS

UTAH

VERMONT